CEDAR CREST COLLEGE
LIBRARY

WITHDRAWN

ESSAYS IN SOCIAL JUSTICE

LONDON : HUMPHREY MILFORD

OXFORD UNIVERSITY PRESS

ESSAYS IN SOCIAL JUSTICE

BY

THOMAS NIXON CARVER, Ph.D., LL.D.

DAVID A. WELLS PROFESSOR OF POLITICAL ECONOMY, EMERITUS,
IN HARVARD UNIVERSITY

CAMBRIDGE

HARVARD UNIVERSITY PRESS

1940

300
C33le

COPYRIGHT, 1915

BY HARVARD UNIVERSITY PRESS

Eighth Printing

PRINTED AT THE HARVARD UNIVERSITY PRESS

CAMBRIDGE, MASS., U.S.A.

TO MY WIFE

21323

PREFACE

ONE of the surest signs of degeneration is the growth of sentimental as distinguished from practical morality, especially when it is combined with an ingrowing conscience. Sentimental morality is the sort which evaluates character and conduct by their ability to satisfy an inner sense of propriety, or to create within us the sensation of approval. Both character and conduct, under this system, come under what economists would call " consumers' goods " whose function is to please. Practical morality is the sort which evaluates character and conduct by their results. The test is thus objective and not subjective. " By their fruits ye shall know them " is robust and wholesome doctrine, though even this may be travestied by defining fruits in subjective terms, under the alluring but delusive name of spiritual goods. An ingrowing conscience is one which leads its possessor to look continually inward upon his own motives and to try perpetually to test them by some supposedly inner knowledge as to what a motive ought to be like. Such a person is like one who would try to guide himself through the world by closing his eyes to the objects around him and following an assumed inner sense of direction.

One school would have us believe that this inner knowledge, or intuition, is like the compass which the ship carries in her midst, which points unerringly to a fixed point outside the ship, and which, accordingly, becomes a safe guide. Another school, the anthropological, demonstrates conclusively that this compass does not point to any fixed point outside the ship, but may point in any and every direction, according to circumstances of time and place. In other words, the human conscience is the product of circumstances, and may lead to any conceivable kind of conduct. But this school goes further and virtually says that it does not matter since there is no fixed point outside the ship toward which the compass can point. We are on an open sea and one direction is as good as another provided we all agree upon it. We shall then all be pleased with the direction we are going, and that is all we need to care about. In other words, any kind of character or conduct which pleases us, which creates the sensation of approval within us, is as good as any other. Whatever we all agree to be right is right.

This book is written on the assumption that there is a fixed point outside the ship by which it must steer, that it makes a great deal of difference in which direction we happen to be headed, and, moreover, that we must be guided by looking out at this fixed point and not by looking in upon our own consciences, for our consciences may be perverted. Character and conduct either of the individual or the state are thus to be evaluated, not in accordance with their power to please, or to create the sensation of approval within us; but in accordance with their power to propel us in the right direction. What is the right direction is a question of fact and not a question of opinion, of likes and dislikes, or of approval and disapproval by an inner conscience.

T. N. CARVER.

CAMBRIDGE, MASS., December, 1914.

CONTENTS

ESSAYS IN SOCIAL JUSTICE

ESSAYS IN SOCIAL JUSTICE

CHAPTER I

WHAT IS JUSTICE?

THE need for justice grows out of the conflict of human
interests. That is to say, if there were no conflict of interests
among mankind we should never have invented the word
justice, nor conceived the idea for which it stands. How
these conflicts arise will form the theme of the next two
chapters. In the present chapter we are concerned with the
concept of justice itself and the test by which one may determine whether a given act or policy is just or unjust.

While the need for justice arises out of the conflict of
human interests, the occasion for the use of the word or the
concept arises only when an attempt is made to adjust conflicts on some other basis than that of might. The unthinking plants and the lowest animals know no such thing as
justice. Every conflict is settled by the right of might.
Possibly some of the higher and more gregarious animals
may have some dim perception of something resembling
justice, though even that is doubtful. Certainly the attitude of the member of a herd or pack toward fellow members is different from that toward those outside the group.
In this respect they resemble human beings. It may be
that the difference is one of degree; but a difference of
degree, if it be wide enough, constitutes a difference of kind.
In fact, most differences are differences of degree. However, we need not waste time discussing a problem of which
we know so little as we do about the mental processes of

animals.   Certain it is that human beings, especially those
who call themselves highly civilized, not only hold an attitude toward members of their own herd or pack, variously
called state, nation, or social group, different from that
which they hold toward members of other groups, but they
are also in the habit of thinking about this attitude, and
wondering what it should be.   When they are thinking
about this they are either thinking about justice or something very closely related to it.

But when men are merely thinking about their attitude
toward their fellow members of a social group, and wondering what that attitude should be, their ideas of justice are
not likely to be very clear or definite.   It is only when some
attempt is made to settle an actual conflict of interests
between individuals that they are forced to think in clear
and definite terms.   Sometimes their conclusions are, to
our ears, extremely absurd, but they are at least definite
and specific.   There is a story of a missionary who had a
watch which was coveted by an influential member of the
tribe where he was located.   This member hired a professional thief to steal the watch, paying him in advance.   The
missionary heard of the bargain, kept guard and, when the
thief appeared, drove him away.   Having already received
his pay, and not wishing to return it to his employer, the
thief absconded.   Thereupon the employer demanded that
the missionary should compensate him for the loss which he
had sustained through the dishonesty of the thief.   He
reasoned that if the missionary had not scared the thief, he,
the employer, would not have sustained the loss.   The
missionary was the cause of the loss and should therefore be
compelled to make it good.

This story is used to illustrate the points already made in
this discussion.   First, there were conflicts of interests.

The man who employed the thief wanted the missionary's watch; so did the missionary. The thief also wanted the reward which he had already received; so did the employer. Second, this caused the employer to ponder over the situation. If he had not felt obliged to treat the missionary differently from the way he would treat an animal or a member of another tribe, he would have taken the watch by force, if he could. He felt obliged to observe certain customs of the tribe. Similarly, in demanding compensation for the loss sustained by the absconding of his employee, he showed some consideration. He did not choose the direct method of knocking the missionary on the head and taking what he wanted. Third, and most important, he worked out a theory of justice to fit this specific case. It may have been an incorrect theory, but it was specific in its application.

Another point, of the very greatest importance, is also illustrated by this story: the man who employed the thief was not restrained merely by his own sense of right and wrong; he was restrained also by his sense of responsibility to a power stronger than himself, that is, to the tribe or the tribal chief. And this sense of responsibility was created by something very material and easily appreciated; that was the physical force which would be exerted to cause him pain, if he disregarded it. He knew perfectly well that he must deal with other members of his group according to rules laid down by that group, otherwise the group would chastise him in some way which he would not like. This represents the final stage in the development of the concept of justice, though the question as to the exact difference between justice and injustice may be far from clear. There exists at least, at this point, some kind of a concept of justice. This point is reached when men have not only thought about how to settle specific conflicts of interest, but when the social group has undertaken to act as an umpire, and to enforce its decisions by superior power.

The groups which undertake to adjudicate the conflicting interests of mankind are known as states [1] or nations. These are groups of individuals which, as groups, undertake not only to settle or adjust conflicting interests among their own members, but to protect and discipline them as well. When a group has no superior or stronger group exercising authority over it, and giving it protection, it is said to be a sovereign group. Such a group may be said to be a law unto itself. It is self-controlled and self-disciplined, subject to no laws except those of the cosmic universe, and it is self-protected, having no defence except its own power and internal efficiency. It stands alone facing a hostile or friendly universe, according to the circumstances of time and place. But in order to maintain its place in that universe, surrounded by rival groups whose interests frequently conflict with its own, it must be strong. How can such a state grow strong ? One way is so to discipline its individual members as to secure as large a contribution from each to the strength of the whole as possible. The state which fails in this will fail in everything, provided another rival group succeeds better. In that event, the rival group will grow stronger and, should their interests ever come in conflict, it will pursue its own interests to the disadvantage of the weaker group.

The term state is in this instance used in the generic sense of a sovereign law-making power, and not as the name merely of one of the component parts of the American Union. But, because of the confusion likely to arise in the minds of American readers through the use of the word state in this double sense, the term nation will be used as the name of a sovereign group. This is in harmony with American, but opposed to European usage.

As between sovereign groups, though there are frequent conflicts of interest, yet the concept of justice is only vaguely and occasionally effective. Here, and here only in the human world, might makes right, or rather, it takes the place of right. The primordial struggle for existence holds sway, practically unmitigated and only slightly softened by concepts of right or justice. The only influence of such concepts is to reduce the savage ferocity of a conquering army to the rules of civilized warfare, to cause the stronger party voluntarily to show pity to the weaker, and to cause it to fear the ill opinion or open hostility of the rest of mankind. These considerations, however, have little influence upon an international bully whose moral sensibilities do not permit it to feel a sense of pity, or to care for the good opinions of the rest of mankind. When conditions arise under which these sovereign groups are subjected to the will of a higher power which has the physical force to compel obedience, then these groups have surrendered their sovereignty to the higher power. That is what the states of the American union did in 1789, though some of them were not convinced of it until 1865; that is what the states of the German Empire did in 1871; and that is what the states of Europe will do when a new Charlemagne arises. Then justice will have a clear and definite instead of an obscure and indefinite meaning in its application to the relations among groups which are now sovereign.

The concept of justice, as applied to the conflict of interests within a nation, has come to play so large a part in our thinking as to influence more or less directly our thinking with respect to international relations. One symptom of this is the frequency with which it is asked: is it right for a nation to do that which it would not permit one of its citizens, or a group of its citizens, to do?

The chief purpose of the nation is essentially that of every living being, viz., to keep on living. It is in no better position to consider, judicially, whether it ought to keep on living or not than is the individual. It can be counted on to decide that question in the affirmative as surely as can the individual. It can, therefore, be counted on to do everything within its power and wisdom to enable it to keep on living. If its existence is threatened, either directly or remotely, it can be counted on to exercise all its power, and to scruple at nothing in its own defence. That is precisely what the individual would do were he similarly situated, that is, were he left to defend himself without any protection from a higher power, and to direct himself without any control by a higher power. The individual who wished to keep on living under such circumstances would, if he were wise, keep himself in the best possible condition. So must the nation. This would require the individual to safeguard the interests of every useful organ or constituent part of his body and to train every useful faculty. The state must do the same. It would also require the individual to discipline himself, to hold every appetite or propensity in check which would, if uncontrolled, weaken him and put him at a disadvantage in the struggle. The state is under the same compulsion, it must not only safeguard and encourage every interest which contributes to the strength of the whole, but it must also restrain and hold in check every interest and every propensity of every citizen which in any way weakens the strength of the whole.

One of the first signs of decadence in a nation is its tendency to forget this stern fact. The greatest and most deadly of all intellectual vices is the unwillingness to see things as they are, or the propensity to believe that to be true which one wishes were true. Under what used to be

miscalled the " canker of a long peace," men begin to wish
that they had nothing to do but to enjoy themselves.   They
therefore succeed in believing that to be true.   As a result
they become impatient of restraint and discipline, they begin
to demand freedom to do as they please, which results in
general irresponsibility and inefficiency, for which rowdy-
ism is the only good name.   It is useless to point out to
them that this is the way to national ruin.   They do not
believe it.   Besides, they think that it will not come in their
own day.   " After us, the deluge," is their cry.

On what principle or principles, according to what rules,
shall the state control and discipline its members, and adjust
their conflicting interests, protecting some and restraining
others ?   That is the problem of social justice.   It has to do
with the internal economy of the nation rather than with its
external relations.   As to the individual, it has to do with
his external relations with his fellow citizens rather than
with his internal adjustments.

Since the first duty of the state is to be strong in order
that it may live, and since it must adjust the conflicting
interests of its citizens, it follows that its duty is so to adjust
these conflicting interests as to make itself strong.   It
must repress and discourage those interests of its individuals
which conflict with its own, and it must support and encourage those which harmonize with its own.   That is
justice.   In the most general terms, therefore, justice may
be defined as such an adjustment of the conflicting interests
of the citizens of a nation as will interfere least with, and
contribute most to, the strength of the nation.

Looked at from another angle the same idea may be
expressed by saying that justice is the name for the moral
obligation of the state, as distinct from the individual, with
respect to its task of adjusting conflicting interests.   Since

the state has this to do, it must find out how to do it.
What *ought* the state to do with respect to these conflicts,
and how *ought* it to do it ?   These are the questions of
social justice.   Since the state is self-ruled, and, what is
more important, self-protected, the only answer it can possibly make to these questions is that it *must* do it in such a
way as to strengthen itself and safeguard its own existence.
This obligation of the nation toward its members is like
that of an umpire toward those whose conflicting interests
he is called upon to adjust, except that the nation is an
umpire whose well-being depends upon the aggregate well-
being of those whose conflicting interests he is adjudicating.
Such an obligation as this no group, certainly no sovereign
group, can avoid.   Its own self-preservation demands it.

The rules of justice, that is, the rules according to which
these conflicting interests are to be adjusted, may be embodied in positive law, or in mere public opinion or social
sentiment.   They may emanate from the sovereign group,
called the nation, in which case they take precedence, in
practice, over all others, or they may emanate from indefinite and intangible groups, variously called "the community," "society," or even "civilization" or "Christen-
dom," in which case they become effective in proportion as
they are embodied in positive law and are enforced by the
sovereign group.

Not only may positive law be wrong and unjust, though
always and necessarily pretending to be just, but public
opinion and social sentiment are equally liable to error.   But
the penalty for mistaken notions of justice is national weakness, and, if they continue and accumulate, national death.
If this were not true, there would be no excuse for a study of
this kind.   How can we be certain that one rule, when
applied, works justice and another injustice ?   The only

way is to find out, if we can, whether the one or the other will strengthen the group, or weaken it. The study must be objective, rather than subjective, that is, we must study the laws of economics and social development, rather than our own sentiments.

At the very outset of this discussion, therefore, it is necessary to do that which ought not be necessary, namely, defend the proposition that social sentiment in its purest form, even though called moral sentiment or intuition, is quite likely to be wrong and unjust. The effectiveness with which a rule is applied to the actual settlement of disputes depends, in a democracy, absolutely upon public sentiment, and the physical force which that sentiment is able to direct and control through governmental agencies. This has led to the not uncommon conclusion that public sentiment, or the popular will, either when expressed directly, or indirectly through constituted agents, is the source of justice. It is merely the source of the power, or physical force exercised by the state which must be invoked in order that a rule may be enforced. The rule and its enforcement may be either just or unjust.

The dictum that " the king can do no wrong " was only one of the many ways in which the idea was expressed that the sovereign will is the source of justice. When the king was supposed to embody in himself the will and sentiments of the people it was easy to conceive that whatever he decreed to be right or wrong must *per se* be right or wrong. But the case is no better when the people themselves express the sovereign will. *Vox populi vox Dei* is no nearer the truth than the formula that the king can do no wrong, in fact it is only another variation of the same error.

The bold assertion that the sovereign people can do no wrong would find, doubtless, as few supporters as the proposition that the sovereign person can do no wrong. Under certain conditions neither can be held accountable to any human power. There is no process, as Burke pointed out, whereby one can indict a whole people. But that the whole people can do no wrong is another proposition. Yet such is the tacit assumption on which a great deal of our popular thinking now proceeds. In considering an act of government, a few will ask the question, Is it just; but many more will ask, Does it express the popular will ? They who raise this question must necessarily assume either that the popular will is necessarily, or *per se* just, or that it is more important that government shall act in accordance with the popular will than that it shall act in accordance with justice. He who consistently believes that the popular will may be wrong is content to judge any act of government on the sole basis of its justice or injustice. If it be just, he will commend it, no matter how universally the popular will opposes it, and if it be unjust he will condemn it no matter how completely it expresses the popular will. In fact he will never ask respecting any policy or proposed policy, Is it popular, or does it really express the popular will ? That would be trivial. He will first try to determine whether it is right, and next, if he be a leader of men, he will try to make the right popular.

Yet, such a view is, in every respect, consistent with democracy. One may believe thoroughly that the popular will is frequently wrong and yet believe that it is less frequently wrong than that of an hereditary monarch, or an hereditary aristocracy, chosen by the " accident of birth " rather than on the basis of merit. A person who believes this may be as ardent a supporter of democracy as any one, and yet, when he is convinced that the popular will is wrong may condemn it and try to change it. But when he is convinced that an act of government is unjust, he will not ask the question, does it represent the popular will; he will condemn it regardless of its popular support.

Not only do many of our most voluminous writers and most loquacious statesmen support, virtually, the opposite view, but the general trend of opinion, at the present moment (A.D. 1914), seems unmistakably to be in the direction of the opinion that the popular will must be right. There is comparatively little interest in efforts to make government more just, there is a great deal of interest in efforts to make it more popular. Most of the movements masquerading under the name " progressive " are designed to popularize government rather than to rationalize its acts or make them more just. If as much effort as is now being expended in trying to contrive a fool-proof government were expended in teaching the people how to run the government they have, and how to distinguish between just and unjust acts of government, more real progress would be made. The great question is not how may we ascertain the popular will. It is rather, how may we ascertain what the popular will ought to be.

As usually happens in similar cases, there is a close relationship between this trend of public opinion and the underlying philosophy of the time. When one suggests that there is a test of right and wrong, of justice and injustice, which transcends public opinion, the likes and dislikes of the people, or even their moral sentiments, one runs counter to some very powerful currents of philosophic thought. This is declared to be unthinkable from the very nature of the case. It is contended either that the moral intuitions of mankind, if given free expression, must necessarily be right, or that right and wrong, justice and injustice, have no meaning outside of human likes and dislikes.

Even Westermarck, in his monumental work[1] begins with this categorical statement: " That the moral concepts are ultimately based on emotions, either of indignation or approval, is a fact that a certain school of thinkers have in vain attempted to deny. . . . Men pronounce certain acts to be good or bad on account of the emotions those acts arouse in their minds, just as they call sunshine warm and ice cold on account of certain sensations which they experience, and as they name a thing pleasant or painful because they feel pleasure or pain. But to attribute a quality to a thing is never the same as merely to state the existence of a particular sensation or feeling in the mind which perceives it."

One might think that as there is an objective quality in sunshine which creates the subjective sensation of warmth, and an objective quality in ice which creates the subjective sensation of coldness, so there might conceivably be an objective quality in goodness which creates the subjective sensation of approval, and an objective quality in badness which creates the subjective sensation of indignation. That would be the reply of the intuitionist. However, it is easy to show that whereas the objective quality of coldness in ice *always* produces the subjective sensation of coldness when brought into contact with the human body, yet the subjective sensations of approval and disapproval are not invariably produced by the same objective facts. In other words, the same act which at one time produces the sensation of disapproval may, at another time and place, produce the opposite sensation. From this it is argued that right and wrong can have no objective character, but are determined wholly by subjective conditions. Something like

[1] *The Origin and Development of the Moral Ideas*, by Edward Westermarck, Ph.D., LL.D. 2 vols. Second Edition, London, 1912.

this is intimated by Westermarck in the further statement:
" Moral concepts, then, are essentially generalizations of
tendencies in certain phenomena to call forth moral emotions."

But are we justified in raising the question: What
phenomena *ought* to arouse the emotion of approval and
what *ought* to arouse that of disapproval in the minds of the
masses of the people ? The author seems to imply that we
are not — that we have no right to raise such a question;
that if certain phenomena actually call forth the emotion
of approval, that settles it; there is no higher court of
appeal; the phenomena are good. If others actually call
forth the sensation of disapproval or indignation, that
settles it; there is no higher court of appeal; the phenomena
are bad. But suppose certain classes of social acts habitually call forth the sensation of approval in the minds of all
the people of a nation or a civilization, but as a result of
these acts, the nation weakens itself or the civilization
destroys itself, leaving the world in possession of other
people or other civilizations in which the sensation of approval is called forth by an entirely different class of social
acts ? Does this affect the case ? In the opinion of the
present writer it does.

Instead of raising the question, ought this class of acts to
arouse the sensation of approval and that class the sensation
of disapproval, it would probably be more to the point to
ask: What will happen to a social group wherein this class
of acts habitually arouses the sensation of approval, and
that the sensation of disapproval ? If, as the result of a
careful inquiry, we find that such a community weakens
itself and endangers its existence by so doing, this conclusion certainly has some practical importance for that
group. Whether we are justified in saying that it ought not

approve and disapprove as it does, we can probably say that the chances are that if it continues so to do, it will eventually cease to be, and its territory will be occupied by a group whose approval and disapproval are differently aroused. These elect groups, whose approval and disapproval are given in such ways as to strengthen them and enable them to grow and flourish, need to be studied pretty carefully. They are of vastly more importance than those groups which have become extinct through their own internal weakness.

Another recent work [1] reiterates time and again the proposition: The *mores* are always right; the *mores* can make anything right, etc. This is virtually an endorsement of Westermarck's position. The terms right and wrong have no meaning beyond the sentiments of universal endorsement or disapproval in the minds of the people. Both writers, and a number of others besides, pile up evidence to show what wide variations there have been in social practices among the people of the earth. It is easy to show that almost everything which we *think* to be wrong has been at one time or another thought to be right by whole communities. In many of these communities the same acts which among us would call forth the sentiments of disapproval, call forth there the sentiments of approval, and the very acts which among us call forth the highest approval, among others have called forth the sentiment of intense indignation. Thus it is easy to show that almost any conceivable kind of conduct has, at one time or another, been *thought* to be right, and the same acts have, at different times and places, been *thought* to be wrong.

[1] *Folkways — a study of the sociological importance of usages, manners, customs, mores, and morals,* by William Graham Sumner. Boston, Ginn and Co., 1911.

But have we a right to raise the question: Are they really right or really wrong ? Is there a test of rightness and wrongness beyond the mere test of approval and disapproval ? The answer of many of these recent writers, especially of the anthropological school, is in the negative.

Their arguments, however, are far from being convincing. Let us take a parallel case. Suppose a biologist were to take the same pains which these anthropological moralists have taken to describe all the individual variations that can be discovered in a given species of plant or animal life. He could make a considerable catalogue regarding the common house-fly, for example. He could find multitudes of freaks and sports, individuals born without wings, with both wings on one side of the body, with eight legs, or only two legs, and a multitude of other peculiarities. If, after he had catalogued a large number of cases, filling a book of considerable size, he should then pronounce the opinion that one kind of a fly was just as good as another because, forsooth, nature produces all kinds, we should have a right to ask what he meant by a good fly. If the fly with both wings on one side is unable to get a living and comes to speedy destruction and disappears instantly from the earth, whereas the flies with wings on two sides survive, we should at least be justified in concluding that nature had some preferences. These were preferences of course in a purely impersonal sense. In other words, one kind of a fly is better adapted to natural conditions than some other kinds.

It seems to the present writer that these anthropological moralists have never gotten beyond the cataloguing of the moral variations of mankind. Finding that nature seems to produce all sorts of moral variations, and being able to catalogue so many as to fill volumes, these writers conclude that one kind of morality is as good as another, if only the people think so, or, if it creates the same sentiment of approval and disapproval.   But if a certain idea of morality unfits the tribe or community for survival, so that it speedily passes from existence like the fly with both wings on one side, have we not some ground for claiming that nature has her preferences, that one kind of morality seems to work better than other kinds, that one scheme of social conduct enables the people who practice it to get on better in the world than certain other schemes ?

Since Darwin, the world is committed to the idea that progress takes place mainly, if not exclusively, by the process of variation and selection.[1]   Whether the variations be small and numerous or occasional and extreme may be open to question.   But without variation of one kind or another there can be no selection, and without variation *and* selection there is no progress.   This, in the opinion of the writer, is as true of moral, social, or economic progress as of biological progress.   It is a universal principle applying to every phase of progress.   This is not bringing morality under the laws of biology any more than it is bringing biology under the laws of morality.   It is merely stating as a universal principle, wider than either morality or biology, the method of trial and rejection, variation and selection, as the method of all evolution and of all progress.   The anthropological school of moralists have never gotten beyond the study of moral variations.   What is now needed is a study of moral selection and survival.

One important service, however, the anthropological school of moralists have undoubtedly performed.   They have finally and completely demolished the whole structure

---

[1] It is astonishing how slow the world is to grasp the real significance of Darwin's work.   There were multitudes of theories of evolution, but Darwin first demonstrated *how* it took place.

of intuitionism. No one with a sense of humor can maintain the existence of moral intuitions as unerring guides after reading such a catalogue of moral variations as is compiled by the anthropological school.

The study of moral variations has probably gone as far as it can profitably. It is high time, in order to give value to that study, that some one should make a study of moral *selection*. By a study of moral selection is meant an attempt to find out what moral variations work best and enable a people to flourish, to grow strong, to people the earth and have dominion over it. To study this problem impersonally, without prejudice or bias, is one of the most difficult tasks in the world. Our likes and dislikes thrust themselves into the problem so persistently that it is much harder to preserve a scientific balance than in any other field of inquiry. " What is the use of flourishing, of multiplying, or even of surviving," is constantly asked, " if the conditions of survival are the doing of things which I dislike so strongly ? " " If the hard-working, frugal, mutually helpful community flourishes, if the community with the despised middle-class virtues expands, while the community with high-toned tastes, which cultivates exquisite loquacity, elegant leisure, and a gentlemanly appreciation of literature, art, golf, and whiskey decays, what does that matter to me; I still prefer the latter," is the common objection to this line of study. But it is depressing to think how little human likes and dislikes count in the long run in social evolution. The world will be what it will be whether we like it or not. If our likes and dislikes are such as to unfit us for survival, we shall eventually cease to count. They whose likes and dislikes fit them for survival will continue to count, and the world will eventually be peopled by them, and their likes and dislikes will eventually be selected for survival.

From this point of view, morality and religion, as the organized expression of moral approval and disapproval, must be regarded as factors in the struggle for existence as truly as are weapons for offence and defence, teeth and claws, horns and hoofs, fur and feathers, plumage, beards, and antlers. The social group, community, tribe or nation which develops an unworkable scheme of morality, or within which those social acts which weaken it and unfit it for survival habitually create the sentiment of approval, while those which would strengthen it and enable it to expand habitually create the sentiment of disapproval, will eventually be eliminated. Its habits of approval and disapproval handicap it as really as the possession of two wings on one side with none on the other would handicap a colony of flies. It would be as futile in one case as in the other to argue that one system was just as good as another. These queer social variations are similar to the biological variations commonly called sports.

As suggested above, morality and justice are not matters of likes and dislikes at all. I may dislike exceedingly a scheme of morality which, if universally practiced within a nation, would make that nation the strongest nation on the face of the earth. Yet in spite of my dislike such a nation will become strong, and there is nothing that I can do about it. I may like exceedingly a scheme of morality and an ideal of justice, which, if universally practiced within a nation, would weaken that nation and make it unable to hold its own in the struggle with other nations, yet in spite of my admiration this nation will eventually disappear. To refuse to see this glaring truth is to commit willful self-murder.

Every one is familiar with the intense struggle for existence that is carried on among the trees of the forest. It is asserted that the struggle is so intense and the issue of life and death is so sharply drawn among the young pines of a thicket, that the cutting of an inch from the top of one of them will doom it to ultimate extinction. Even that slight difference puts it at a disadvantage in the struggle for light, and it never regains what was lost, but falls farther and farther behind and is eventually killed by its less unfortunate rivals. Now let us imagine that trees were conscious beings, and capable of evolving systems of morality. Let us suppose further that one set of trees possessed a system of morality which stimulated growth and helped them in the struggle for soil and light, while another set of trees possessed a system of morality which retarded growth and hindered them in the struggle. In each group of trees the sentiment of approval or disapproval would be called forth, but by an entirely different class of acts. In the one case the class of acts which call forth approval help the trees in their struggle for existence. In the other case the class of acts which call forth approval hinder them in this physical struggle. Is there any doubt as to which of these systems of morality would ultimately dominate the forest ? Those trees which happened to possess the system of morality which helped them would survive, and those which happened to possess the system which hindered would perish, and with them would perish their system of morality.[1]

Over against the opinions of the anthropological school of moralists who, as said above, have never got beyond the study of moral variations, we may set such a moral prophet as Thomas Carlyle, who saw far beyond the variations in moral approval, and whose prophetic soul perceived the great principle of moral selection. This stern old Scotchman had small patience with the idea that whatever the people happen to like is good, or whatever they happen to think to be right is right.

Unanimity of voting, — that will do nothing for us if *so*. Your ship cannot double Cape Horn by its excellent plans of voting. The ship may vote this and that, above decks and below, in the most harmoniously exquisitely constitutional manner: the ship, to get around Cape Horn, will find a set of conditions already voted for, and fixed with adamantine rigor by the ancient Elemental Powers, who are entirely careless how you vote. If you can, by voting, or without voting, ascertain these conditions, and valiantly conform to them, you

[1] *The Religion Worth Having*, by the author, Boston, 1912.

will get around the Cape: if you cannot, — the ruffian winds will blow you ever back again; the inexorable icebergs, dumb privy councilors from Chaos, will nudge you with most chaotic " admonition "; you will be flung half-frozen on the Patagonian cliffs, or admonished into shivers by your iceberg councilors, and sent sheer down to Davy Jones, and you will never get round Cape Horn at all! Unanimity on board ship; — yes, indeed, the ship's crew may be very unanimous, which doubtless, for the time being, will be very comfortable to the ship's crew, and to their Phantasm Captain, if they have one: but if the tack they unanimously steer upon is guiding them into the belly of the Abyss, it will not profit them much! — Ships accordingly do not use the ballot-box at all; and they reject the Phantasm species of Captain: one wishes much some other Entities — since all entities lie under the same rigorous set of laws — could be brought to show as much wisdom and sense, at least of self-preservation, the *first* command of Nature. . . .

If a man could shake out of his mind the universal noise of political doctors . . . and consider the matter face to face . . . I venture to say he would find this a very extraordinary method of navigation, whether in the Straits of Magellan or in the undiscovered sea of Time. To prosper in this world, to gain felicity, victory, and improvement, either for a man or a nation, there is but one thing requisite, — that the man or nation can discern what the true regulations of the Universe are in regard to him and his pursuit, and can faithfully and steadfastly follow these.

Carlyle's favorite idea of the absolute certainty of justice in spite of the wrongs of tyrants and the mistakes of democracy accords perfectly with this modern notion of moral variation and selection. However popular an idea of justice may be, if it does not accord with the eternal laws of right and wrong, if it be not in harmony with the order of the universe, it will come to naught. But more specifically, we know, under the operation of Darwin's law of variation and selection, the method by which it will come to naught, namely, it will fail in competition with sounder systems which happen to harmonize a little more closely with the decision of these " ancient Elemental Powers." The scourge of God is prepared for the whipping of the nation which weakens itself. But this scourge is not wielded by invisible hands which work in darkness.

Another writer, who in many respects differed from Carlyle, namely, James Anthony Froude, resembled him in the conception of this great primal moral fact. In his essay on " History as a Science," he asks the question: " What, then, is the use of History and what are its lessons ? . . . First, it is a voice forever sounding across the centuries the laws of right and wrong. Opinions alter, manners change, creeds rise and fall, but the moral law is written on the tablets of eternity. For every false word or unrighteous deed, for cruelty and oppression, for lust or vanity, the price has to be paid at last, not always by the chief offenders, but paid by some one. Justice and truth alone endure and live. Injustice and falsehood may be long-lived, but doomsday comes at last to them, in French revolutions and other terrible ways."

Perhaps it would be better to say that whatever is written on the tablets of eternity *is* the moral law.

Again, in the same essay, the same writer declares: " One lesson, and only one, history may be said to repeat with distinctness; that the world is built somehow on moral foundations; that, in the long run it is well with the good; in the long run it is ill with the wicked."

Instead of saying that history teaches that the world is built on moral foundations, it would be as well to say that whatever history really teaches *is* morality *per se*. That the good *are* they with whom it is well in the long run and the bad are they with whom it is ill in the long run.

But the modern critic asks: Is the world built on moral foundations ? Is there a moral order of the universe ? On the contrary, it is asserted that science is unable to perceive anything resembling a moral order. The difficulty with these queries and contentions is that we fail to get the right point of approach. We are trying to apply *our* sense of approval and disapproval to the laws of the universe, beginning with the assumption, somewhat resembling that of the anthropological school, that whatever we think to be right, or more accurately, whatever creates in us the sensation of approval, is for us right. And then, finding that the universe does not always conform to this principle, that is, the universe does not always create within us the sensation of approval, therefore we are unable to perceive a moral order. In short, since it only means that the universe does not create within us the sense of approval, it does not settle anything; it merely raises the question as to whether it is the universe or our moral sense which is wrong.

If, however, we could get away from this anthropological, as well as from the intuitional viewpoint, and look upon the whole moral problem as a problem of adaptation and adjustment, we should reach a different conclusion. The ultimate problem of any variety of life, including the human race, is that of adjustment to the material universe. All other problems are subordinate to that, and all values are derived from their relation to this ultimate problem. Anything which facilitates the adjustment of man to the universe is, for man, good. Anything which hinders that process of adjustment is, for him, bad. Any class of actions which help in this process of adjustment *ought* to create in us the sensation of approval whether they do or not, and any class of actions which hinder in this process *ought* to create the sensation of disapproval whether they do or not. Otherwise there is no room for the existence of moral sentiment. That is the function of the moral sentiments and they are abortive when they fail in that function. From this point of view it would be silly to ask is there a moral order of the universe, for whatever the order of the universe happens to be, that *is* the moral order. Instead of saying that nature is non-moral or that science is unable to discover a moral order in the universe, we should say that nature is the final authority on morality, and our opinions, likes and dislikes, approvals and disapprovals, must be modified to suit that final authority. That nature is non-moral or that the scientist is unable to discover anything resembling a moral order is virtually to say that nature does not seem to conform to our preconceived notions of morality, or that the scientist is unable to discover in the order of the universe anything resembling what he has been taught to regard as the moral order.

If one had been taught a peculiar system of hygiene and afterwards discovered that nature seemed to pay very little attention to his system, he might then say that nature was non-hygienic, that nature did not know anything about physiology, or that science was unable to discover a hygienic order of the universe, all of which of course would be extremely silly. It would not, however, be one whit less silly to say that nature knows nothing of morality. If we once perceive that morality is merely social hygiene, and that anything is moral which works well for society in the long run, which prolongs its life and enables it to grow and flourish and hold its own in competition with other societies, and beat out all those which are organized on immoral bases, we should no more think of questioning the moral order of the universe than we now do of questioning the hygienic order. We should then say frankly that whatever the order of the universe is, that, *per se*, is the moral order, likes and dislikes, approvals and disapprovals to the contrary notwithstanding. We should then say that whatever social customs and conventions are found to fit into the order of the universe, and whatever private conduct is found to permanently strengthen the social group, that is *per se* morality.

This view agrees with that of the intuitionist in that it assumes that there is a moral order.   It differs in that it denies that this moral order is intuitively understood.   We must discover the moral order by experience and observation, precisely as we discover the hygienic order.   This happens also to be consistent with the highest form of religious thought which the world possesses today.   The most thorough-going religionist is he who believes that the universe is not only created by the divine will, but is momentarily recreated by the perpetually creative activity of that will; that all the phenomena of nature, so-called, are merely manifestations of divine activity; that, like the moving picture which is reproduced on the screen rather infrequently, but frequently enough to deceive the physical eye, so the material universe is recreated by the divine creative energy every mathematical instant of time, so frequently, in other words, as to deceive the mental eye and create the illusion of permanency.   " Therefore the observed uniformities commonly called natural laws are merely the observed uniformities of the operation of the divine will; that the moral laws, like the laws of nature, are the expressions of that continuously creative activity; that the laws of natural selection are identical with the laws of divine approval; and that the process of exterminating the unfit or the unadapted is only the manifestation of divine disapproval." [1]

But whether one be a religionist of this most thoroughgoing kind or a thorough-going materialist who sees nothing back of the physical processes, and regards the universe

[1] *The Religion Worth Having,* pp. 83–85.

only as a huge impersonal machine, grinding out its impersonal results without rhyme or reason, one's conclusion must be very much the same, namely, that they who conform to the machine, or to the divinely guided universe, will get on and flourish, and they who do not conform will perish and disappear. In either case that which will be, will be. Instead of saying, therefore, that whatever is, is right, which would carry with it the conclusion that whatever was, was right, we should say that whatever inevitably tends to be is right, for the right is that which inevitably tends to be under the laws of variation and selection.

Again, a new interpretation is put upon the dictum that that is right which is capable of becoming universal. Instead of interpreting this to mean that that is right which we with our present likes and dislikes, approvals and disapprovals, would like to see made universal, we must interpret it to mean that that is right which is capable of making itself universal whether we like it or not, of winning out in the struggle with other conceptions of right, and of forcing itself upon the world by the sure process of selection which, as indicated above, is the only method by which progress takes place.

The foregoing argument has been designed to show that the duties and obligations of the state, while they may be derived from the expressed will of the people, are not finally determined by that expressed will. While it would probably be inexpedient to say that the state should act contrary to the expressed will of the mass of the people, for that involves a very different question, it is at the same time false and dangerous in the extreme to say that whatever the state does in harmony with the supposed will of the people must *per se* be right.

This raises, of course, the question as to which is the safest method of finding out what is right and what is wrong for the state to do. If the mass of the people are less likely to be mistaken than any individual, such as the king, or any small aristocratic group which might be selected, then as a practical expedient the state should follow the will of the people; that is to say, it is less likely to do wrong if it follows this guide than if it follows any other that, humanly speaking, can be designed. Nevertheless the point must be insisted upon with the clearest emphasis that, though the will of the people may be the safest guide, still even that guide may fail and the state may be going directly toward perdition while following this guide implicitly. The only comfort would be that if it followed any other guide it would head toward perdition with still greater certainty.

Another variation of the same general theory is found in the doctrine that the closest possible approximation to practical justice is to be found in the general trend of judicial decisions as they are given out in the actual adjudication of conflicting interests. This may mean that the probability of error is less when we follow this general trend of expert opinion as given out by men who are charged with the task of administering justice than when we follow any other guide. That is reasonable, but it leaves undecided the question as to what nation to choose as the basis of study. The judiciary of our country does not always agree with that of another, and the general trend of judicial opinion will depend somewhat upon the country, or the judicial system, selected as authoritative. On the other hand, it may mean that the general trend of judicial opinion is the embodiment of the mature and enduring opinions and sentiments of the people on matters of justice. Admitting this to be true, the question still remains, are the mature and enduring opinions and sentiments of the people at large necessarily sound on such questions ? This would be answered in the affirmative both by the intuitionist and the anthropological schools. The former would say that since every man has an intuitive knowledge of right and wrong, at least in their general aspects, therefore in the universal opinions and abiding sentiments of mankind we necessarily have a criterion of what is right and what is wrong in the settlement of conflicting interests, that is, in matters of justice. But the anthropological school would deny that there are any universal opinions or abiding sentiments as to what is right and wrong, in this or any other field, thus destroying the basis for the intuitionist's conclusion. The present writer agrees with the anthropological school on this point.

But the anthropological moralist would say that there is no such thing as a universal principle of justice, that that is just in any one nation which that nation, in the mass, unites in approving, and that unjust which it unites in disapproving. Therefore, if one can find out what are the matured and enduring opinions and sentiments of any nation with respect to justice, one has found out all there is to be known about justice for that nation. Since judicial opinion is the best expression of those matured and enduring opinions and sentiments, it is only necessary to study these decisions. The present writer cannot agree with this opinion, believing that even the matured and enduring sentiments of a whole nation on the subject of justice may be wrong.

It may be argued, however, that where a nation is actually progressing, where it is improving its material condition, where its people are uniformly satisfied with the treatment they receive, where the arts and sciences are advancing, and all the other earmarks of genuine progress are present, there is a strong presumption in favor of the proposition that justice prevails. Justice is that system of adjusting conflicting interests which makes the group strong and progressive rather than weak and retrogressive whereas injustice is a system of adjusting conflicting interests which makes a nation weak and retrogressive rather than strong and progressive. But there are other factors besides justice and injustice. With a new and rich continent to exploit, with untold natural resources waiting to be developed, a nation may be rich and prosperous, for a time, and its people uniformly well satisfied with the situation, in spite of many injustices. Therefore, while growth in power, national progress and general satisfaction create a presumption that justice exists, this presumption falls far short of proof. If one could once be certain that practical justice did actually prevail in a nation, one would then be justified in assuming that the trend of judicial opinion would give him the principles of ideal justice. But this amounts very nearly to saying that if one is certain that judicial decisions are just he can then find out from these decisions what justice is. This means virtually that if one assumes that judicial decisions are, in the main, just, one has already assumed the thing which one is starting out to discover.

There probably never was a time when the people who had their way did not think they were progressing. They have always thought that the step which they have decreed was a step of progress, yet when viewed in a historical perspective we are now able to see that they have frequently gone wrong, and what they thought was progress was retrogression. Yet from the standpoint of the anthropological school we have no right to raise this question. If the steps they were taking created within them the sensation of approval those steps were right and proper, and nothing

else is involved. From the point of view here outlined, however, if the steps they were taking were, in Carlyle's language, " leading them into the belly of the abyss," they
were not progressing but retrograding. *The purpose of this
work is not, therefore, to find what political steps are necessary
in order to satisfy our likes and dislikes, our sentiment of
justice, or to create within us the sensation of approval; but to
find out what political and social acts will facilitate our adjustment to the material universe in which we find ourselves, and
make our society a strong rather than a weak society.*

This is the problem of the student. We must then trust
to the preacher of righteousness to create such mental and
spiritual conditions within the people as to enable these acts
which facilitate the process of adaptation to create the
sentiment of approval, and those which hinder adaptation
to create the sentiment of disapproval among the people.
The dictum " Righteousness exalteth a nation " means,
from this point of view, that whatever in the long run exalts
a nation *is* righteousness, and the purpose of the preacher of
righteousness is to adjust the sentiments of the people to
this fact, so that very class of acts which actually exalt and
build up a nation shall create the sensation of approval in
their minds, and every class of acts which make for weakness
and degeneracy shall create the sensation of disapproval and
indignation. It is only by this process that our people and
our civilization shall eventually prove their fitness for survival, or that we can ever justify our claim to be the chosen
people. Who are the chosen people is not a historical
question. It is a question of fact, adaptation, and survival.
What is the true church will never be determined by
archaeological and historical investigation. It will be
determined by the laws of selection and survival. What is
the true system of morality, will never be determined by the

test of popular approval, but we shall determine whether the popular mind is sound or not by waiting to see whether the things which the popular mind approves work or not, whether they make our people the strongest people in the struggle for survival.

What ought the state to do ?   What ought the people to approve in the way of social control ?   What schemes of social control, what social institutions, what systems of economic organization, production, distribution *ought* to meet the approval of the masses of the people ?   This is the real question of social justice, not what *do* the people actually approve, or what would the reader or the writer or any one else *like* to see in the way of a social system.   Self-preservation has become the first law of nature for the state rather than for the individual.   Justice is an essential part of the program of self-preservation.   But we must not delude ourselves into thinking that the state which does that which creates the sensation of approval within us will, in some inscrutable way, be preserved.   Rather must we labor to discover what will preserve the state and then train our consciences to approve that.   If we do otherwise we shall ourselves be involved as individuals in the destruction which overwhelms the state of which we are a part.

> " For the strength of the pack is the wolf
> And the strength of the wolf is the pack."

Lest this should be misinterpreted as a glorification of militarism, the author wishes to point out that, in the long run, any nation which develops militarism beyond that which is necessary to defend its territory against actual invasion, or its commerce against actual destruction, weakens rather than strengthens itself.   But in our advocacy of peace we must not forget that it is national suicide not to be able to defend ourselves, so long as there are international bullies abroad in the world. There is no reason for believing that the Attillas, the Genghis Khans, the Tamerlanes, and the Napoleons have all disappeared from the world. In order to be strong, therefore, it is essential, first and primarily, that as much of our energy as possible shall be directed, and directed as intelligently as possible, toward productive ends, and secondarily, that as much energy shall be put into the military arm of the nation as is necessary for purposes of actual defence. But on this point we must not be too economical. To err on the side of too much preparation for defence means, at most, only a moderate financial loss. To err on the side of too little may mean national death. To err on the side of sybaritism, either material or spiritual, that is, on the side of too little production and too much seeking of pleasure, either physical or spiritual, leads certainly to death. " For strait is the gate and narrow is the way that leads to eternal life " for a nation as well as for an individual.

It is as necessary to be careful in defining strength as in defining goodness. That is strength which in the end brings survival. That is weakness which in the end brings extermination.

That the meek shall inherit the earth is probably a scientific statement. It means that the unmeek, the proud, the haughty, shall be exterminated. If so it will be precisely because meekness, that is teachableness and willingness to mind one's own business, is strength, while pride and vanity are weaknesses.

If meekness is strength it is precisely because it is a quality which makes a strong nation when it is possessed by all its citizens. If pride and vanity are weaknesses, it is precisely because they make a weak nation when they characterize the citizens.

When the superman of our own wild west rode into a cow town to attempt one of his Gargantuan stunts, and began by announcing that he was a bad man and was looking for trouble, — that he was half horse and half alligator and ate people alive, — or that he was a mean hog and didn't care where he rooted, — he was promptly hanged to a telegraph pole by the quiet and peaceable citizens who did not want to have their business of branding calves and selling steers interfered with. It was precisely because they were quiet and peaceable, and attending to the important business of raising cattle, that the community grew strong. If they had all been of the superman type, the community would have been weak, because neither cattle-raising nor any other useful, strength-sustaining occupation could have flourished.

" Only by pride cometh contention," said the wise man. A proud and contentious spirit, either in an individual or a nation, creates enemies. It is not prosperity but ostentation which creates enmity against the prosperous; it is not power, but swaggering, which creates hatred against the powerful. The meek will become not only rich and powerful, but, so long as they retain their qualities of meekness and usefulness, they make friends rather than enemies, and that adds to their strength and prosperity. They who are rich in goods, but poor in spirit, who are powerful for war, but meek and gentle in spirit, they of whom it can be said, " In thee shall all the nations of the earth be blest," stand the best chance, so far as one is now able to see, of inheriting the earth. The wise man also said, " After pride cometh shame," and " Pride goeth before destruction and a haughty spirit before a fall."

However, it is the present purpose, merely to affirm that virtue and strength are identical, and that strength is not to be defined according to some of our own perverse notions, but according to its ability to make itself universal.

CHAPTER II

THE ULTIMATE BASIS OF SOCIAL CONFLICT[1]

SINCE justice has been defined as a principle for the adjustment of conflicting interests among men, our first problem is to examine the nature of this conflict of interests and inquire into its ultimate source. The thesis which we shall try to expand in this chapter is that the ultimate basis of all social conflict is found in economic scarcity of one form or another. Around this fact of economic scarcity with its inevitable conflict of interests are grouped practically all our moral ideals, our social, political, and legal institutions. Moreover, it is the basis of all real values whether they be classified as economic, moral or aesthetic.

Whatever else it may mean in art or morals there is no doubt whatever that in economics the word value means power in exchange. Be it understood that power in exchange is not the same as a ratio of exchange. Power in exchange implies motivation, control over human conduct, the ability to call forth expenditures of energy, — to direct human enterprise, to influence human choices. Value is the *power* which an article or a service possesses of commanding other desirable things in peaceful and voluntary exchange. Why a thing has this power is the first problem in the study of economic value.

Whether it be universally agreed to or not, it is none the less true that utility and scarcity, and these alone, are

[1] The substance of this chapter has previously appeared in an article in the *Harvard Theological Review*, vol. i, no. 1.

necessary to give value to a thing which is capable of being transferred, whether that thing be a commodity or a service. If it is *both* useful and scarce it will have value, and it will have value under no other conditions whatever. By utility is meant power to satisfy a want. Whether that want be fundamental or trivial, wholesome or pernicious, does not matter so far as commercial value or power in exchange is concerned. The proposition that utility, or the power to satisfy a want, is essential to value becomes sufficiently obvious when it is translated into the proposition that nothing has economic value unless somebody wants it. Moreover, nothing has moral value unless somebody needs it. Where wants and needs coincide, economic and moral values are identical.

By scarcity is meant insufficiency to satisfy wants. However abundant a thing may be, speaking absolutely, if there is not as much as is wanted in any time and place it may be said to be scarce in that time and place; and however rare it may be, speaking absolutely, if there is as much as is wanted, or more, it cannot be said to be scarce. The proposition that scarcity is essential to value becomes sufficiently obvious when it in turn is translated into the proposition that a thing has no value when everybody has as much as or more than he wants of it. At this point we may distinguish between rarity and scarcity. Mosquitoes may be said to be rare in the winter time, but cannot accurately be said to be scarce since nobody wants any more than there are. On the other hand, grass can hardly be said to be rare in the summer time, and yet if there is less than the cattle growers want it may be said to be scarce and that is why it has value. To sum up, whenever and wherever people want a thing and want more of it than they have got, they will be willing to give something in exchange for it, or make some sacrifice in order to get it. It will therefore possess value or power in exchange, and it will possess value under no other conditions whatever. It will have a positive influence in directing human enterprise, in determining human choice, in supplying human motives to conduct. So much by way of definition.

The question, Why do things have the power to satisfy wants ? would lead us back through physiology and psychology quite to the borders of the unknowable. The question, Why are they scarce ? would lead us also toward the unknowable, but by a somewhat different route. Into this philosophical hinterland of his science the economist has generally refrained from bursting lest he should be found poaching upon the preserves of the philosopher; but there are some things in this region which, when seen through the eyes of the economist, may come to have a new significance.

Of course the first and most obvious reason for the scarcity of goods is that nature has not provided them in sufficient abundance to satisfy all the people who want them in the time and place where they are wanted. Of some things, it is true, she is bounteous in her supply; but of others she is niggardly especially in certain times and places. Things which are so bountifully supplied as to satisfy all who want them do not figure as wealth, or economic goods, because we do not need to economize in their use. But things which are scantily supplied must be meted out and made to go as far as possible. That is what it means to economize. Because we must practice economy with respect to them they are called economic goods or wealth. Toward other things our habitual attitude is a non-economic one, but toward this class of things it is distinctly economic. In fact the whole economic system of society, the whole system of production, of valuation, of exchange, of distribution, and of consumption, is concerned with this class of goods — toward increasing their supply and making the existing supply go as far as possible in the satisfaction of wants.

The fact that there are human wants for whose satisfaction nature does not provide in sufficient abundance — in other words, the fact of scarcity — signifies that man is, to that extent at least, out of harmony with nature. The desire for fuel, clothing, and shelter, grows out of the fact that the climate is more severe than our bodies are fitted to endure, and this alone argues a very considerable lack of harmony. The lack is only emphasized by the fact that it is necessary for us to labor and endure fatigue in order to provide ourselves with these means of protecting our bodies against the rigors of nature. That labor also which is expended in the production of food means nothing if not that there are more mouths to be fed, in certain regions at least, than nature has herself provided for. She must therefore be subjugated, and compelled to yield larger returns than she is willing to do of her own accord. And that expanding multitude of desires, appetites, and passions which drive us as with whips; which send us to the ends of the earth after gewgaws with which to bedeck our bodies, and after new means of tickling the five senses; which make us strive to outshine our neighbors, or at least not to be outshone by them — these even more than our normal wants show how widely we have fallen out of any natural harmony which may supposedly have existed in the past.

That there is a deeper harmony lying hidden somewhere beneath these glaring disharmonies is quite possible. Certainly no one can positively assert that it is not so. It may be true, as some profoundly believe, that these natural discomforts, with the necessity for work which accompanies them, furnish a discipline which is necessary for our highest good. Being thus driven by a *vis a tergo* toward our own highest good, we may be in harmony with our surroundings in ways which do not appear to our immediate sense of self-interest. But this whole question lies within the field of philosophical conjecture, and nothing positive can be affirmed on either side.

Our leaning toward a theory of a deep-lying harmony is easy enough so long as we contemplate only the civilized races of the temperate zones. They are obviously better off than the tropical races, which are *apparently* less out of harmony with their environment. But our faith is likely to receive a shock when we contemplate the hyperboreans. They, if any, are under the chastening hand of nature; they, if any, are driven by hard necessity; if discipline is what men need, they have it; and yet they do not progress according to any standard which we can understand. Even the comparison of the races of the temperate zone with those of the tropics lends doubtful support to the theory, because it is by no means certain that there is any less conflict between man and nature in the tropics than elsewhere. The climate is milder, it is true, and nature is more profuse in her supply of food; but she is also more profuse in the supply of living enemies of man, and living enemies, especially the invisible ones, are quite as dangerous and as difficult to guard against as inhospitable weather. Saying nothing of beasts of prey and venomous creatures, the hook worm, the mosquito, and the divers sorts of harmful bacteria all imperil the lives of the dwellers in the tropics quite as much as the east winds do the lives of our New Englanders. While these tropical enemies are as dangerous, they are even more difficult to guard against than those with which we have to contend. The amount of intelligence which is required to see the necessity of clothing and shelter in our climate is small as compared with that which was required to see the necessity of exterminating the mosquito, to take a single illustration, in the fever-haunted tropics. On the whole, therefore, it would be quite as easy to maintain the thesis that the civilized races are less out of harmony with their natural environment than the uncivilized races — in other words, that the most civilized races occupy those parts of the globe where the necessity for work is least — as it would be to maintain the opposite thesis. If that thesis be sound, the theory of a deep-lying harmony between man and nature could scarcely stand. The truth probably is that the more civilized races occupy those regions where the advantages to be gotten by work are most obvious to the average intelligence. This leaves us without any light whatever upon the question of an underlying harmony.

Whatever our belief upon that point may be, there is not the slightest doubt that men are sometimes cold and hungry and sick; and that these discomforts would be much more frequent than they now are, if men did not work to prevent them. But work causes fatigue. Obviously the individual cannot be expected to see in this situation any sign of a complete harmony between himself and his material environment. So far as the individual can see and understand, the lack of harmony between himself and nature is a very real one.

Viewed from this standpoint, the whole economic struggle becomes an effort to attain to a harmony which does not naturally exist. As is well known, the characteristic difference between the non-economizing animals, on the one hand, and man, the economizer, on the other, is that in the process of adaptation the animals are passively adapted to their environment, whereas man assumes the active rôle in attempting to adapt his environment to himself. If the climate is cold, animals must develop fur or blubber; but man builds fires, constructs shelters, and manufactures clothing.   If there are enemies to fight against, the animals must develop claws or fangs, horns or hoofs, whereas man makes bows and arrows, or guns and ammunition.   The whole evolutionary process, both passive and active, both biological and economic, is a development away from less toward greater adaptation, from less toward greater harmony between the species and its environment.

That phase of the disharmony between man and nature which takes the form of scarcity gives rise also to a disharmony between man and man.   Where there is scarcity there will be two men wanting the same thing; and where two men want the same thing there is an antagonism of interests.   Where there is an antagonism of interests between man and man there will be questions to be settled, questions of right and wrong, of justice and injustice; and these questions could not arise under any other condition. The antagonism of interests is, in other words, what gives rise to a moral problem, and it is, therefore, about the most fundamental fact in sociology and moral philosophy.

This does not overlook the fact that there are many harmonies between man and man, as there are between man and nature.   There may be innumerable cases where all human interests harmonize, but these give rise to no problem and therefore we do not need to concern ourselves with them.   As already pointed out, there are many cases where man and nature are in complete harmony.   There are things, for example, which nature furnishes in sufficient abundance to satisfy all our wants; but these also give rise to no problem.   Toward these non-economic goods our habitual attitude is one of indifference or unconcern. Where the relations between man and nature are perfect, why should we concern ourselves about them ? But the whole industrial world is bent on improving those relations where they are imperfect. Similarly with the relations between man and man; where they are perfect, that is, where interests are all harmonious, why should we concern ourselves about them ? As a matter of fact we do not. But where they are imperfect, where interests are antagonistic and trouble is constantly arising, we are compelled to concern ourselves whether we want to or not. As a matter of fact, we do concern ourselves in various ways; we work out systems of moral philosophy and theories of justice, after much disputation; we establish tribunals where, in the midst of much wrangling, some of these theories are applied to the settlement of actual conflicts; we talk and argue interminably about the proper adjustment of antagonistic interests of various kinds, all of which, it must be remembered, grow out of the initial fact of scarcity — the fact that there are not as many things as people want.

That underneath all these disharmonies between man and man there is a deep underlying harmony of human interests is the profound belief of some. But this belief, like that in a harmony between man and nature, is not susceptible of a positive support. It rests upon philosophical conjecture — and faith. To be sure, it is undoubtedly true that most men, even the strongest, are better off in the long run under a just government, where all their conflicts are accurately and wisely adjudicated, than they would be in a state of anarchy, where every one who was able did what he pleased, and what he could if he was not able to do what he pleased. This might possibly be construed to imply a harmony of interests, in that all alike, the strong as well as the weak, are interested in maintaining a just government. But the argument is violently paradoxical, because it literally means that interests are so very antagonistic that, in the absence of a government to hold them in check, there would be such a multiplicity of conflicts, wasting the energies of society, that in the end everybody even the strongest, would suffer. This is an excellent argument in favor of the necessity of government, but it is the poorest kind of an argument in favor of the universal harmony of human interests.

Fundamentally, therefore, there are only two practical problems imposed upon us. The one is industrial and the other moral; the one has to do with the improvement of the relations between man and nature, and the other with the improvement of the relations between man and man. But these two primary problems are so inextricably inter-mingled, and they deal with such infinitely varying factors, that the secondary and tertiary problems are more than we can count.

But whence arises that phase of the conflict with nature out of which grows the conflict between man and man ? Is man in any way responsible for it, or is it due wholly to the harshness or the niggardliness of nature ? The fruitful-ness of nature varies, of course, in different environments. But in any environment there are two conditions, for both of which man is in a measure responsible, and either of which will result in economic scarcity. One is the indefinite expan-sion of human wants, and the other is the multiplication of numbers.

The well-known expansive power of human wants, con-tinually running beyond the power of nature to satisfy, has attracted the attention of moralists in all times and places. " When goods increase, they are increased that eat them: and what good is there to the owners thereof, saving the beholding of them with their eyes ? " is the point of view of The Preacher. It was the same aspect of life, obviously throwing man out of harmony with nature, which gave point to the Stoic's principle of " living according to nature." To live according to nature would necessarily mean, among other things, to keep desires within such limits as nature could supply without too much coercion. Seeing that the best things in life cost nothing, and that the most ephemeral pleasures are the most expensive, there would appear to be much economic wisdom in the Stoic philosophy. But the pious Buddhist, in his quest of Nirvana, overlooking the real point — that the expansion of wants beyond nature's power to satisfy is what throws man inevitably out of harmony with nature and produces soul-killing conflicts — sees in desire itself the source of evil, and seeks release in the eradication of all desire.

Out of the view that the conflict of man with nature is a source of evil grow two widely different practical conclusions as to social conduct. If we assume that external nature is beneficent and that man is at fault, the conclusion follows as a matter of course that desires must be curbed and brought into harmony with nature, which is closely akin to Stoicism, if it be not its very essence. But if, on the contrary, we assume that human nature is sound, then the only practical conclusion is that external nature must be coerced into harmony with man's desires and made to yield more and more for their satisfaction. This is the theory of the modern industrial spirit in its wild pursuit of wealth and luxury.

Even if the wants of the individual never expanded at all, it is quite obvious that an indefinite increase in the number of individuals in any locality would, sooner or later, result in scarcity and bring them into conflict with nature, and therefore into conflict with one another. That human populations are physiologically capable of indefinite increase, if time be allowed, is admitted, and must be admitted by any one who has given the slightest attention to the subject. Among the non-economizing animals and plants, it is not the limits of their procreative power, but the limits of subsistence, which determine their numbers. Neither is it lack of procreative power which limits numbers in the case of man, the economic animal. With him also it is a question of subsistence, but of subsistence according to some standard. Being gifted with economic foresight, he will not multiply beyond the point where he can maintain that standard of life which he considers decent. *But* — and this is to be especially noted — so powerful are his procreative and domestic instincts that he *will* multiply up to the point where it is *difficult* to maintain whatever standard he has. Whether his standard of living be high or low to begin with, the multiplication of numbers will be carried to the point where he is in danger of being forced down to a lower standard. In other words, it will always be hard for us to make as good a living as we think we ought to have. Unsatisfied desires, or economic scarcity, which means the same thing, are therefore inevitable. It is a condition from which there is no possible escape. The cause lies deeper than forms of social organization; it grows out of the relation of man to nature.

These considerations reveal a third form of conflict — perhaps it ought to be called the second — a conflict of interests within the individual himself. If the procreative and domestic instincts are freely gratified, there will inevitably result a scarcity of means of satisfying other desires, however modest those desires may be, through the multiplication of numbers. If an abundance of these things is to be assured, those instincts must be only partially satisfied. Either horn of the dilemma leaves us with unsatisfied desires of one kind or another. We are therefore pulled in two directions, and this also is a condition from which there is no possible escape. But this is only one illustration of the internal strife which tears the individual. The very fact of scarcity means necessarily that if one desire is satisfied it is at the expense of some other. What I spend for luxuries I cannot spend for necessaries; what I spend for clothing I cannot spend for food; and what I spend for one kind of food I cannot spend for some other. This is the situation which calls for economy, since to economize is merely to choose what desires shall be gratified, knowing that certain others must, on that account, remain ungratified. Economy always and everywhere means a threefold conflict; a conflict between man and nature, between man and man, and between the different interests of the same man.

This suggests the twofold nature of the problem of evil. Evil in the broadest sense merely means disharmony, since any kind of disharmony is a source of pain to somebody. But that form of disharmony which arises between man and nature has, in itself, no moral qualities. It is an evil to be cold or hungry, to have a tree fall upon one, to be devoured by a wild beast or wasted by microbes. But to evils of this kind, unless they are in some way the fault of other men, we never ascribe any moral significance whatever. It is also an evil for one man to rob another, or to cheat him, or in any way to injure him through carelessness or malice, and we do ascribe a moral significance to evils of this kind — to any evil, in fact, which grows out of the relations of man with man. But, as already pointed out, this latter form of evil — in other words, moral evil — grows out of, or results from, the former which may be called non-moral evil. Any true account of the origin of moral evil must therefore begin with the disharmony between man and nature.

Let us imagine a limited number of individuals living in a very favorable environment, where all their wants could be freely and fully gratified, that is, where there was no scarcity nor any need for economy. Under a harmony with nature so nearly perfect as this, there could arise none of those conflicts of interests within the individual, since the gratification of one desire would never be at the expense of any other; nor could there arise any conflict of interests among individuals, since the gratification of one individual's desire would never prevent the gratification of another's. There being no conflict of interests either within the individual or among different individuals, there could never arise a moral problem. That would be paradise. But suppose that wants should expand, or new wants develop; or suppose that, through the gratification of an elemental impulse, numbers should increase beyond any provision which nature had made. Paradise would be lost. Not only would labor and fatigue be necessary, but an antagonism of interests and a moral problem would arise. Human ingenuity would have to be directed, not only toward the problem of increasing the productivity of the earth, but toward the problem of adjusting conflicting interests. Questions of justice and equity would begin to puzzle men's brains.

It would be difficult to find in this illustration any suggestion of original sin or hereditary taint of any kind. The act which made for increase of numbers, instead of being a sinful one, for which punishment was meted out as a matter of justice, would, on the contrary, be as innocent of moral guilt as any other. But *the inevitable consequence* of it would be the destruction of the pre-existing harmony, giving rise, in turn, to a conflict of human interests. Nor does the illustration suggest or imply any " fall " or change in human nature, but rather a change of conditions under which the same human qualities would produce different social results. Moreover, the illustration does not depend for its validity upon its historical character; that is to say, it is not necessary to show that there ever was a harmony between man and nature so nearly complete as the illustration assumes to begin with. The fundamental basis of conflict is clearly enough revealed by the illustration when it is shown to be inherent in the nature of man and of the material world about him.

This theory of the origin of evil is already embodied in a well-known story, which need not be interpreted as having a historical basis in order to have a profound meaning — more profound, probably, than its most reverent students have seen in it. Once upon a time there was a garden in which lived a man and woman, all of whose wants were supplied by the spontaneous fruits of the earth. There was no struggle for existence, no antagonism of interests; in short that was paradise. But the gratification of a certain desire brought increase of numbers, increase of numbers brought scarcity, and paradise was lost. Thenceforward man was to eat his bread in the sweat of his brow. The struggle for existence had set in. Man had to contend against either natural or human rivals for the means of satisfying his wants, and every form of greed and rapacity had a potential existence. When his eyes were opened to these inherent antagonisms, that is, when he became a discerner of good and evil, of advantages and disadvantages, both near and remote, he became an economic being, an adapter of means to ends, a chooser between pleasures and pains. In short, the process of industrial civilization, of social evolution, had made its first faint beginning. The human race was caught in a network of forces from which it was never to extricate itself. It was adrift upon a current which set irresistibly outward — no man knew whither.

In this antagonism of interests, growing out of scarcity, the institutions of property, of the family, and of the state, all have their common origin. No one, for example, thinks of claiming property in anything which exists in sufficient abundance for all. But when there is not enough to go around, each unit of the supply becomes a prize for somebody, and there would be a general scramble, did not society itself undertake to determine to whom each unit should belong. Possession, of course, is not property; but when society recognizes one's right to a thing, and undertakes to protect him in that right, that is property. Wherever society is sufficiently organized to recognize these rights and to afford them some measure of protection, there is a state; and there is a family wherever there is a small group within which the ties of blood and kinship are strong enough to overcome any natural rivalry and to create a unity of interests. This unity of economic interests within the family group is sufficient to separate it from the rest of the world, or from other similar groups among which the natural rivalry of interests persists. Saying nothing of the barbaric notion that wives and children are themselves property, even in the higher types of society it is the desire to safeguard those to whom one is bound by ties of natural affection, by sharing the advantages of property with them, which furnishes the basis for the legal definition of the family group.

Closely associated with the right of property — as parts of it in fact — is a group of rights such as that of contract, of transfer, of bequest, and a number of other things with which lawyers occupy themselves. It would be difficult to find any question in the whole science of jurisprudence, or of ethics, or politics, or any of the social sciences for that

CEDAR CREST COLLEGE
LIBRARY

matter, which does not grow out of the initial fact of economic scarcity and the consequent antagonism of interests among men. This reveals, as nothing else can, the underlying unity of all the social sciences, that is, of all the sciences which have to do with the relations between man and man; and it shows very clearly that the unifying principle is an economic one. Even the so-called gregarious instinct may very probably be the product of the struggle for existence, which, in turn, is the product of scarcity — the advantage of acting in groups being the selective agency in the development of this instinct. But that question, like a great many others, lies beyond the field of positive knowledge. This does not necessarily constitute economics as the "master science," with the other social sciences subordinate to it; but it does signify that, if there is such a thing as a master science, economics has the first claim to that position among the social sciences. The economic problem is the fundamental one, out of which all other social and moral problems have grown.

Though it lies somewhat beyond the scope of the present paper, it would be interesting, nevertheless, to follow up our conclusion with an examination of the possibilities of escape from the situation which is imposed upon us by economic scarcity. The method of stoicism, or the repression of desires, now going under the name of " the simple life," and of industrialism or the multiplication of goods, have already been mentioned. Complete escape, by either of these methods, seems to be cut off, in the first place by the refusal of desires, especially the elementary ones, to be repressed, and, in the second place, by the utter impossibility of increasing goods to a point which will provide for every possible increase in population when population is unchecked by economic motives. If economic motives continue to operate as a check upon population, that is in itself an evidence of continued scarcity.   But if they do not operate, and the procreative instincts are given free play, there is absolutely no limit to the increase of population.   Any one who has ever been initiated into the mysteries of geometrical progression will not entertain the slightest doubt on this point.

But even under the conditions of economic scarcity there would be no antagonism of interests between man and man if human nature were to undergo a change by which altruism were to replace egoism.   If I could develop the capacity to enjoy food upon my neighbor's palate as well as upon my own, as I have already developed the capacity to enjoy it upon the palates of my children, and if my neighbor could develop a like regard for me, obviously there could be no antagonism of interests between us on the subject of food.   Let this capacity become universal, and the moral problem would be solved.   That would be the Christian's Millennium.   Whether this way of escape lies open or not, in other words, whether such a change in human nature is possible or not, is a problem for the psychologist or the religionist.   Support for the affirmative of that question comes from a somewhat unexpected quarter, namely, from the writings of the late Mr. Herbert Spencer, who must be classed among the premillenarians.   The closing words of his *Principles of Sociology*, which are, in fact, the final conclusion of his whole system of Synthetic Philosophy, are as follows: . . .   " On the one hand, by continual repression of aggressive instincts and exercise of feelings which prompt ministration to public welfare, and on the other hand, by the lapse of restraints, gradually becoming less necessary, there must be produced a kind of man so constituted that while fulfilling his own desires he fulfils also the social needs. . . . Long studies, showing among other things the need for certain qualifications above indicated, but also revealing facts like that just named, have not caused me to recede from the belief expressed nearly fifty years ago that — ' The ultimate man will be one whose private requirements coincide with public ones. He will be that manner of man who, in spontaneously fulfilling his own nature, incidentally performs the functions of a social unit; and yet is only enabled so to fulfil his own nature by all others doing the like.' "

This conclusion differs from that of the ordinary premillenarian only in the method by which the end is to be reached. According to Mr. Spencer's argument, it is not to be by evangelization, but by the sterner process of exterminating the unsocial and preserving the social elements in the population, until the whole population is made over into a new type. The execution and imprisonment of criminals, thus preventing them from breeding more of their own kind, undoubtedly work in this direction, but they leave us a long way short of the goal. That we may approach it indefinitely seems reasonable, but that it is ever attainable, either by the method of biological evolution or of evangelization, or by both combined, is by no means a foregone conclusion. It is certainly a long way off. Meanwhile what are we to do ?

We may escape from some of the worst features of the situation by working along several lines at the same time. Every improvement in the arts of production, whereby a given quantity of labor is enabled to produce a larger quantity of the means of satisfying wants, tends, of course, in some degree to alleviate scarcity. If this can be supplemented by the doctrine of the simple life, made effective especially in the lives of the wealthier classes, so much the better; for then there will be fewer wants to satisfy. If this result can be still further strengthened by a rising sense of the responsibilities of parenthood, whereby the reckless spawning of population can be checked, especially among those classes who can least afford to spawn, the discrepancy between numbers and provisions will be kept at a minimum. Again, a more widespread spirit of altruism, or even a milder and more enlightened egoism such as that which moves the farmer to take delight in the sleek appearance of his horses, or the English landlord to take pride in the comfortable appearance of his tenants and cotters, would go a long way toward softening the antagonism of interests among men.

In spite of all these methods, however, there will still be antagonistic interests to be adjudicated. The state must therefore continue to administer justice. But every improvement in our conceptions of justice, as well as in the machinery for the administration of justice, whereby a closer approximation to exact justice may be secured, will make for social peace, though the mere adjudication of conflicting interests will not remove the conflicts themselves nor their cause. That lies deeper than legislatures or courts can probe.

These conclusions sound commonplace enough, and are doubtless disappointing to those who hope for a new earth through some engine of social regeneration. The old world is already pegging away, and has been for a very long time, upon all the plans which have been mentioned in this paper. But after all, the old world is wise — much wiser than any man, though there are some men who think otherwise. Whether we agree with Burke or not that there are not many new discoveries made in moral philosophy, we must at least admit that many of the fundamental facts in sociology have been known and understood for a very long time.

While it is the contention of this chapter that economic scarcity furnishes the ultimate basis of all social conflict, he would be blind indeed who did not realize that there were many counteracting influences which in many cases overcome the conflict of interests and lead to forms of combination in spite of the underlying conflict. In modern civilized society this counteraction is strongest perhaps within that small social group which goes under the name of the family. Here the ties of blood and kinship resulting in intense love and affection are so strong as to overcome and generally to obliterate the underlying conflict of interests. While it is still true that even in this small circle economic scarcity creates an underlying conflict of interests, that is to say, the satisfaction of the physical wants of one member of the family interferes with a like satisfaction of the physical wants of another, nevertheless, affection is normally so strong as to overcome this and enable one to take more delight in the satisfaction of the physical wants of another member than in his own. This, however, by no means eliminates the conflict. It merely transfers the scene of conflict from the objective to the subjective field. The father would enjoy the consumption of certain luxuries on his own palate, but he also enjoys the consumption of these luxuries on the palates of his children. But one form of enjoyment interferes with the other. He then experiences a conflict within himself and must choose which form of satisfaction he will enjoy. Happily for society and civilization, he is very likely to choose the satisfaction of his family affection rather than his physical appetite.

But family affection is not the only counteracting force. As the individual looks out upon the world with himself at the centre of his field of view, he will see the antagonism of interests as an all-pervasive fact in a world of scarcity.

Within a series of concentric circles he will see that this all-pervasive conflict is balanced against, softened, or modified by a considerable variety of counteracting forces.   Within the smallest of these circles, namely the family, the counter-acting forces, which may be called natural affection, so completely overcome the basic conflict, in the normal case at least, as to cause it to be lost sight of and to create a kind of community of interests among the individuals within the group.   In a wider geographical group known as the state there is another counteracting force called patriotism or loyalty, much weaker than natural affection but still strong enough to modify without obscuring the all-pervasive conflict.   The tooth and claw conflict which pervades outside of the widest of these circles is, within this circle, modified into what is known as economic competition.   Outside the group called the state or the nation, but including what we may call the civilized world, is another group within which a still weaker tie, namely the feeling of kinship in a common culture, modifies the all-pervasive struggle.   The somewhat humane laws of war, laid down in our international codes, slightly, though very slightly, soften and modify the war of tooth and claw.   Though the conditions of international rivalry are getting more and more to resemble economic competition, there are still conditions of latent warfare, but of warfare according to civilized principles.   Outside this circle called civilization lies another circle including all mankind, within which the conflict is also softened, but still more slightly, by the feeling of a common humanity.   The condition is still one of latent warfare, and is softened by none of the ameliorations prescribed by international law. Nevertheless our attitude toward the least civilized human beings is measurably different from our attitude toward the animal and vegetable creation.   Outside this circle of human life lies the whole non-human universe where, generally speaking, there is no counteracting force, and where the normal condition is one of the appropriation of the weaker by the stronger.

Of course there are other circles and groups such as the church, the lodge, the trade union, where varying degrees of counteraction are found, but the more characteristic groups are probably those already named. The circles described are those which surround the average civilized man. The width of the circles within which the varying conditions named would be found would depend upon the degree of socialization of the individual. At the bottom of the scale, showing the minimum of socialization, would be the cannibal, whose attitude of appropriation would include the whole world, human and non-human, outside a very narrow circle, say his own tribe. At the opposite end of the scale, showing perhaps an abnormal degree of socialization, would be the religious vegetarian who regards even the animals as in a sense his brothers and will not assume toward them the attitude of appropriation. It is doubtful if anyone could be found who would go to the still greater extreme of refusing to appropriate to his own use even vegetables. If there were such an individual, he would speedily be exterminated, and leave none of his seed behind to preserve in the world his extreme ideal of socialization.

There may possibly be an individual here and there in whom the feeling of humanity is so strong as completely to overbalance the general antagonism of interests and to lead him to treat all mankind as the normal individual treats the members of his own immediate family, that is to say, who would have an affection for every man of whatever race, tribe, culture, religion or language equal to that which the average man has for the members of his own family circle.

If we had a world made up of such individuals then we should have a kind of communism throughout the world similar to that which now prevails within the family. Such communism, of course, would not depend upon political or legal institutions or any kind of positive law. But because such individuals are so rare in the world as to be negligible for practical purposes, communism does not exist and could probably not be created by any kind of political or legal arrangement.

Certain other bases of conflict, such as the desire to be conspicuous on the one hand and envy of the conspicuous person on the other, the desire for power on the one hand and the resentment against the powerful on the other, are not only secondary to the basic conflict already described, but really grow out of it. The only conspicuous form of antagonism which is not directly associated with the fact of scarcity is that between the factor of scientific curiosity on the one hand, leading us to take delight in the discovery of new things, and on the other the factor of mental inertia, leading us to resent new ideas. These two factors, which are present in every person but combined in different proportions, sometimes produce a conflict within the individual and sometimes between different individuals. This is really the basis of the so-called conflict between science and religion, which is nothing more or less than the conflict between the scientific spirit or the spirit of scientific curiosity which is continually seeking to find out new things, and the religious spirit which is continually seeking to get itself adjusted to a system of thought upon which it can rest undisturbed. So far as religious opinions themselves are concerned, they are in most cases merely old scientific theories which once rested on evidence but are now retained in spite of evidence and hold their ground because of the unwillingness of their supporters to reconstruct the whole body of their beliefs and opinions. The theory of the origin of this particular form of conflict has also its mythical setting. This is embodied in the story of the box of Pandora, whose curiosity, or desire to pry into things, let loose a swarm of plagues upon the earth, just as the theory of the origin of evil due to the conflict of economic interests is embodied in the story of the Garden of Eden. It happens, however, that all our modern problems of economic and social justice grow out of economic rather than religious conflict. The mythical setting of our problem is therefore found in the partaking of the forbidden fruit rather than in the gratification of the spirit of prying curiosity as illustrated by the box of Pandora. However, both these stories when properly interpreted have a most striking significance for the modern economist.

CHAPTER III

THE PRINCIPLE OF SELF-CENTERED APPRECIATION COMMONLY CALLED SELF-INTEREST

So long as a man has a preference for certain persons over others, so long will he work in the interest of those for whom he has a preference and, where there is a conflict of interests, against the interests of those for whom he has no preference. The stronger his preference for certain persons as compared with others, the more strenuously will he work in the interests of the former. If the one for whom he has a preference happens to be himself, then he may be said to be selfish or self-interested. If those for whom he has a preference are members of his own family, his close neighbors and his intimate friends, then he will commonly be regarded as generous. But this kind of generosity results in his working in the interests of those people who happen to come within the circle of his preference. If their interests conflict with those of people living outside that circle, then he will work against the interests of the latter. The stronger his preferences for those living inside the circle the more strenuously will he work for their interests and against the interests of others. In other words, that which generally goes under the name of generosity produces just as strenuous rivalry and competition as that which commonly goes under the name of selfishness. The only difference is that it tends to become group rivalry in the one case and individual rivalry in the other. Rivalry in some form is inevitable and ineradicable except among people, if such there be, who have no preferences whatever. These would scarcely be human.

As suggested in the last chapter, self-interest is one of the original factors in the problem of social conflict. It cannot be said, under the view therein set forth, to have been an exciting cause of the conflict, but rather one of the underlying conditions which made conflict inevitable whenever or wherever scarcity should arise. It may be regarded as a part of our general animal inheritance, along with hunger, thirst, and sex.

Just what is implied in the term self-interest is not very clearly understood and it is doubtful if it has ever been set forth fully and completely. It is not necessary here to enter into a hair-splitting discussion of the old philosophical riddle as to whether altruism is only another form of selfishness. Since according to this sophistry the altruistic individual is presumably altruistic because he prefers to be so, and since he gratifies his preference he is to be accounted selfish. Such philosophical claptrap results from an overemphasis upon motive rather than upon conduct. It may be true, from the purely subjective standpoint, that the man who gets more delight from the taste of food upon the palates of his children than upon his own is as selfish as the man who gets no pleasure at all from the taste of food on any palate but his own, but there is no doubt as to which will make the better father, and that is the only thing that matters in the least. There is no doubt that the man who takes some pleasure in the happiness of his neighbors is a better neighbor than the man who takes no pleasure in such things. The qualities which enable one to function properly as a neighbor and a member of society are the ones which must always receive social approval in a sound social body, and those which prevent proper functioning must meet with disapproval, however the names of these qualities may be juggled by the methods of subjective analysis.

Only conduct counts.   Motives derive their sole value from the conduct which they produce.

Discarding all subjective quibbles, we may state as tentative definitions that benevolence is a quality which results normally, without compulsion, in conduct advantageous to others, and that selfishness is a quality which normally, and without compulsion, results in conduct primarily advantageous to self.   If by complete benevolence is meant the quality which gives absolutely no preference to self as compared with any other being, then it is safe to say that such a thing does not and never did exist.   Nor does such a thing as complete selfishness exist if that term means a quality which shows absolutely no regard for the interests of any other being than self.   Both benevolence and selfishness, as actual facts in the world, must be found somewhere between the two extremes, one of which allows no preference whatever for self as compared with any other being, and the other of which allows no interest whatever in any other being. Every one, however benevolent, will show some preference for self where his interests conflict with those of some other being, perhaps distantly removed from himself, though he might gladly die for some few who are peculiarly near himself.   And every one, however selfish, will show some regard for some other being, perhaps very closely related to himself.   He would not be a benevolent man, but an angel of love who would not decline to go hungry to relieve the slightly greater hunger of some man of another race, color, and language, whom he never saw; and he would not be a selfish man, but a devil of hate, who would not deny himself at least a trifling luxury in order to save from starvation some near relative or near neighbor.   Neither angels of love nor devils of hate actually exist in human form, though there are doubtless pretty close approximations to both.

From this it will appear that the real difference between the benevolent and the selfish man is a difference of degree. The benevolent man may be said to have a mild or moderate preference for self and the selfish man to have a strong or immoderate preference for self.   To put it in another way, the benevolent man may be said to have a wide circle of beings in whom he is interested, or to be so much interested in them that he will deny himself things of considerable

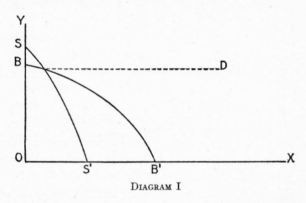

DIAGRAM I

importance to meet their slightly greater needs;   whereas the selfish man may be said to have a narrow circle of beings in whom he is interested, or to be so little interested in them that he will only deny himself things of little importance in order to provide for their much greater needs.   One's benevolence may be said to increase directly with the width of the circle in which one is interested and with the intensity of one's interest in those within the circle, whereas one's selfishness may be said to increase with the narrowness of the circle and with the feebleness of one's interest in those within the circle.

This may be illustrated by means of Diagram I.

Along the line OX measure the radius of the circle of one's
interests, with oneself at the centre O.   Along the line OY
measure the intensity of one's interest in each person within
that circle.   Assume, further, that the line OS measures
the intensity of S, the selfish man's interest in himself, while
the line OB measures B, the benevolent man's interest in
himself.   They in whom S and B are interested are ranged
along the line OX, those nearest these two persons being
the ones in whom each is most intensely interested, and
those farthest away being the ones in whom each is least
interested.   The radius of the circle of S's interests would
then, we shall assume, be measured by the line OS' and that
of B's by the line OB', and the curve SS' would represent
the intensity of S's interest in other beings, while the curve
BB' would represent that of B in others. S becomes
satanic in proportion as the curve SS' approaches the line
SO, while B becomes divine in proportion as the line BB'
approaches the dotted line BD.   Being human, their curves
are found somewhere between these two extremes.

Let us now see exactly what is meant by the width of the
circle of one's interests, or by the terms nearness to and distance from self.   In some way it will occur at once that the
width of the circle has something to do with the number of
people who are included in it.   If the circle of the benevolent man's interests is wider than that of the selfish man, it
means that the one is interested in a larger number of people
than the other.   In either case, those within the circle of
one's interests will be found to be in some sense nearer to
self than are those who are outside that circle, and those
within the circle in whom we are most interested will be
found to be, in some sense, nearer to self than those in whom
we are least interested.   But in what sense can we use such
a geometrical term as " nearer to " to express a moral or

social fact ? In the first place, it can be used in a strictly geometrical sense, meaning physical or geometrical propinquity. They who are nearer to one in space usually, though not always, command more of one's attention and interest than they who are farther away. We normally care more for members of our own household than for members of other households, more for our near neighbors than for our distant neighbors, using the words near and distant with respect to space.

Again, we may use the words near and far with respect to time, and say that they who are near to us in point of time command more of our attention and interest than they who are far from us. We are more interested, for example, in our contemporaries, other things equal, than in those who have lived or are to live in remote times, in our immediate parents than in our remote ancestors, in our immediate children than in our remote descendants.

But there is another, and very important sense in which these terms are used which is not so easily expressed as are the concepts of space and time. They may be used with respect to similarity and dissimiliarity. Other things equal, we care more for those who are like ourselves than for those who are unlike ourselves. That is to say, we normally care more for our own flesh and blood than for others, for our near relatives than for our distant relatives, for our own fellow citizens than for foreigners, for those who profess our own religion than for pagans, for human beings than for animals, for the higher than for the lower animals, etc. etc.

This may all be summed up by saying that we are more interested in those who are near to ourselves in point of space, in point of time, and in point of similarity and dissimilarity than in those who are distant from us in these three senses. It will, of course, inevitably happen that these three concepts of nearness will often be in conflict. They who live near us in point of space may happen to be distant from us in point of dissimilarity. In this case the ties of kinship may prove stronger than the ties of neighborhood, or vice versa; that is, in case of conflict, we may side with those who are near of kin though distant in space, rather than with those who are near in space but remotely of kin, or vice versa. We are frequently, for example, more moved by the sufferings of an animal which is near by in point of space than by the equal sufferings of a human being who is distant, though if both were equally near in point of space we should be more deeply moved by the sufferings of the human being, since he is nearer in point of similarity. Because of these distinct factors in the determination of our interests, all of which may be working in harmony or in conflict, the problem of determining the actual circle of one's interests becomes a perplexing problem in permutations and combinations.

To this general characteristic of human nature, which might be called the law of human preferences the term self-interest is generally applied. But it is doubtful if this term accurately names the fact, because each individual is interested, usually deeply interested, in others besides himself. Self-interest only implies a preference, mild in the case of the benevolent man, extreme in the case of the selfish man, for self as compared with the rest of the world in general. Besides, every individual shows some preferences in his regard for the rest of the world, caring more for some than for others, those for whom he cares most centering, in some sense, around himself. A more accurate term with which to describe this principle would be self-centered appreciation. And accordingly, as an improvement in nomenclature, self-centered appreciation is here offered as a substitute for the principle of self-interest.

Let us now see exactly what is meant by a preference for self as compared with some one else. In order to be as concrete as possible, let us begin by considering the interest which one has in the utilization of his income, remembering, however, that there are other interests in life besides income. It will be generally agreed that as a man's income increases, other things equal, his appreciation of each dollar

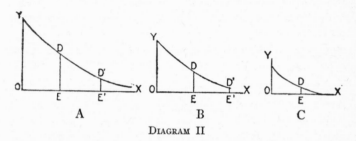

DIAGRAM II

will diminish. That is to say, if he has only three hundred dollars a year, he will guard each dollar pretty carefully because the loss of a single dollar would deprive him of something necessary for his subsistence. Moreover, he will not spend a dollar for things for which he does not have a strong desire. But if, with the same disposition, his income were three thousand dollars, each dollar would mean somewhat less to him than when he had only three hundred dollars. Again, if it should be still further increased to thirty thousand a year, each dollar would be still less highly appreciated. This principle may be illustrated by Diagram II.

Let his income be measured along the line OX beginning at O, in diagram A while his appreciation of a dollar is measured along the line OY. As his income increases, his appreciation will fall, and this fall will be represented by some sort of a descending curve, say the curve $YDD'X$. That is to say, where his income is measured by the line OE, his appreciation of a dollar is represented by the line DE; but when his income is enlarged to OE', then his appreciation of a dollar is represented by the line $D'E'$.

In a similar way, diagram B may represent his appreciation of his *neighbor's* need of an income, or the need of some one peculiarly near to himself in some of the sense noted above. If the other man's income were as large as his own, that is, if each had an income of OE, he would not be inclined to divide with the other man. His appreciation of *the other man's* need of a dollar would be represented by the line DE in diagram B, while his appreciation of his own need of a dollar would be represented by DE in diagram A. However, if his income were much larger than the other man's, say that his is OE in diagram A, while the other man's is OE in diagram B, in which case his appreciation of his own need of a dollar is represented by the line $D'E'$ in diagram A, and of his neighbor's need of a dollar by the line DE in diagram B, he then appreciates the other man's need of a dollar somewhat more highly than his own and, acting accordingly, gives him a portion of his own. In this case, he would ordinarily pass as a benevolent man, but he would still be somewhat self-interested or self-centered.

Again, if some one whom he does not ordinarily recognize as his neighbor, or as near to himself in any sense, say some person living a long way off, and belonging to a different branch of the human race, is brought to his attention, he may appreciate that person's needs according to diagram C. If their incomes are equal, he will ordinarily pay no attention whatever to the distant person's needs. But if he has a larger income, say OE', and it is brought to his attention that the distant person has no income at all and is starving, he may surrender one of his many thousand dollars in order that the distant person may have one dollar's worth of goods to keep him alive. In the diagrams, his appreciation of his own need of a dollar is represented by the line $D'E'$ in diagram A, while his appreciation of the distant person's need of a dollar is represented by the line OY in diagram C. Even in this case he would ordinarily pass as a benevolent man, doubtless more benevolent than the average man in any community past or present, yet he would be decidedly self-centered. The only being who would not be at all self-centered would be one whose appreciation of the needs of his near neighbor and also of his most distant neighbor would be represented by curves exactly as high as the curve in diagram A. Such a man would be willing to divide his income equally not only with his nearest neighbor, but also with his most distant neighbor, distance being reckoned not only in terms of space and time, but in point of dissimilarity as well.

This problem of comparative valuation or appreciation of things near by and far away, present and future, has many ramifications and applications. Every student of economics knows how large a part the valuation or appreciation of present as compared with future goods has played in the theory of capital and interest. It is sometimes roughly assumed that present goods are preferred to future goods. Because of this preference, present goods will commonly command a higher price than future goods, or, which amounts to the same thing, money being left out of account, a given quantity of present goods will exchange for a somewhat larger quantity of future goods.

It is highly improbable that present goods should ever *actually* exchange for future goods of the same kind and quality, but something like this is *virtually* done whenever one purchases goods which will not be ready for consumption until some future time.   The wine merchant, who sells aged wine which is ready for consumption and with the proceeds buys new wine which must be stored several years, is virtually exchanging present goods, the aged wine, for future goods, the new wine.   If it were not true that people, generally speaking, prefer present goods to future, there would be no great difference in the price.   But because they do have such a preference, the wine merchant is able to live on the difference in price.   He saves the customers from the necessity of waiting.   This would be no service to them did they not dislike to wait.   Something of the same kind happens when one buys a tool or a piece of machinery to be used in production.   No one wants the tool for its own sake, any more than the connoisseur wants new wine.   He wants it for the sake of the consumable products to which it is the necessary means. To get these consumable products he must wait as well as work.   Because he dislikes waiting as much as he dislikes working, and because both are equally necessary, both must be paid for with equal certainty and for equally good reasons.   The way in which the owner gets his pay for waiting is by being able to buy the tool for something less than its future earning capacity.   That is, he purchases the tool with money which represents present goods, and re-ceives the tool, which represents future goods.   The present goods which he pays are less in quantity than the future goods which he receives, though their present values are equal.   By waiting until those present goods become past and the future goods present, he finds himself in the pos-session of more goods, and more value than he paid out. This surplus is interest.

On the subject of interest, the present author has else-where written as follows: [1]

[1] *The Distribution of Wealth*, New York, Macmillan, 1905, pp. 231–232.

All tools are, as we have seen already, alike in that they are not wanted for their own sakes, but for the sake of the incomes which they will earn. Incomes consist, in last analysis, of consumers' goods, and these goods are the sole reason for desiring the possession of income-bearing goods. But all tools are also alike in that their cost of production must have been borne by some one before they begin to return their incomes. The maker of a tool must himself wait for the income to mature, or he must sell it to some one else, in which case it is the buyer who waits. His waiting consists in giving up the opportunity of buying present consumers' goods, and receiving in return the means of securing consumers' goods at some time in the future. It is virtually an exchange of present consumers' goods for future consumers' goods which they will bring him, he really exchanges for the latter goods. It is the same whether he lends money, or invests in machinery, or deposits in a savings bank. They are all forms of waiting, or of saving as it is sometimes called. The man who buys a plough to use on his farm is saving as truly as the man who deposits a like sum in a bank or hides it in his stocking. Waiting or saving is quite as essential to the existence of capital as labor itself, for if there were no saving there would be no capital.

But it must not be inferred that all saving involves sacrifice. There would be some saving were there no interest at all, — that is, if capital did not earn any more than enough to replace itself. It is even probable that a considerable amount would be saved if, instead of savings affording a surplus, men were obliged to pay rent for vaults in which to store them or even to hire others to take their surplus wealth and use it for them. In so far as it is true that men estimate present higher than future consumption, it only applies to the consumption of corresponding increments of income. A man with an income of $10,000 a year derives less utility from the consumption of the last than from the first thousand. He may receive so small an amount of pleasure from the consumption of the last thousand dollars that he will prefer to save it for the purpose of satisfying a more pressing want in the future. It is upon this principle that men lay up for a rainy day or for old age. This may be illustrated by Diagram III on the next page.

In Fig. 1 and 2 of that diagram, let the amount of a man's income be measured along the horizontal lines AB and $A'B'$. Let the utility of different increments be represented by the perpendicular lines, those in Fig. 1 representing the present utility of present increments of goods, while those in Fig. 2 represent the estimate which we now put upon the utility of the same or equivalent increments of goods a year hence. In other words, we discount the future at a rate corresponding to the ratio between the perpendicular lines in Fig. 1 and the corresponding lines in Fig. 2.   It is evident, then, from the diagram, that increment No. 10 would be saved, in order that it might be applied to the satisfaction of want No. 1 in the future.   Similarly, No. 9 of the present would be saved because No. 2 of the future is higher. The same may be said of No. 8 of the present, because it does not quite come up to No. 3 of the future.   But here saving would stop; for there would be a loss in abstaining from the consumption of No. 7, in order to apply it to No. 4 of the future.

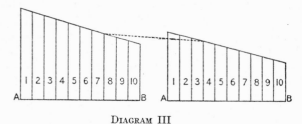

DIAGRAM III

We may conclude, as a result of the foregoing analysis, that even after we eliminate from our consideration all other beings than self, there is yet a possible distinction between one's present and one's future self.   It is always, of course, the present self which esteems or appreciates all interests, whether they be present or future.   And the present self estimates or appreciates present interests somewhat more highly than it does future interests.   In this respect the present self appreciates the interests of the future self according to a law quite analogous to, if indeed it be not the same law as that according to which it appreciates the interests of others.   This aspect of the problem lends some justification, perhaps, to the custom of certain leading ethicists of using the impressionistic and, on the whole, useless term " conjunct self " to describe the fact of one's special interest in other beings bound to one by the ties of kinship, race, religion, etc.   The same diagrams may, as a matter of fact, illustrate the one case as well as the other.

The following series of diagrams may serve to illustrate and summarize the whole theory of self-centered appreciation. To understand their meaning it is necessary to read the formulae across as well as up and down. Reading across formulae I, II, III, and IV, and referring each part of each formula to the diagram above it, we get the law of self-centered appreciation in all its essential variations. I, for example, relates to the individual's appreciation of his own present and future needs. II, relates to his appreciation of his own needs as compared with those of his contemporaries and others removed in point of time. III, relates to his appreciation of his own needs as compared with those of his neighbors and others removed in point of space, while IV, relates to his appreciation of his own needs as compared with those of others near to him in point of similarity as well as those removed from him in point of dissimilarity.

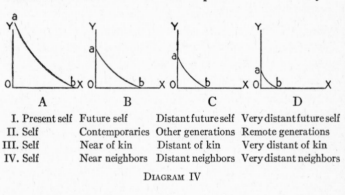

	A	B	C	D
I.	Present self	Future self	Distant future self	Very distant future self
II.	Self	Contemporaries	Other generations	Remote generations
III.	Self	Near of kin	Distant of kin	Very distant of kin
IV.	Self	Near neighbors	Distant neighbors	Very distant neighbors

DIAGRAM IV

In each of the diagrams, A, B, C, and D, let the line OX measure the quantity of means of satisfying a desire of any kind, and the line OY the intensity of one's appreciation of the importance of each unit of that quantity. Then the curve ab in each diagram will represent the diminishing appreciation of each unit of the supply, as the supply itself increases. But in diagram A in each case the curve *ab* represents the diminishing appreciation of each unit of the supply when applied to the satisfaction of the desires of the self or of the person doing the appreciating. But in each of the other diagrams the curve *ab* represents the diminishing appreciation of each unit of the quantity of the means of satisfying the desire when applied to the satisfaction of other persons than the one whose appreciation is measured. I, for example, may be doing the appreciating, in which case the curve *ab* in diagram A will represent my appreciation of the importance of different units of my income when applied to my own gratification. But in each of the other diagrams, the curve represents *my* appreciation of the importance of satisfying other people's desires, or, as in the first case, of the desires of my future as compared with my present self.

With this understanding, then, it can be made perfectly clear just what my benevolence would consist in if my supply of the means of satisfying a given desire were measured as in diagram A by the line *OB*. The last unit of that quantity would have a negligible utility for me, that is, I could surrender it with no sacrifice whatever. At the same time, if my near neighbor possessed absolutely none of it, I should have interest enough in him to appreciate his need, at least, to such an extent as would be measured by the line *OA* in diagram B. Since by depriving myself of one unit at the point *b* in diagram A without any loss whatever I can satisfy myself to the extent of the line *OA*, diagram B, by contributing to B's supply, I would very easily choose to allow B to have at least one unit of my supply, rather than to keep it myself. I do this, of course, because I personally get more gratification from the consumption of that unit by B than I would by its consumption by myself. From one point of view I could be said to be acting selfishly, and from another point of view I could be said to be acting generously. As will be seen clearly by the foregoing argument and the above diagrams, there is an element both of benevolence and self-ishness in every such act. The difference between the benevolent and the selfish man would be shown by the difference between the curves *ab* in the different diagrams A, B, C, and D. The greater the difference between the height of the curve in diagram A and in the other diagrams, the greater the selfishness.

So far in this chapter we have been engaged exclusively in the discovery of what is; that is, in the analysis of the actual facts of appreciation and valuation as applied to the problem of benevolence and self-interest. It is tolerably clear, let us hope, that every normal human being is self-centered in his system of valuation, but that no human being is absolutely selfish. Let us next consider the part which this principle of self-centered appreciation plays in the economy of that part of the universe which consists of human beings. In the first place, let us assume that the great problem of the human race, as of every other species of life is to keep on living. This, in turn is the problem of adaptation and adjustment to the material universe in which it finds itself. Everything else derives its value from its relation to this one ultimate problem; everything which facilitates the process of adjustment is good, and everything which hinders this process is bad; the final test of adaptation is the test of survival, the issue being one of life and death. That is good which promotes life in the long run, but there is no life in the long run that is not adjusted or adapted. In the world of variation and selection, the one great crime is unadaptation. Nature's verdict is " Adapt or die." She cherishes her darlings, the adapted; but the unadapted she disinherits.

It is from this point of view that we must evaluate everything, both morally, commercially, and aesthetically; obviously, then, the question whether this principle of self-centered appreciation is good or bad depends upon its relation to this great and final problem of adaptation. Specifically, the problem may be put thus: Imagine several different communities of men, each community made up of individuals in whom the principle of self-centered appreciation has different degrees of development. In one community at the extreme end of the scale we have men who approximate to absolute selfishness. At the opposite end we have a community whose men approximate to absolute benevolence, that is, where there is no self-centered appreciation at all. Between these two extremes we have communities made up of men who are self-centered in varying degrees. Each community, let us assume, follows out its own distinctive development, organizes itself according to the instinct and predilection of its individuals. In each community, the normal impulses coöperate either in the direction of multiplication of numbers or of race suicide, according again to the development of the self-centered principle. In those in which the processes of multiplication go on rapidly there will grow up the necessity of expansion of territory and this will sooner or later create conflict between the groups for possession of territory over which to expand. The problem is, which group in all probability will succeed best in expanding, in securing territory, defending its boundaries, and finally, in crowding the other communities off the face of the earth. The community that succeeds in this final test will be the community with the best moral and social organization. It will be the best moral and social organization because of its ability to meet this final test of goodness and for no other reason whatever.

The community in which absolute selfishness prevails would lack cohesiveness, though it would have certain other elements of strength. Such coöperation as took place would only be on the basis of a truce. No individual having any interest whatever in any other individual none would submit to the slightest inconvenience whatever, or have the least consideration for the rights of any one else except under compulsion. There would doubtless be a considerable multiplication of numbers if the male part of the population had its way, because the gratification of the sexual instinct would have free play without any hindrance, provided, of course, the males were strong enough to catch and hold the females. On the other hand, the selfish interests of the female population would impel them toward race suicide in order to avoid the painful processes of childbirth. Such children as were born under this process would be turned upon the world without much protection, and the spawning process, rather than the family building process, would be the normal method of multiplication. It is fairly clear that such a community as this could never hold its own against a community which could organize and work together because of an *esprit de corps*, of neighborliness, of interest in one another's welfare. It takes some degree of interest in others even to prompt parents to sacrifice for their offspring, or to give time, attention and labor to their care. The community in which the parental instinct has some degree of development has an advantage over the community in which there is no such development, for the child, during the growing period, would have protection, care and nourishment. Again, the neighborhood spirit, the group spirit, the national spirit, involves expansion of interest beyond the immediate ego of each individual, and it is fairly certain, therefore, that the community at the selfish end of the scale would never prove its fitness.

On the other hand, the community at the opposite extreme of benevolence would have certain advantages, but also certain serious handicaps.   Since no individual would have any preference, either for himself as compared with others, or for his own family as compared with other families, or his own neighbors as compared with others, or even for the members of his own community as compared with the members of the above-mentioned selfish community, there could be no group spirit.   The members of this community would have to appreciate the interests of the troglodytes at the opposite end of the scale, i. e., in the community of egotists, as much as their own.   They would have to strive as hard to enable the troglodytes to gratify their animal propensities as they would try to gratify their own higher instincts.   Therefore, they would be laboring as zealously for the survival of the troglodyte as for their own survival.   It seems probable that this alone would so handicap this group of saints as to give them a short duration.

The oriental saint who gave his body to feed the tiger because the tiger was hungry may have been a very amiable person, but it is improbable that a community made up of such persons would have a long duration.   Such a principle of life is calculated, not to convert tigers into saints, but to convert saints into tigers, not to fill the world with saints, but to fill the world with tigers.   In other words, that extreme form of benevolence is the very food on which the extreme forms of selfishness fatten.

It is, therefore, obvious that the community that meets the final test of fitness must be self-centered, at least to the extent of preferring itself as a community to other communities, of preferring its own survival to that of other communities. In other words, its members must have more interest in their own group than in other groups. Thus we can eliminate from our consideration, as nature herself would speedily eliminate them, both extremes in the scale.

But there are questions of internal economy still somewhat dependent upon a development of this self-centered appreciation. Even in the same community there are certain to be, under the biological processes of reproduction, great variations among individuals, some with intellectual and others without intellectual proclivities, some with a higher degree of moral purpose than others, some with greater powers to contribute to the success of the group than others. If, however, with these biological variations there are no individual preferences, but each individual has the same regard for all other individuals within the group, not even preferring his own kin, or his own kind in point of moral or intellectual quality, there will still be difficulties to be overcome. In the first place, that extreme form of moral development which regards the interests of others without any modification or qualification whatever, will also be self-destructive. There is the high moral purpose which approves high moral purpose in others and condemns low moral purpose, and therefore prefers those individuals possessing high moral purpose to those lacking it. There is also another kind of high moral purpose which would not attempt to make any such discriminations, but would say, " The meaner the man, the more he is to be pitied, and the more I should exercise myself to benefit him." Logically it would be driven to say, " But am I fit that I should pretend to say how he shall be benefited ? If he wants certain things I must exercise myself to enable him to get them, and not attempt to discriminate too closely." The former type of high moral purpose will not make too sharp a discrimination between hating sin and hating the sinner. The latter type will attempt to make that impossible distinction, that is to say, while it will pretend to hate sin, it will at the same time pretend to love the sinner. Moreover, it will express this love for the sinner, not in trying to reform him against his will, but in trying to make him prosperous and happy in spite of his sinfulness. This resolves itself ultimately into the problem of the saint and the tiger, with the same fatal results to sainthood. But there are other more concrete advantages in favor of self-centered appreciation or for the expression of individual preferences among one's fellow citizens.

We may state this argument categorically as follows:

1. Every interest ought to be safeguarded and provided for by the person who is able to safeguard and provide for it most effectively.

2. Generally speaking, but with a few exceptions, every interest can be safeguarded and provided for more effectively by the person who knows that interest most intimately.

3. Generally speaking, but with a few exceptions, the individual of mature years and sound mind knows his interests more intimately than he knows the interests of other people.

4. Generally speaking, but with a few exceptions, the individual of mature years and sound mind knows the interests of his contemporaries better than those of later generations, and of near generations better than those of remote generations.

5. Generally speaking, and with few exceptions, he knows the interests of his near of kin better than those of his distant or his very distant of kin.

6. He knows the interests of those who are like-minded with himself better than he knows the interests of those who are unlike-minded with himself, that is, those whose moral and mental qualities, purposes, and ideals are similar to his own, than he does those whose moral and mental qualities, purposes, and ideals are different from his own.

Now from these general propositions, from which there can obviously be no great degree of dissent, it follows that, generally speaking, if Jones and Smith be both of mature years and sound mind, Jones can ordinarily look after Jones' interests more effectively than he can look after Smith's, and Smith can ordinarily look after Smith's interests more effectively than he can look after Jones'. If circumstances should arise under which Smith can look after Jones' interests better than Jones can, then it is wise economy of effort for Smith to look after Jones, but these circumstances will ordinarily be rare. In the first place, Jones may be in peculiar circumstances where it is impossible for him to do for himself as well as Smith could do for him. In the second place, he may not know his own interests as well as Smith knows them, in which case it would be a wise economy of effort for Smith to look after Jones.

In general terms, the success of the process of adaptation, or of safeguarding and providing for human interests, depends upon the economizing of human energy. Human energy is economically expended when it is directed by close and intimate knowledge, rather than by a distant and indirect knowledge. If one man knows his own interests better than other men, it then occasions less waste of energy if he looks after those interests which he knows best, leaving other individuals to do the same thing. In the case of children, or of mature persons of unsound mind, or persons who lack training for certain exigencies of life, it frequently happens that others know their interests better than they themselves do, in which case it is an economical expenditure of human energy for others to safeguard and provide for the interests of these who are incompetent.

This, therefore, is the general conclusion to which we are driven, namely, that the success of our community depends upon the wisest economy and direction of the fund of human energy embodied in its population.   Every waste of energy handicaps it in the struggle.   Every economy of energy strengthens it for the struggle.   It would be a waste of energy for an individual to attempt to safeguard and provide for interests which he did not know as well as someone else. The nearer he keeps to himself in his effort to safeguard and provide for the interests of others, the more clear will his knowledge be of the work to be done or the interests to be provided for.   With this general principle in mind, then, it is only a question of fact how wide a circle of interests should the individual attempt to safeguard and provide for, and what relative importance should he give to the interests which are near to the centre of the circle, that is, himself, and those which are distant from the centre, that is, distant from self.

This question of fact no one can determine on general principles.   Each individual must determine for himself. It would be a clear waste of my energy if I should attempt to do as much for the dwellers in central Africa as for my near neighbors.   If I should be as deeply distressed over the hardships or the injustices suffered by those distant neighbors whom I cannot economically reach as by my near neighbors whom I can, I should be wasting a great deal of energy in fruitless sorrow over distress which I am either unable to help, or able very inadequately and with great waste of energy to mitigate.   But if there are people in my own neighborhood or my own town who are in distress, it is less waste of energy for me to sympathize with them because I can reach them with less effort, and my energy can be made effective at the point where help is needed.   Nevertheless, if my neighbors are comfortably well off, and could be only mildly pleased by any benevolent efforts which I might put forth, whereas there is a famine in some distant country where people are starving to death and where a few dollars of my surplus income would save many lives, then obviously it would be a waste of energy again if I should confine all my ministrations to my well-to-do near neighbor and refuse to help my distant perishing neighbors.

It is extremely probable that the physical factors governing the economical expenditure of human energy in providing for human interests, account for the psychological fact of self-centered appreciation.   In the age-long struggle for existence, those groups or human types have survived whose mental and moral qualities have enabled them to utilize their energy most economically and effectively. They who show preference for those near to themselves as compared with those distant from themselves have normally been able to utilize their energy with less waste. Therefore the world is now peopled by men who are able to utilize their energy economically and effectively because their appreciation of the interests to be safeguarded is self-centered.

While it is thus physically demonstrable that a greater economy of human energy is secured under the principle of self-centered appreciation, it is still a difficult question to determine just how far that principle should be carried.   In an age when geographical knowledge was very limited and the means of communication likewise, a normal adjustment to the situation would probably require a rather narrow circle of interests on the part of each individual, and this for the obvious reason that his power to help others is very limited and circumscribed. Having become, let us say, psychologically and morally adjusted to that situation, we now find ourselves in a new situation where geographical knowledge is extended and the means of communication very greatly improved. Our natural impulses which we have inherited from a previous state still give us a rather narrow circle of interests, whereas our opportunities are so great that it would not be wasteful but probably economical of our energies if we should widen out our circle of interests to correspond with the circle of our opportunities. Therefore, we doubtless need some moral readjustment, that is to say, we need to breed up a race of people, or train them, as the case may require, with a circle of interests corresponding roughly to the circle of their opportunities.

But it is easy to attempt to stand so straight as to lean over backward. All our valuations take the form of motivation. We now evaluate benevolence simply because we need to stir up the benevolent motives to more effective action. We are likely to forget that values are never absolute but only relative. A good thing may be overdone. Benevolence being somewhat less abundant than it ought to be under our present situation, we need to cultivate it. It might, however, become so overabundant as to need to be repressed. This is parallel with many other forms of cultivation. There is many a flower so underabundant as to make it desirable that it should be increased. We first place a high value upon it and then following that evaluation we try to produce it.

But in economic valuation and production it is well understood that if this same flower should become overabundant it would become a weed and have to be repressed.

Negative valuation followed by negative production means repression.   The same law of value must be applied to the moral qualities.   A certain quality in human nature is deemed to be less abundant than it ought to be, therefore we place a value upon it, and following this valuation try to encourage it or cultivate it.   As a result of this evaluation we call it a virtue, but the same thing might, like the flower, become overabundant in which case we should place a negative value upon it or call it a vice and try to repress it.   Then benevolence according to the foregoing argument might conceivably be overabundant and become such a waster of human energy as to endanger the very life of society, in which case the survival of that society would require that a negative valuation be placed upon benevolence or a positive valuation upon self-centered appreciation. A new vogue would be given to such expressions as " Charity begins at home," " He is good to everybody but his own family."   The oriental saint who gave his body to feed the tiger, instead of being called a saint would then begin to be called a sinner.

CHAPTER IV

THE FORMS OF HUMAN CONFLICT

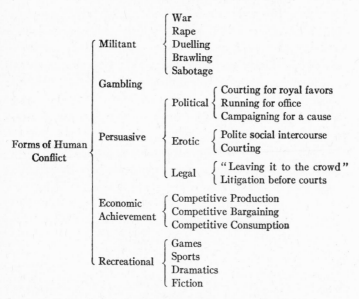

In Chapters II and III the sources of conflict have been shown to be, — first, scarcity of desirable things, second, self-interest or self-centered appreciation. There being fewer of certain things than people desire — people uniformly preferring their own satisfaction or that of those near to them to the satisfaction of other people — the conflict of interests is unavoidable. This conflict shows itself, however, in a great variety of forms, the chief of which are outlined in the foregoing diagram.

By the Militant form of conflict is meant any form in which one's success depends upon one's power to destroy, to harm, or to inflict pain or injury. One strives to get what one wants by inflicting injury upon one's rivals, and in order to succeed in this form of conflict, one must develop one's powers of destruction.

Under Gambling is included every method of securing what one desires by leaving it to chance. It is a cheaper and less destructive method than any of the militant forms of conflict, though it is not likely to result in any closer approximation to justice.

Under the Persuasive forms of conflict are included every method by which one furthers one's own interests by the exercise of one's powers of persuasion. Under this method one must beat one's rival by competing with him in some kind of persuasive contest, by argument, debate, or oratory; by manners, dress, or personal popularity; or by ogling, demagogy or political claptrap.

By the method of Economic Achievement is meant any conflict or competition in which one strives to get what one wants either by producing it, or by bargaining, or by conspicuous consumption.

Under the Recreational forms of conflict we include every attempt to amuse ourselves by engaging in some kind of a contest, by observing a make-believe contest as it is placed on the stage, or by reading the story, real or fictitious, of some of the multifarious forms of conflict outlined above.

One conspicuous fact about human conflict in general is that no one is absolutely confined to any of the methods outlined in this diagram. He who is beaten in one form of conflict may, unless restrained by conscience or social force, resort to another form to regain what he has lost. Generally the tendency is to resort to the more primitive rather than to the less primitive form. That is to say, a gambler who is beaten in the game may attempt by the use of knife or pistol to regain what he has lost. In other words, he reverts from the gambling to the militant type of conflict. The courtier who has failed to get the favorable ear of the king, having been beaten by a rival, may challenge his successful rival to a duel, as may also the defeated candidate for office in a democracy, or the defeated suitor for the hand of a lady. These are all cases of reverting from a less primitive to a more primitive form of conflict. A political party which is beaten in a general campaign for a cause is also under temptation to start an insurrection, as has happened many times in history, attempting to regain by war what has been lost in politics.

In the field of Economic Achievement there is an equal tendency to revert to a more primitive form of conflict. They who are beaten in economic competition are under temptation to go into politics in order that they may win back, if possible, in that form of conflict what they have lost in the other. If they are beaten in both the economic and the political fields, they are still under temptation to revert to sabotage, which is one of the militant forms of conflict. This temptation is peculiarly strong because of the fact that they who are in a strong position economically are almost of necessity in a weak position in politics, or, contrariwise, they who are in a weak position economically are almost of necessity in a strong position in politics or war.

The reason for this is that, other things equal, the fewer there are in a given competitive group, the stronger is their economic position, but the weaker their political or militant position. If there are only a few men capable of producing a certain commodity, and the commodity is, therefore, scarce, or if there are only a few capable of rendering a given service, the commodity or the service of each one will be in great demand. The supply is less than is demanded and they who control the limited supply are necessarily in a strong economic position. But the very fact that they are few in numbers makes them weak politically in the sense that they control fewer votes than others. Contrariwise, if there are a very large number capable of producing a given commodity, or rendering a given service, so that the commodity or service is very abundant, it will, other things equal, sell at a low price. The very fact of the numerical strength of the members of this competing group puts them in a weak position economically. They are pretty certain to be beaten in the economic form of competition. But the very source of their economic weakness is the source of their political strength. They have an excellent opportunity, therefore, to win back by political agitation what they lost in economic competition. Even if they fail in political agitation, they still have a chance (or are likely to think they have) if they are numerous enough, to win by the militant form of conflict, that is, by reverting to violence, sabotage, the general strike, or some other militant method.

In a later chapter on the Redistribution of Human Talent we shall attempt to show the economic advantages of such a redistribution of talent as will make one competing group approximately as numerous, relatively to the demand for it, as any other competing group. What has already been said in this chapter ought to be sufficient to prove that the same thing would be politically expedient; that is to say, if one competing group becomes so very numerous, relatively to others, as to put it at a very great disadvantage in economic competition, it will have a strong temptation to revert, first to political and later to those militant forms of conflict that mean the destruction of the state and of civilization itself.

In view of the multiplicity of forms in which the conflict of human interests may show itself, it must appear futile even to attempt to repress all forms.   We may repress certain forms but in so doing we are likely to increase the intensity of others.   If we repress, for example, all the militant forms of conflict, the combative instincts of mankind together with the conflict of interests will cause them to compete or contest with one another in the other fields.   There being more contestants in these other fields, the contest will become more intense.   If we repress both militancy and gambling, we still further tend to concentrate and intensify the conflict in the remaining fields.   If it were possible to stop all economic competition, as is sometimes proposed, by universal public ownership and operation, we should not lessen the combative instinct nor the rule of self-interest. We should merely concentrate it in the political field.   In fact, under such a system as this, every business or industrial position would become at once a political position.   We would show our rivalry and our preference for ourselves by struggling more intensely than we now do for political office or preferment.   Every one would, in other words, become a candidate for some political office, there being no other way to make a living.   Incidentally it may be re- marked that this would be an exceedingly wasteful form of competition, more wasteful than economic competition. When two farmers compete with one another in producing corn, more corn is likely to be grown as the result of that competition.   When two candidates compete for a given office, the time which they spend in campaigning is wasted, — it produces nothing.

On the other hand, if we could suppress the ordinary political methods of competition, we should only intensify the economic methods. For example, if instead of distributing the offices on the basis of the number of votes secured by various contestants, each office could be awarded for superiority in production, then contestants would strive to produce as much as possible rather than to get as many votes as possible. This would probably secure better public officials than we can possibly get by the voting method, but what is more important, the energy used in this kind of a campaign would result in more goods, more utilities, whereas that which is used in the present type of political campaign is wasted. However, this is not the main contention. The main contention is that conflict is so universal and so deeply imbedded in human nature that it cannot possibly be repressed. We can direct it into one field or another. It is to be regarded as any other great natural force, like wind or water power. One cannot stop the wind nor the flow of water, but one may harness these great natural forces to useful ends. That is what is done when we close the militant field for the exercise of human conflict and open the field of economic achievement. This is not an approval or endorsement of the spirit of conflict. One needs neither to approve nor condemn any more than one would approve or condemn wind, water power, gravitation, or any other natural force. One needs only to take account of it and try to make the most of it.

Few realize how deadly the erotic form of persuasive conflict is. When one realizes that a man or woman can be killed by old age as effectively as with an axe or a gun, and also realizes what the mating process signifies, one will begin to get an idea of the deadly nature of this conflict. The man or the woman who fails in this conflict is done for as effectively as if he or she had failed in a militant conflict. His or her life comes to an end and leaves no replica behind in the form of offspring. This, to the mind of the philosopher is as tragic an event as though he or she were killed in war. The fundamental instincts of both men and women agree with the mind of the philosopher in this respect. Therefore, this erotic conflict is waged as relentlessly and with as little consideration or quarter as any other form of warfare.

Of the three forms of economic competition the most advantageous and least harmful is that of competitive production; production is service. Competitive production is, therefore, rivalry in the performance of service. In competitive bargaining we have more opportunities for harm because there are so many opportunities for deception and fraud. Most of the charges brought against the competitive system apply to competitive bargaining rather than to competitive production. However, a mutual exchange of service or commodities on a fair and equitable basis is a highly useful operation. If A has something which he does not want but B does, and B likewise has something which he does not want while A does, it is obviously to the advantage of both to effect an exchange. However, in the actual process of exchange we may normally expect both A and B to higgle for an advantage and both are under temptation to deceive, and deception is always immoral. Because of the persistence of this temptation, a great deal of our law and legal procedure is concerned with the task of preventing deception without interfering with legitimate exchange. It is a difficult problem; but because a thing is difficult is no reason for not doing it.

When we come to the field of competitive consumption, however, there is little that can be said in defence of it. It is the result of the lowest and least defendable quality in human nature. It is the result of the desire to outshine our neighbors, or to avoid being outshone by them. The desire to show off, to attract notice, and all the other tendencies which are summed up under the one word "vanity" are at work here.

While this is by far the worst form of economic competition, producing more evils than any other, having less that can possibly be said in its defence, it is a striking fact that comparatively few of our modern social reformers have given any attention to it whatever. They have attacked business competition, competition in production, competition in exchange, but are singularly silent on competition in consumption. The older preachers of righteousness of a somewhat narrow and orthodox school preached incessantly against vanity and luxury. In this respect they were wiser economists and more rational reformers than the so-called liberal school of the present day. Their teachings on this particular subject would do vastly more for society and for the poor themselves than all the radical leaders of the present day. Further consideration of this topic will be postponed to Chapter XV on the Responsibility of the Rich for the Condition of the Poor.

CHAPTER V

ECONOMIC COMPETITION

It is time to stop talking about protecting the weak against the strong. There is no better ground for this than for the Nietzschean proposal to allow the strong to do as they please. What the state must do is to protect production against predation. Whether the predacious individual be weak or strong does not enter into the case, neither does the question as to whether the productive individual be strong or weak. However strong the productive individual may be, it is a waste of energy for him to have to defend himself and his products against the predacious individual. The state can do it more economically. However weak the predacious individual may be, he must be restrained.

Of all forms of human conflict, economic competition is the highest. In no other form of conflict does success depend so much upon production or service and so little upon destruction or deception. There are three forms of economic competition: competitive production, competitive bargaining, and competitive consumption. Competitive production always works well; competitive bargaining sometimes works well and sometimes badly; competitive consumption always works badly. Of these three forms of economic competition, therefore, the highest is competitive production, the lowest is competitive consumption, while competitive bargaining occupies a middle position.

Most of the opponents of economic competition propose to substitute for this form of conflict another form, namely, political competition. The more the state absorbs the enterprises now carried on by private initiative, the more will political competition displace economic competition. Political competition is a lower form. Before pursuing this topic further, let us examine the fundamental factors involved in all human conflict.

That the chief purpose of all living beings is to keep on living is too obvious to need discussion. The universal struggle for existence has occupied the attention of all students of the problems of life, both human and sub-human, for many generations. Some of the most revolutionary and far-reaching scientific generalizations of modern times have grown out of this study. It is clearly perceived by every student that economic competition is, in some way, a part of this universal struggle. It is not always understood just how it relates itself to that struggle as it is carried on in the sub-human world. There is abroad a very uncritical and undiscriminating opinion to the effect that there is no essential difference between economic competition and the brutal struggle for existence as studied by the zoölogist.

In assuming the universality of the struggle for existence, however, it is not necessary to exclude such facts as love, friendship, play, and mutual aid, either among men or animals. These are facts which cannot be denied, and they must have a place in any philosophy of life that is worth a moment's consideration. In the effort of living beings to keep on living these benign agencies have a place as well as the sterner facts of war and slaughter. In a preliminary and superficial way it may be suggested that the key to the problem of harmonizing such unlike things as love and war, friendship and strife, mutual aid and mutual slaughter, is found in the observation that human interests are sometimes harmonious and sometimes antagonistic.[1] Where they are

[1] Cf. Chapter I.

harmonious, love, friendship, and mutual aid promote the effort to keep on living. Where they are antagonistic, some form of struggle is inevitable. It may take any one of a multitude of forms. The rivals may, in an unthinking way, absorb the limited supply of nutriment, moisture, or light, leaving the less successful competitors to perish of starvation; it may take the form of a conscious and deliberate extermination of rivals by the method of slaughter, or it may take on the idyllic, but none the less deadly form of gracious social intercourse which accompanies courtship, and leaves the less fortunate competitors to go unmated and eventually to perish without reproducing themselves. From this point of view, love and friendship are only specialized forms of battle and slaughter.

But economic competition relates to those rivalries which grow out of the desire to possess those things which are generally classed under the name of wealth. Just what is to be included under this term varies from time to time and from place to place. When wives were regarded as property, were evaluated commercially, and bought and sold, they were wealth, and the rivalry for their possession took the form of economic competition. Where they are no longer regarded as property, nor evaluated commercially, nor bought and sold, they are not included under wealth; but they are regarded as something very much better. Under these conditions there is frequently a rivalry among men for their possession, and, where this rivalry is not restrained by law or custom, it is even more deadly than economic competition; but it is not economic competition.

The very nature of wealth involves a conflict of interests and consequent rivalry. Nothing is ever regarded as wealth, commercially evaluated, or bought and sold, unless it be scarce. A thing is scarce only when there is less of it available, in a given time and place, than is wanted. Where there is less of it than is wanted, if some one gets all he wants, some one else must necessarily get less than he wants. Instantly there is rivalry for the possession of the scarce article.

In an unrestrained and brutal state of existence, there are no limits to the form which this rivalry may take. The rivals may strive with tooth and claw, or with manufactured implements of destruction, or they may strive to win the desired article by useful and meritorious service; but strive they will in one form or another. Not every form of struggle for wealth is economic competition. The only forms to which that name can accurately be applied are those wherein some form of service, real or imagined, is a condition of success. These alone are economical forms of rivalry, all others are uneconomical. They consist in contributing to social production as much as is acquired by the competitor. Rivalry in acquisition becomes rivalry in production; all other forms of rivalry in acquisition being more and more suppressed by enlightened governments.

A glance at the diagram at the beginning of Chapter IV will reveal, in a general way, the difference between economic competition and the unrestrained, brutal struggle for existence. In the absence of some kind of social control or legal restraint, any or all the methods there outlined are followed. Wherever there is any kind of social control or legal restraint, an effort is made to distinguish between the economic and the uneconomic, and to suppress the uneconomic methods, particularly the destructive methods, of acquiring wealth. In fact, the enlightenment and efficiency of a system of government or social control may be tested by the accuracy with which it makes that discrimination, and the success of its efforts to suppress the uneconomical methods.

By an economical method of acquiring wealth is meant a method by which an individual succeeds in proportion as he contributes to the wealth of the community. By an uneconomical method is meant a method by which the individual impoverishes others in proportion as he succeeds himself. The more people there are in a community acquiring wealth by uneconomical methods, and the more successful they are, the poorer they tend to make the community; but the more there are acquiring wealth by economical methods, and the more successful they are, the richer they make the rest of the community.

The fact that we can make such a distinction as this between the economical and the uneconomical ways of making a living shows how far we have progressed beyond the brutal struggle for existence. Neither brutes nor unrestrained human beings make any such distinction. All the grosser and less refined of the destructive ways of acquiring the means of subsistence are practiced by brutes. The only reason they do not practice the more refined methods is that they do not know how. But unrestrained and uncontrolled human beings have not even the limitations of ignorance.

It will be observed that every special method named in the list of destructive methods, is practiced, even by the most civilized nations, in their dealings with one another, whenever their interests seriously conflict, or are thought to conflict. But within the nation, citizens are not allowed to practice these same methods in their dealings with one another. The reason is that the sovereign human group, which we commonly call the state or nation, is unrestrained and uncontrolled by any power higher than itself. It does as it pleases, and, consequently, it does precisely what any living being, either brute or human, would do under the same conditions, if it were unrestrained or uncontrolled by a higher power.   Every sovereign group is a law unto itself. It is undisciplined except by the laws of the universe, it is uncontrolled, except by the impact of cosmic forces, and it is unprotected except by its own internal efficiency.   But in the interest of this internal efficiency, upon which its life depends, when it is brought face to face with another sovereign group, it must discipline and control, as well as protect its citizens.   The sovereign group which should fail in any of these respects would soon lose its only protection, namely, its own internal efficiency, and would soon be conquered and eliminated.

The only place in the human world where we find the primordial struggle for existence, such as characterizes the sub-human world, is in the rivalry between sovereign groups. Each such group, as already pointed out, stands alone, uncontrolled, unprotected, a law unto itself.   That which goes under the name of international law is not law at all.   It is, rather, international good breeding.   It has no sanction except that which exists among gentlemen in support of gentlemanly behavior.   Any one who cares nothing for the good opinion of his fellows, and who feels strong enough to be free from the fear of a thrashing, is quite free to violate any and every rule of gentlemanly behavior.   Recent events have shown that precisely the same condition prevails among nations with respect to international law.

Whenever international law becomes *law*, with adequate sanctions, and a power behind it which can and will enforce it, the only change effected will be that those groups which we now call sovereign will have lost their sovereignty.   In their stead will be a great international state, if such it may be called, which then becomes sovereign.   It will still be under the same stern conditions of existence as are the sovereign states of the present. Its attitude toward the groups which remain outside the pale of international law, that is, outside the territory of the great international state, will be the same as that of a sovereign state of the present toward others. When this great international state is formed, subjecting to its will all the peoples living within it, establishing something more than a Roman peace throughout the civilized world, it will be an evil day for the "lesser breeds without the law," that is, for those races which are not capable of living up to the standards prescribed by this great civilized state. Civilized peoples having ceased wasting their energies in fighting among themselves, will have more to devote to the conquest of the rest of the world.

Wherever the primordial struggle for existence is found, either in the human or the sub-human world, the only unpardonable sin is weakness. Neither pity nor the sense of justice will preserve the weak from extermination or exploitation. The only virtue is strength. Nature cherishes her darling, the strong, and whips the weak to death. But how can a sovereign human group, i. e., a nation, strengthen itself for this inevitable and unmitigated struggle ? That is the question which transcends all others in importance. The nation which listens to other advice, and allows other questions to divert its attention from this supreme one, will pay the penalty with its life. The heavens are brass to its prayers for mercy if it neglect obedience to this supreme law of self-preservation. The nation which deludes itself with other theories, which listens to the siren voice of enervating pleasure, which gives itself to motionless contemplation and sentimental moral speculation, will go the way of all such nations. The primrose path leads to national even more certainly than to individual perdition.

Wherever this primordial struggle is carried on, among individuals or groups, among men, animals or plants, the supreme command of nature is, be strong! This is the whole of the law. To disobey this is to disobey every other command. Strength comes with self-discipline. To the sovereign social group this command enjoins the enforcement of discipline within. Murder must be suppressed because the group that permits it weakens itself. Thieving, swindling, monopolizing, and all other destructive activities must be suppressed for the same all-sufficient reason, and for no other reason whatsoever.

May it not sometimes be the duty of a nation, as of an individual, to be crucified rather than to survive ? It can be the duty of an individual to be crucified only for a principle which, if universally adopted within his group, will make that group strong. To be crucified for any other purpose is to die as the fool dieth. Obviously this reason why the individual should be willing to suffer crucifixion could not possibly apply to the group. The individual should die if, thereby, the group may live; but the sovereign group has but one duty and that is to live.

What may sometimes look like the death of the group is merely the flitting of sovereignty from a smaller to a larger group. When many small nations were, as is commonly said, " swallowed by the Empire of Rome " in order that a Roman peace might be established, they were, in most cases, made a part of a larger group, which then exercised sovereignty. If a new international empire, with its capital at The Hague, should be established, the nations which now exercise sovereignty would not cease to live, they would merely surrender their sovereignty and submit to the laws and discipline of this larger group. They would become what our American states became after the adoption of the Constitution. None of these groups ceased to live as groups. They merely accepted the protection, on the one hand, and the authority, on the other, of the Federal Government.

But how shall a nation grow strong ? One way is to secure the maximum economy of its fund of human energy. When human energy, or labor power, is allowed to go to waste, either in idleness, or in non-productive effort, the nation weakens itself to that extent. One of the most effective ways of preventing idleness is to establish the rule that only he who works shall eat, and, further, that each shall be allowed to possess in proportion as his production exceeds his consumption. When applied specifically to the pursuit of wealth it is the duty of the state, as pointed out in Chapter VII, to identify acquisition and production. Referring in anticipation to the program at the beginning of Chapter X, a nation must discriminate sharply and accurately between the economic and the uneconomic ways of acquiring wealth, and suppress absolutely all uneconomic ways. When men can acquire wealth in no other way whatsoever except by producing it or its equivalent, or rendering a positive service commensurate with it, then they will strive to acquire it by these productive and useful methods. Instead of enriching himself at the expense of some one else, each individual will then find it impossible to enrich himself except by enriching the nation.

This means in a most distinct and important sense that, in order that the sovereign group may be successful in the unmitigated, primordial struggle which it must of necessity wage, it must discipline its individuals and prevent them from waging such a conflict among themselves. It must repress all destructive methods of acquiring wealth within its own jurisdiction by means of a criminal law. That is what criminal law is for. A crime is that which weakens the group. The more crimes there are committed the weaker the group becomes, other things equal.

When farmers rival one another in growing corn, there is a struggle among them, but it is not the unmitigated brutal struggle. It is the kind of a struggle which increases the corn crop and strengthens, to that extent, the group. There is no reason why the state should repress that kind of a struggle, or even regulate it beyond seeing that each one acts fairly and does not try to win by destroying other men's crops or interfering with their work. But when they quarrel over line fences, one trying to move his fence over on another man's land, there is a struggle which produces nothing. What one wins another loses, and there is no net gain. All the energy expended in this kind of a struggle is, from a social point of view, wasted. It, therefore, tends to weaken rather than strengthen the group. Therefore it is to the interest of the group to suppress, as promptly as possible, this kind of a struggle, — not to regulate it, not merely to see fair play, and let the stronger win; but to settle it. Therefore we have courts of law to take such quarrels out of private hands and settle them. It is even more important that such a quarrel be settled than that it be settled justly, though this is very important. To settle it justly is to give the land in dispute to the man who had earned it, i. e., who had given an equivalent for it. Otherwise the other man would acquire wealth uneconomically, that is, without having contributed anything for it.

From this point of view, it will appear that the purpose of a just government is not, strictly, to protect the weak and restrain the strong, though there is a sense in which that may be true. If by the weak are meant those weak in body, and by the strong those strong in body, it is one purpose of government to prevent the strong from imposing upon the weak by means of his bodily strength alone. If, however, the strong is able to contribute more to the strength of the state through superior production or service, the state must allow him to profit by his success, and if the weak is unable, because of bodily weakness to contribute anything to the strength of the state, he must fail. The state may support him, but it must be called charity and not justice. At any rate, it would be suicidal for any state to make it a practice to restrain the strong in this sense, from performing superior service lest he should succeed better than the weak, with his inferior service.

In this restrained economic struggle or competition, a new definition of strength is virtually adopted, and a new standard of fitness for success in the struggle is put into effect. In the unmitigated brutal struggle, weapons of destruction are quite as important as serviceable qualities. Success comes to whomsoever is able to fight successfully where there are no rules of the game. The state must lay down rules for the struggle among individuals, and, in proportion as it approximates to justice, these rules will make productivity, or usefulness to the state, the condition of success. The struggle thus becomes a struggle to see who can become most useful or productive, and the prizes are awarded accordingly.

In this struggle strength succeeds on condition that it be used in service, and it fails if it is not. Weakness, of the kind which can render little service, is sure to fail and has and deserves no protection against the normal consequences of that kind of weakness. In this kind of a regulated struggle, it becomes literally true that greatness depends upon service. " And whosoever will be chief among you, let him be your servant " — not a servant in the sense of one who is in servitude under your beck and call, but a servant in the sense of one who contributes most largely to the life and strength of " you all," i. e., the whole of society.

Under these conditions, if any state can reach them, economic success would be an accurate measure of economic merit. The more men there were getting rich, and the richer they got, the better it would be for the whole. A large crop of multi-millionaires would then be a favorable sign because it would mean that there were a large number of individuals, each of whom had contributed millions to the wealth of the state. This fact, however, would probably not make them popular, nor protect them from the envy and covetousness of the weak.

There is no denying that, even under these ideal conditions there would be a real and intense struggle among individuals within the state. What we are laboring to show is that it differs in the most fundamental qualities from the unmitigated brutal struggle for existence. The enemies of the competitive system not only fail, but refuse to see this important difference. To fail to see this difference is to fail to see the difference between production and destruction, between service and harm. Brutes and sovereign human groups sometimes succeed by means of implements of destruction, and in proportion to the harm they do. Under economic competition men succeed only by means of instruments of production, and in proportion to the service they do.

Here the philosophy of Nietzsche is at fault. While it is a wholesome tonic against the debilitating effect of the " cult of incompetence " and self-pity with which the modern world is afflicted, it fails to see that the primordial struggle has been transferred from the individual to the group, and that the super-man must therefore give way to the super-group. All that he says regarding the strong man, applies to the strong group. Men who did not use team work, and fight in groups, would easily succumb to those who did. But the very idea of team work, or group action, involves a restraint upon and discipline of the individual. The super-man would threaten the strength of his group, and, without his group, he would be a helpless Gulliver among organized Lilliputians, however strong he as an individual might be. In short, his own safety would require him to submit to the discipline which his group found necessary to its own preservation.

Against the over-hasty conclusion that any kind of individual conduct which pays the individual is, therefore, good conduct and justified by the laws of natural selection, it is only necessary to mention the fact that, in the case of the human species, the struggle for existence is primarily and dominantly a struggle among groups. In the process of adaptation it has become a struggle among those territorial groups, exercising sovereignty, called states or nations. It is only among these sovereign groups that the primordial character of the struggle persists; every other group, and every individual struggle is under discipline of one kind or another, according to the character of the state of which it or he is a part. This large fact is well summed up in one of Kipling's "Jungle Book" rhymes, — ' For the strength of the pack is the wolf, And the strength of the wolf is the pack.' It is the pack as a whole which struggles to maintain itself in the midst of the jungle, and, in order to succeed and survive, it must discipline its members. The pack, like the state, is itself sovereign and therefore undisciplined except by the forces of nature and the competition of rival packs. That is a good wolf, from the standpoint of the pack, whose conduct, however unprofitable to himself, is such as to strengthen the pack and help it to succeed. That is a bad wolf whose conduct, however profitable to himself, is such as to weaken the pack as a whole and interfere with its success. From the standpoint of the individual wolf, that is a good pack which is so organized and disciplined as to dominate the jungle. The average member of such a pack is better off than the average member of a pack so badly organized and disciplined as to be overcome by the hostile forces of the jungle. That pack is best fitted to succeed and to dominate the jungle which rewards with honor, power, and authority those individuals whose conduct contributes most to the success of the whole, and penalizes those individuals whose conduct contributes least to the success of the whole, or interferes most with that success. Substitute " man " for " wolf," " society " for " pack," and " world " for " jungle," in the foregoing sentences, and we shall have, in a nutshell, the whole theory of rational morality.[1]

Under a state which accurately distinguishes between the economic and uneconomic ways of getting wealth, and effectively suppresses all of the latter, it follows of necessity that every individual will be forced, with respect to wealth, to act in his own self-interest precisely as he would if he were animated by the most completely altruistic motives and patriotic sentiments. If as an altruist he saw that there was a great and intense need for a certain product or service, he would feel impelled to supply it. As a self-interested person he would find it profitable to do the same. If as an altruist he saw that he could use the price for which his product or service would sell in supplying other needs, he would exact the price and use it thus. As a self-interested person he would find it profitable to do the same. If as an altruist he saw that he could, by reducing his consumption, use his surplus income in purchasing tools, rather than consumers' goods, thus turning the productive forces of the community into the tool-making rather than the luxury-producing industries, and thus, in turn, increasing the productive power of the community, he would thus reduce his consumption and increase his investment. As a far-sighted or wisely self-interested person he would find it advantageous to do the same thing. If as an altruist he saw that he could, by exacting a price for the use of his new tools and using this price in purchasing still other tools, he could still further increase the productive power of the community, he

[1] From *The Religion Worth Having*, by the Author.

would exact the price, that is, interest on his capital, and reinvest it. As a self-interested person he would find it to his advantage to do the same. And so on, throughout the whole list of possibilities, the wisest philanthrophy and the wisest self-interest would lead to identical conduct, until we reach the missionary field where the people are to be given services which they do not want and will refuse to pay for.

Here, and here only, will altruism and self-interest lead to different conduct. Altruism would insist on performing services for the people which they do not want,—which they even resent. It would, of course, be very "undemocratic" on the part of altruism, to assume that it knew what was good for the people better than they knew themselves. Self-interest would say, "who am I that I should pretend to know what the people want better than they themselves do. I shall give them the product or service for which they ask and are willing to pay." This would be very democratic of self-interest, as democracy is popularly conceived, which always assumes that the people know better than any one else, what is good for them.

This appeal to self-interest to do for the community precisely what altruism would do, is in no sense whatever, an attempt to set up self-interest as the sole motive to action, or to refuse to appeal to altruism and patriotism even in matters of wealth. The appeal is to both. Every human being has a certain amount of altruism and patriotism about him, and can always be appealed to, more or less powerfully on this basis. It is quite proper to make this appeal and turn this sentiment to the public good. On the other hand, no human being is free from self-interest or, as it was previously called, self-centered appreciation, and there is no one who cannot be appealed to on this ground. If he can be appealed to on this ground also, as well as on the ground of altruism or patriotism, we have a double appeal moving him in the direction of public service. It is like harnessing two great natural forces and compelling them to work together toward the same end. Where this can be done successfully, it would be silly to attempt to dispense with one and depend upon the other alone.

At this point it is well to be on our guard against a common interpretation of Adam Smith's famous dictum regarding a beneficent order of nature under which the individual is led, " as by an invisible hand, to promote the public interest while trying to promote his own." Adam Smith saw clearly, as has every clear-headed student of the problem since his day, that under the competitive system, properly safeguarded, men are led by their self-interest to do many things which result in good to society. In fact it would not be difficult to show that, in the mass, most of the good and useful things that are done in any progressive community are done through self-interest. The few really good things which are done through pure altruism are so conspicuous because of their unfamiliarity, as to attract notice.

But it is a mistake to assume that this beneficent order of nature exists, or can possibly exist, in the absence of very careful and strict government supervision and interference. Government and government alone prevents competition from lapsing into the brutal struggle for existence, where self-interest leads to uneconomic as well as to economic, — to destructive as well as to productive activity on the part of the individual. But where governmental interference is wisely and efficiently directed, so that men are not allowed to follow their self-interest in the direction of destructive, harmful, or uneconomic activities, they will still follow their self-interest. Since the only ways left open to them are the productive, useful, and economic activities, their self-interest impels them into these activities. Thus it is that, *under proper government interference and control*, men are led as by an invisible hand, to promote the public interest while trying to promote their own.

The perception of this great truth made a deep impression upon the minds of those philosophers who first grasped its significance. To them it seemed so beneficent as to become identified almost with the divine order of the universe. Therefore they were accustomed to regard it as the natural order of things. By a natural order of things, however, they did not mean a state of things which could exist where there was no government, much less a state of things which had ever existed in any primitive or idyllic community, but rather a state of things which seemed to fit so well into the universal scheme of things, cosmic and social, as to produce the maximum of harmony and the minimum of friction. From this point of view, their essential position has never been successfully assailed, though a different terminology has been substituted for theirs. Instead of calling it the natural order, we should now be content to say that it is the best and most workable scheme of economic organization that has ever been invented. In fact, it has not been *invented* at all, but is the result of a gradual adjustment to circumstances, meeting each situation with the best wisdom available.

Let it not be understood, however, that merely because government supervision and control are necessary to the maintenance of the competitive system as distinguished from the unmitigated struggle for existence, that all government interference is, therefore, justifiable. Speaking broadly, it would not be so very unsafe to say that government interference is almost as frequently harmful as beneficial. It is only when it is wisely planned that it can be justified. To be wisely planned is, essentially, to distinguish accurately between economic and uneconomic activities, and to suppress the latter efficiently.

The reliance upon the motive of self-interest as one means of harnessing men to useful work does not necessarily mean the reliance upon greed. They who object to this principle of government sometimes make the mistake of using opprobrious words where nothing really opprobrious is involved. The desire to possess goods for oneself, one's family, and others in whom one is specially interested is not an unworthy desire, though it is, by the high-souled partizans of another system, characterized as greed. In its place it is sometimes proposed to substitute the desire for social esteem, or some other agreeable motive. But if the desire to possess goods is greed, then the desire for social esteem is vanity. As between greed and vanity there is little to choose. Besides, the appeal to the desire for goods does not, in the slightest degree, interfere with the appeal to the desire for social esteem. They are equally self-interested. If we can appeal to both, we have a more powerful combination of motives than if we appeal to one alone. There is thus the same reason for appealing to both forms of self-interest, in order to induce strenuous production, that we found in favor of appealing to both self-interest and altruism.

But is rivalry of any kind desirable ? Is it in harmony with our ethical principles ? In the first place it is inevitable if we have a population dominated by self-interest, or what was more accurately called self-centered appreciation in Chapter III. If there is any degree of preference for self as compared with others, for one's family as compared with other families, for one's neighbors as compared with other neighbors, then the individual having such preferences will strive more zealously for his own interest than for others, for the interest of his family than for other families, for the interest of his neighbor than for other neighbors.   This attitude is absolutely inevitable if we once have the sociological background which I have called self-centered appreciation.   The only question, therefore, is as to the method by which the individual shall express his preference for self, for his family, or for his neighbor as compared with others.   He may express this preference by striving to produce as much as possible for his own consumption or for the consumption of his family, even trying perhaps to do better by his family than other men can do for theirs.   He may strive through political methods for a better office, or a better position in the state than other men are getting, or to rise as high in the bureaucracy as possible.   If his field of endeavor lies not in the field of independent economic enterprise, but in the field of politics, he is certain to compete with his fellows if he has any preference of the kind described.   Rivalry is inevitable where you have any such sociological background.   Or in the absence of social control he may show his preference by uneconomical methods such as war, robbery, etc.

Since rivalry of some kind is unpreventable under any social system where you have any degree of preference for oneself or those near to oneself over others, it is a waste of time to consider the question whether there ought to be any rivalry or not.   There is rivalry.   The only question is which form of rivalry is least harmful or most beneficial.   There are three characteristic forms of rivalry still recognized: war, politics, and business.   In a militant state, military rivalry is the dominant form.   Success in life will be determined largely by the possession of military qualities. The method of attaining success will be through the exercise of fighting power.   But fighting is destructive and not productive.   In a state which is predominantly political, that is, where most of the functions are performed through politics or by the state, and most of the good positions in life are secured by political methods, there, of course, political rivalry becomes the dominant form.   There the individual's success will depend mainly upon his ability in politics, which, in last analysis, depends upon his vote-getting power.   But in a state which is predominantly industrial, where there is little scope for military ambition, where the functions of the state are kept down to normal limits, and the great mass of men are engaged in industrial pursuits, guided and dominated by private business enterprise, the characteristic form of rivalry will be business rivalry.   Here one's success will depend, not upon his fighting power nor upon his vote-getting power, but upon his ability to supply goods or service which people are willing to purchase.

We may rule out of consideration the military form of rivalry as being destructive, and therefore not to be encouraged except where national protection is necessary. Certainly, within the nation, duelling and other antiquated relics of militancy are not to be considered.   We are concerned, therefore, with the comparison between the political and the economic forms of rivalry.   Is it better that the state should take over most of the industrial functions, thus narrowing the field of business competition and enlarging the field of political competition ?   For if the state runs most of our industries as it now runs the post-offices, then most of our industrial positions will be filled as postal positions are now filled.   One's success in getting desirable positions will depend upon the same qualities which now advance him in the civil or governmental service.   But if most of our industrial enterprises are left in the hands of individuals, then the rivalry will be business rivalry and one's success in getting desirable positions will depend upon the qualities which bring success in business. The question as to the relative desirability of these two forms of rivalry depends upon which is the more accurate method of selecting men for desirable positions, the political method or the business method. Under the political method, generally speaking, the man's advancement will depend upon his ability to convince voters of his fitness for the place. Under business competition, a man's success will depend primarily upon his ability to convince buyers of the value of his products or services. It would seem, therefore, that this question depends upon whether the voter votes more intelligently than the buyer buys. The question is: Does the average man when he votes spend his vote as intelligently as he does his dollar when he buys products or services? If he is more likely to be prejudiced in his votes than in his purchases, or is more likely to vote ignorantly than he is to purchase ignorantly, one should conclude that buying is a more accurate test of merit than voting, and vice versa. Suppose that a private individual should produce and put on the market a good product which appeals to the buyer, but the producer is a member of an unpopular race or an unpopular religious body, that is, that there is a great deal of prejudice against him and his class; is this prejudice as likely to interfere with the sale of his product or his services as it is to interfere with his getting votes for a desirable position? It would seem not. To that extent, at least, buying is a less inaccurate method of determining merit than voting, that is, the racial and religious prejudices are less likely to be factors in buying than in voting. If that be true, the man who succeeds in getting the money of purchasers is in this respect, at least, more likely to have earned that money than is the man who gets their votes through racial or religious prejudices likely to have deserved their votes.   Thus far, at any rate, the argument is in favor of the business rather than the political form of rivalry.

Again, as to the matter of ignorance or intelligence: Does the average purchaser purchase as intelligently or more intelligently than he votes ?   Does he know as accurately what he is getting for his money as he does what he is getting for his vote ?   Doubtless many improvements can be made in our balloting system.   Any one who will examine himself or his own experience will probably agree that he votes very unintelligently, that is to say, he knows very little about the candidates whose names appear on the ballot, and he has very inadequate methods of finding out about them.   Though the writer has tried consistently to do his duty as a voter, he has to confess that in a majority of cases the candidates for whom he votes are absolutely unknown to him and that, therefore, a man who could not read at all could vote quite as intelligently as he can in more than half the cases.   In other words, in more than half the cases, voting with him is wholly a matter of guess work, and he has no adequate means of finding out in advance what he is voting for, in the way of men, and seldom in the way of measures.   If this be the experience of the average man, it would seem to imply that the average man votes very unintelligently, and that therefore there is little reason to expect that the individuals who get his votes have earned them or deserved them.

It is also doubtless true that we buy unintelligently, yet so far as the author's own experience is concerned, though he is frequently deceived in his purchases, he is perfectly clear that he is deceived less frequently than in his votes, that he knows more accurately what he is purchasing than what he is voting for. If this be true of the average person, then it would follow, as the day the night, that the man who gets our dollars more frequently deserves them than the man who gets our votes. In other words, that business success is a less inaccurate test of merit than political success. If that be the case, then the economic form of rivalry is superior to the political form, in that in business rivalry merit wins more frequently or less infrequently than in the political form of rivalry. It is therefore the author's deliberate opinion that the process of buying and selling, when it is properly safeguarded, is a better method of testing the economic value of men than is the process of voting.

There are, however, some services which have to be rendered and which we cannot possibly get by the process of buying and selling, or, through business rivalry. We could not have several governors trying to rule the state and giving the governed the option of paying for the service of the one he liked best. This, however, is the result of what is known as territorial sovereignty in government. The only absolute monopoly in the world is government. The individual has no choice in the matter except by the process of migration, and even that may be forbidden by the government of the territory in which he happens to be born. Where you have an absolute monopoly there can obviously be no such thing as business or economic competition, for the two are contradictory. Then the only method by which the governed can have a voice in the determination of the kind of service which he is to receive is by the ballot. Where there is no territorial sovereignty, or territorial monopoly, but where rivals may really be in the field offering their services, he who would secure a service may take his choice and give his vote, that is, his money, to the one that satisfies him best.

Thus business and industry which have not become monopolistic are all extremely democratic, in that sense more democratic in fact than any government can ever possibly hope to be.   Balloting is only a clumsy device to try to make government partially democratic.   But it is, even at its best, less democratic than industry is already.   If industry once became as absolutely monopolistic as government is, then they who are served by the industry would be helpless to control it without the ballot — as helpless as they are to control government without the ballot.   Even then they would have less control of that industry than they now have over competitive industry through their ability to purchase or to withhold their purchase, that is, to give or to withhold their industrial, as opposed to their political, votes.

This leads us to a consideration of a statement which is so frequently set forth in the ephemeral literature of the day, by popular writers and speakers, to the effect that as the nineteenth century achieved political democracy it remains for the twentieth century to achieve industrial democracy. They who have this point of view have apparently never gotten beyond the idea that balloting and democracy are synonymous.   We have heard a great deal of preaching in our day regarding the idolatry of wealth, of the worship of the almighty dollar.   We have heard apparently little of the worship of the almighty ballot, and yet of the two forms of idolatry the latter is not only more vicious, but more silly.

Two things and two things only are essential to real democracy.   The first is an open road to talent, that is to say that every man shall have an opportunity to rise to positions of power and responsibility in proportion to his ability, regardless of birth, privilege, caste, or other social barriers.   The son of the peasant may become the ruler in government or the employer in business by sheer force of his own merit, if he happens to possess merit. The second essential of pure democracy is that they who are in positions of power and responsibility shall be made sensitive to the needs, the desires, and the interests of those over whom they exercise power and responsibility. Irresponsible power, power upon which there is no automatic check, power which may be abused, while they against whom it is misdirected have no effective remedy, is thus incompatible with democracy. Be it understood that power, responsibility, and authority are themselves entirely compatible with the highest conceptions of democracy, if only power is made sensitive and responsible. Even the leader of a mob exercises power and authority, but the mob has it also within its power to refuse to follow the leader. There is thus an effective check upon his abuse of power so far as the members of the mob themselves are concerned. The victim against whom the mob is exercising its force, having no such effective or automatic check, is helpless, so that the mob is only democratic on one side, but exceedingly autocratic on the other. The mob is, therefore, less democratic than an orderly government in which all equally can enforce a check upon the abuse of power. Not only they who follow and support the person in authority, but they against whom the authority is directed must, under the machinery, have equal and effective methods of imposing a check upon the abuse of power.

Given these two conditions, namely, an open road to talent and a keen sense of responsibility on the part of those who exercise power and authority, and you have every essential of the principle of democracy, whether there be any balloting or not. It happens, however, that in matters of government the ballot is the most effective method through which responsibility can be secured, or through which those in authority can be made sensitive to the desires and wishes of those over whom they exercise responsibility.   But according to both these tests, industry was democratic long before government became so, and moreover, industry is today more democratic than any government on the face of the earth, even though the ballot is not used in industry.

The simple fact is that industry is more democratic without the ballot than government can possibly be made even with the ballot.   First as to the open road to talent; that has always existed in industry in a higher degree than in politics.   However meritorious a man may be in politics, if his opinions are in advance of those of the majority he gets no advancement.   A very small and select minority may approve his work in industry and reward it.   He secures his advancement as the result of this without waiting for the crude majority to approve.   It is true even here he may fail through being so very far in advance of his times as not to secure the support even of the elect minority, but it is obviously easier for an advanced person to secure the support of a small and highly-intelligent minority than to transform this into a majority, which would require that much less intelligent people should be convinced.   Even under the best of democracies the man of genius stands a better chance outside of than in politics, whereas, of course, in an aristocratic or autocratic government he stands no chance at all.

It is of course also true that a trickster who would not succeed at all in politics, may succeed in business by deceiving a small and select body of imbeciles.   However, he must, even in business unless he violates the criminal law, succeed in giving even these few people something which they *think* they want.   Any field of endeavor in which men succeed in proportion to the number of desires they can satisfy, necessarily involves the opportunity for abuse so long as there are evil desires to be satisfied.   Individuals come more nearly getting what they want from business men than they do from politicians and government agents. If they happen to want evil things of course they get them from business caterers, unless the law in some way restrains and forbids them to get what they want, as in a prohibition state.   This in itself implies greater democracy in business and industry than in government.

This suggests also the second test, namely, that of sensitiveness.   The man who offers his services in the way of production in the field of business and industry is absolutely dependent upon the good will and favorable opinion of the purchasers from whom he solicits custom.   They have a better check upon him than they have upon their rulers.   If I, for example, am dissatisfied with the service I am getting from an elected official, I am helpless unless I can convince a majority.   I cannot reject the service nor refuse to pay for it.   The government may collect taxes for a purpose which I disapprove altogether, or it may be expending money in ways which I disapprove.   I am still helpless unless I can convince a majority of my fellow citizens that I am right; whereas if a man who produces goods for my satisfaction displeases me, I can reject his services and refuse to buy.   I have a more direct and effective check upon him than I have upon any public official.

The reason for this important difference is the principle of territorial sovereignty, which makes government the one absolute monopoly.   All who live within its territory are its subjects and must accept its service and pay for it whether they like it or not.   Being such an absolute monopoly, the quasi purchaser of the service of government is not a purchaser at all, because he cannot do other than accept, and, whether he accepts or not, he must pay for it in the way of taxes. Since this is true, he would have absolutely no check upon the power or authority of rulers did he not have the ballot. The ballot, therefore, is only a clumsy invention to make government somewhat sensitive, or to approximate in government to the sensitiveness which exists without the ballot in industry. If we could conceive of an industry which had reached such a stage of monopoly as that which government always possesses, we should then have to resort to the ballot in the control of that industry. If the power of a great monopoly, say the Standard Oil Company, were multiplied a hundred fold, so that it not only controlled the sale of oil, but could compel every individual in the country to purchase so much oil every year, whether he wanted it or not, a thing which no private monopoly has ever been able to do, it would then be in about as strong a position as government is. If it were in that position, then it would lack sensitiveness, unless people were given a ballot to enable them to control its management.

While no industry has ever attained such a monopoly as this, there is, therefore, no such overwhelming need for the ballot in the control of industry as exists in the case of government. Still industries sometimes develop monopolistic tendencies. They then begin to lose something of their sensitiveness to the desires of the people to whom they cater. This is true where they make such advances toward absolute monopoly as to practically control the field for the sale of a certain product. Though the individuals are still free to reject the product or to buy other partial substitutes for it, still some control must be exercised over such partial monopolies, and this control can only be exercised through politics and the ballot.   This control must eventually take the form of price regulation in order to take away their control of markets.

Incidentally, this would destroy most of the trusts.   No trust exists by virtue of its superior productive powers. Every one depends for its existence upon its superiority in buying or selling, that is upon its power over prices.   Take away this power and enable the outside concerns to match their productivity against that of the trust, and outside competition will increase and force the trust to break up into its most effective *productive* units, as distinguished from the most efficient *bargaining* units.

This means, however, that the necessity for the ballot as a means of directly controlling the policy of an industry arises only when an industry begins to take on some of the qualities and characteristics of government.   Enough has doubtless been said to show how purely shallow and senseless it is to repeat such vague generalities as " the democracy of industry " when industry is already more thoroughly democratic than government has ever been or can ever possibly become.

In short, the more nearly any industry approaches that condition of complete monopolization which characterizes all government, the more we shall find it necessary to resort to the ballot to exercise a check upon the power of the monopoly as we now use it to exercise a check upon government.   Concretely, this means government control. But government control merely means playing the vote-getting monopolist against the money-getting monopolist. The politician, that is, the vote-getter, cares no more for the people than does the trust magnate.   He merely wants their votes as the trust magnate wants their money.   He wants their votes in order that he may further his own interests just as the trust magnate wants their money in order that he may further his own interests.   If it came to a detailed comparison, it is impossible to predict which would suffer most.   But when one is played against the other, one bidding for the people's votes and the other bidding for their money, the people themselves may profit as the result of this new kind of competition.   When they can no longer play one against the other, that is, when they are completely in the hands of either the one or the other, they will be helpless indeed.   That is to say, when politicians cease baiting trusts and corporations, on the one hand, and when, on the other, there is no field of enterprise outside of publicly owned industry in which the private individual may pursue his interest, but must seek it in the public service, then will the people suffer.   In the one case, monopoly will crush all initiative.   In the other, the successful vote-getter will place his heel on the neck of the man who opposed his candidacy and who must come to him for a job in the public service after he is elected to a high position.

Again, the dollar is less likely to be influenced by class prejudice or race hatred than the ballot.   No one refuses to buy cotton grown by a negro, though many would refuse to vote for him for a public office.   No one refuses to buy clothes of a Jew though there are people who would refuse to vote for him.   In short the negro, the Jew, or a member of any other unpopular class stands a better chance of getting what he deserves in business than he does in politics.   Suppose cotton planting were handled as a government enterprise; negroes might be given positions as field hands, but on one, however capable or meritorious would be likely to get a position which a white man wanted, except where negro votes outnumbered the white.   There the conditions would be reversed provided the negroes would vote together.   In those communities where there is a prejudice against the Jew, he would seldom secure a desirable position under the political form of competition, except where Jews had large voting strength.   But in business he can rise to the highest positions if he possesses the ability to render good service. Gentiles will buy his products or services, thus enabling him to secure their dollars, who would not give him their votes.

Against the general conclusion that the acquisition of money is as accurate a test of public service as the acquisition of votes, or that the purchasing of products or services is as accurate a test of popular approval as voting, it may be argued that, in political elections, one man has as many votes as another, whereas in purchasing one man has many more dollars than another.   In voting, therefore, one man has as much influence on the general result as another, whereas in purchasing one man has a much larger influence than another.   This argument is entitled to some consideration, and is undoubtedly good as far as it goes.   It does not follow, however, that the one-man-one-vote principle is necessarily superior to all others.   It may be the most easily workable, but something is to be said, in principle at least, for a system of cumulative voting.   Suppose that it were possible, which it is not, to allow each man a number of votes in proportion to his usefulness, or his contribution to the public welfare, ideally this would be superior to the one-man-one-vote method.   The only reason for not adopting it is that, in the matter of votes, it would be impossible to estimate, even approximately, how many each man deserved.

In the matter of dollars, however, under a sound economic system, where competition is controlled as it ought to be controlled, the number of dollars possessed by a man would depend upon the number he had earned; that is the same as saying that the number would depend upon his usefulness or his contribution to the public welfare.   To the objection that we have not yet reached that state, the reply is that we still have that as an ideal, toward which we are trying to progress.   Therefore we will do well to assume that we can reach it, rather than to surrender to lower ideals.   Having a definite ideal or standard toward which we are to work, it is well to adjust the various details of our social system to that standard as rapidly as possible, rather than to adjust them to inferior standards which must, in their turn, be uprooted.

Much has been written on the waste of competition, — meaning economic competition.   These wastes are considerable and not to be minimized.   No device was ever invented which would run without friction.   The real question for the inventor is, therefore, to find a system where the friction or waste of energy is least.   The same principle must guide the statesman.   He cannot eliminate waste altogether.   Under the most perfect social system there would be some apparent waste of human energy, and it would be possible to write startling treatises on the cost of the system, whatever that system might be.

As between the economic and the political forms of competition, the latter is vastly more wasteful in proportion to what is accomplished.   When two farmers compete in growing corn, as previously pointed out, or two manufacturers compete in the making of goods, or two merchants in providing convenient service, there is more corn, there are more goods and better services provided for the group. But when two candidates run for office, there is no more public service rendered.   One gets the office and the other has wasted all his time and energy spent in campaigning.   So long as there is no other satisfactory method of filling offices, this is a form of waste which must be borne. It is part of the cost of having a representative government and we must not refuse to pay it. Incidentally it may be remarked that only rich countries can afford democratic government. A poor country must, perforce, be content with a cheaper form. The cost of government is not discovered by studying the tax rate. That is the least item in its cost. It must be discovered by studying its political campaigns, and calculating the amount of time and energy spent in palaver which might otherwise have been spent in production. The cost of *filling* the offices rather than of *paying* the officers, is the chief burden of democratic government. If all positions were political offices, as they would be under universal public ownership, the cost of filling these offices by the methods of political campaigning would be so enormous as to stagger the imagination. Under a benevolent despotism, such as exists in the Panama Canal Zone, where neither campaigning nor candidacy was permitted, the cost would be very low.

We now come to the question of the morality of the competitive spirit. Is it true, as some high idealists would have us believe, that competition is in spirit incompatible with ethics and religion, that we ought neither to run for office, thus engaging in political competition, nor engage in business competition ? We have tried to show that, where the principle of self-interest or self-centered appreciation is present, competition in one form or another is inevitable and cannot possibly be avoided, — that as between the two forms, namely, political and economic competition, economic competition is less wasteful and more accurate as a test of fitness, that industrial competition is more in harmony with the spirit of true democracy than is political competition. But is any form of competition compatible with the ideal of Christianity or of Christian ethics ?

In the first place, it would seem that those who hold the view that competition is antagonistic to the spirit of Christianity would find it impossible to engage in a game of tennis or croquet, for there is certainly competition here. In fact, if we look at the matter fairly and squarely, we should find that it would be very difficult even to amuse ourselves without some form of competition. But the answer will probably be made that it may be proper to compete in minor matters, but that it is wrong to compete for the necessaries of existence. I do not think that the difference is logically brought out by this contrast. Even in sport competition may take on an extremely unethical and irreligious tone, and in industry it may be as harmless and benign as the competition which takes place in a friendly game of golf. Whenever and wherever sports are engaged in primarily for the sake of a prize, where the contestants regard victory as the one desirable thing in terms of which everything else is evaluated, even sport becomes vicious. Then the rule is, anything to win; everything is evaluated in terms of its relation to the one desideratum, namely, victory. It is this, and this only, which tends to make sport vicious, unethical, or unchristian. This spirit will spoil any form of competition.

He who stands between me and the one desire of my heart is my enemy and I shall kill him if I can. For if there is one desire of my heart in terms of which everything else is evaluated, then everything which interferes with that desire I shall consider as a positive injury to myself. Everything which will contribute to that single and overmastering desire has a positive value to me. This rule applies to every form of competition or rivalry, whether it be sport, love, war, or business.

If the prize of success in business, say money, is the one desire of my heart, in terms of which everything else is evaluated, then everything which interferes with the fulfillment of that one desire is to me hateful. He who stands between me and the fulfillment of that desire is my enemy. On the other hand, where I engage in a game for the sake of the game and not for the sake of the prize, then he who plays the game against me and does his best to beat me, is not my enemy but my friend. Similarly in business competition, if I am animated by the spirit of the productive life, if my desire is for production rather than consumption, if I am " playing the game " not for the sole purpose of accumulating certain prizes of success, namely, consumers' goods, then he who plays the game against me and tries to beat me is my friend and not my enemy. My feelings towards him will not be unethical and unchristian. If, however, I am playing the game for the sake of the prize, for the sake of consumption, he becomes my enemy and not my friend and my feelings toward him are eminently unethical and unchristian.

From this point of view it will be perfectly clear that the evil is not to be found in competition itself, but the spirit which dominates it. This spirit in turn is determined by the philosophy of life of the competitors. They who regard the possession or consumption of wealth as the great end of life and industry will necessarily appraise everything in terms of its effect upon their possession and consumption. Anything which, or any person who interferes with or reduces their possession or consumption will be hated. Any person who promotes that possession and consumption will be prized or possibly loved. This philosophy of life may for euphony be called the pig-trough philosophy, and the manners and morals of the pig-trough will dominate the activities of the people who possess it. On the other hand, we have what may in contrast be called the work-bench philosophy of life, which regards action and not possession, production and not consumption, as the prime object. They who possess this philosophy will appraise everything according to its relation to action and productivity. That only is hateful which interferes with productive action. That only is lovely which promotes productive action. If I possess this philosophy, my enemy is not the man who plays against me in a game, but the man who refuses to allow me to play at all. Likewise in business my enemy is not the man who tries to win in industrial competition, but who tries to keep me from working or competing at all.

Thus it will be seen that the fundamental question which must be settled before anything else can be settled is the question of the philosophy of life which dominates the competitive process. If the world is dominated by the pig-trough philosophy, competition is not only inevitable, but it will invariably take on the morals of the pig-trough and become unethical and unchristian. But it would be futile to attempt to correct this by doing away with industrial competition so long as the same philosophy of life dominated individuals. So long as we had learned books written on the " economy of happiness " and the " efficiency of consumption," in which everything is expressed in terms of consumers' satisfactions, so long as it was conceived to be the chief end of industry and human effort to enable men to fill their bellies with the husks of material wealth, the rivalry would be unethical and unchristian no matter what form it took, whether it were political rivalry, military rivalry, or economic rivalry. Merely changing the machinery of government, or the methods of holding property, or of conducting industry, would in no way alleviate the grim and deadly character of that rivalry.

But let the community become dominated by the work-bench philosophy, under which productive action rather than consumption, either graceful or ungraceful, is the end, then competition in whatever field it may be carried on, or in whatever channel it may be directed, loses its unethical and unchristian character and comes to be the very expression of the highest ideals of Christian ethics. Incidentally it will be found that every single statement or pronouncement by the founder of Christianity on the subject of wealth, industry, and property is in the strictest harmony with this point of view. Not a single word did he ever utter in condemnation of private property or large possessions or large accumulations; but on every occasion he showed his disapproval of selfish consumption.

He who does less well than he can does ill. He who spends a dollar in selfish gratification when he might spend it for tools or productive services, does less well than he can. This is the logic back of every pronouncement of the Nazarene regarding wealth.

CHAPTER VI

HOW OUGHT WEALTH TO BE DISTRIBUTED?[1]

Why there should be hard-working poor men and idle rich men in the same community is a question which no one has answered and no one can answer satisfactorily. That is why the opinion is so prevalent that the world, economically considered, is so very much out of joint. However, though there is such general unanimity that wealth ought not to be distributed as it now is, there is a wide diversity of opinion, where there is any definite opinion at all, as to how it really ought to be distributed.

Fundamentally all these theories of distributive justice may be grouped under three heads, though there are innumerable variations under each of the three. The first may be called the aristocratic theory, the second, the socialistic theory, and the third, the democratic or liberalistic theory. By the aristocratic theory is meant the theory that the good things of this world belong more particularly to one distinct group or class than to another, that these, the elect, have a prior claim over all others to the resources of the earth and the products of industry. By the socialistic theory is meant the theory that wealth ought to be distributed according to needs; and by the democratic or liberalistic theory is meant the theory that wealth ought to be distributed according to productivity, usefulness, or worth.

The aristocratic theory is the most difficult of the three to discuss adequately, because no one definitely affirms it.

[1] The substance of this chapter was published in the *Atlantic Monthly* for June, 1906.

Nevertheless, there are many who tacitly assume it, and show by their attitude that they accept it in one form or another. Moreover, it is the theory upon which the civilized world has actually proceeded during a considerable period of its development. There are too many variations of this theory to be catalogued here. They range all the way from the caste systems of the old world, with their hereditary titles and laws of primogeniture, up to the idea, somewhat prevalent even in America, that the world belongs to the white race. The Mosaic land legislation, under which the land returned at every jubilee to the heirs of the original owners, was aristocratic rather than democratic in that it assumed that these had a superior right over all others to the land. In this country, for example, such a system would have created a landed aristocracy of the most exclusive sort, because no immigrant, nor the heir of any immigrant, could ever have become a land owner in the strict sense. The Spartan commonwealth, sometimes referred to as a socialistic community, was in reality extremely aristocratic, because it was a kind of military camp maintained by a small ruling class in the midst of a subject population. Even in the most democratic countries of the present there is a remnant of the aristocratic theory left in the form of hereditary rights to property. This is aristocratic rather than democratic, in that it assumes that one person, by accident of birth rather than individual merit, has a better right than another to the accumulations of the past.

As with all political and social theories, the justification or condemnation of the aristocratic theory of distribution must be determined by its results viewed in the light of the circumstances of time and place. It can scarcely be doubted that this theory, as practiced in the early stages of civilization, was a powerful factor in promoting the first steps of social development.   Even the crudest case imaginable, that of the primitive despot, — the strong man who by the strength of his arm and the weight of his club subjugated his neighbors to his will and robbed them of their substance in the form of tribute, — even he may have been an unconscious and unmeritorious agent of progress.   Fundamentally like this primitive form of despotism is every form of aristocracy, autocracy, or monarchy, though sometimes religious fear or a superstitious belief in some form of divine right is combined with physical force as a means of class domination.   Though all such things seem odious in the light of our present civilization, yet to the scientific observer who neither praises nor condemns they seem to have been factors essential to certain stages of progress. One or two familiar principles will help to make this clear.

It is a well-known fact, for example, that grass tends to grow as thick as the conditions of soil, heat, moisture, and the presence of enemies will permit.   If for any accidental reason the grass in a certain plot of ground should be thinner than these conditions will permit, its power of multiplication is so great that it will speedily increase in density until the equilibrium is restored.   Nature seems everywhere intent on preserving some such balance or equilibrium as this, for the same rule applies to all forms of life, including the human species, at least in its lower stages of development.   " Nature," wrote Malthus, " has scattered the seeds of life abroad with the most lavish hand.   She has been comparatively sparing of the means of subsistence."   With the human species as with other forms of life, nature tends to preserve an equilibrium between population and subsistence, or between the demand for nutriment and the supply of it.   This equilibrium may be stated in terms as follows: In the absence of disturbing causes the population tends to

become so dense as to require all its energy to procure subsistence enough to sustain that energy.   A community
which possesses enough energy to more than procure subsistence enough to sustain that energy, may not inaccurately
be said to possess surplus energy.   But nature tends to dissipate any such surplus, first by rapid consumption, and
finally through rapid multiplication of numbers.   Whenever any branch of the human species succeeds in achieving
something more than its own maintenance, that achievement may be called a storing of surplus energy, for no such
result is possible except where nature's process of dissipation is arrested, — that is, where human energy can be used
for other purposes than its own sustenance.

Since nature, considered apart from social control of
some kind has made no provision for the storing of surplus
human energy, but everywhere tends to preserve a balance
or equilibrium, it becomes pertinent to inquire how it has
happened that such a result has been achieved in some few
cases.   In a perfectly natural state, and in the absence of
some artificial means of arresting the process of dissipation,
the life history of human beings, like that of other forms of
life, would be summed up in the words: They are born to
breed and die, generation after generation in endless and
unprofitable repetition.   For the vast majority of human
beings who have peopled this planet, that is all that can be
said for or about them.   But in a few scattered instances,
sections of the race have achieved something more, — have
left something as a mark of their having existed.   Their
achievements may have been nothing more than a few
monumental tombs or a few rude altars to their unknown gods; they may have been magnificent temples and
royal palaces; higher still, they may have been systems
of religious philosophy, national literatures, or bodies of

scientific knowledge. The explanation of these results can never be complete unless it accounts for the fact that the universal dissipation of energy was by some means arrested, that something was saved from the vital processes in order that human energy might be stored in these products of civilization.

Now, one of the most effective, and probably the earliest, of the agencies for the storing of human energy was the despot. When that primitive bully subjugated his neighbors and demanded a share of their produce as tribute, he simply reduced the amount of subsistence left for them. If they could not live on what remained, nature had a way of restoring the equilibrium by thinning them out. But the despot himself would be in possession of a surplus. The chances were that he would waste this surplus in riotous living, thus himself becoming an agent of dissipation. But in a few cases, either through the surfeiting of his primary appetites, through the substitution of vanity for greed, or through the fear of things dark and mysterious, the whim seized him to build himself a tomb, a palace, or a temple, or to maintain priests to save his soul, musicians to sing his praises, or artists to represent him in heroic attitudes. In such cases the race had done something more than provide for the primary appetites of hunger, thirst, and sex. This is, in substance, the beginning of every ancient civilization. Instead of a single despot it was sometimes, as in Judea, the machinations of a priestly class; in other cases, as in Greece, the united power of a race of despots ruling over a conquered people; again it was all these agencies combined which produced the result. Without these agencies of exploitation the mass of the people would in all probability have continued indefinitely wasting their surplus in sloth or gluttony, or dissipating it through rapid multiplication, living, as they had always lived, like the insects of an hour, only to breed and die.

Odious as despotism is, it is probably justified by such results as these. The grandeur of ancient Egypt was the result of the exploitation of the masses and the embodiment of their energy in permanent forms — energy which would otherwise in all human probability have been dissipated in the manner common to all life. The religious philosophy of the Hebrews could hardly have been developed in the absence of a priestly class supported by tithes. The brilliant civilization of Greece was based on slavery, and the magnificence of Rome upon the exploitation of conquered peoples. Possibly none of these results were worth what they cost, for the cost was oppression in one form or another, and oppression is always hateful. But whatever the cost, the results *were* achieved, and if we are called upon to choose between the oppression which achieves such results and the primitive communism under which wealth is dissipated and life kept down at a low level because it is all at the mercy of the most gluttonous consumers and the most rapid breeders, we could not go so very far wrong if we were to choose oppression. The thought of injustice is not pleasing, but neither is that of a community living a profitless round of animal existence for the sole apparent purpose of reproducing their kind. It was doubtless this aspect of human life which led Thomas Carlyle to his conclusion that the real benefactor of his fellows was not necessarily the man who freed them from oppression, but the man who mastered them (by the force of his own personality, to be sure, and not by hereditary titles and sham prestige) and made them do what they ought to do.

Vastly more important than the building of magnificent tombs, temples, and palaces, or the development of esoteric philosophies and literatures, is the development of a high standard of living among all the people. This, of course, is something that no form of oppression or class domination can do. The civilization built up under these forms is always and everywhere a civilization under which the few are lifted on the backs of the many into a high plane of existence. Though this is doubtless better than no civilization at all, yet it does not satisfy our ideals. The social problem of the future is to work out a system under which all the people may, without constraint or oppression, each one remaining the master of himself, live on a high level. It is needless to point out that such a result has not yet been achieved, and that it furnishes a prospect so pleasing that such a scheme as socialism seems like a pitiful makeshift in comparison.

The effort to maintain a high standard, or any standard at all above the minimum of subsistence, toward which as an equilibrium point humanity in a natural state tends, has led to some interesting expedients, some of them purporting to be democratic, but all of them departing essentially from the democratic principle. Especially significant is a custom which is said to have prevailed among the primitive Italian villages, viz., that of enforced migration from time to time of chosen bodies of youth. These youth, selected by lot, were, according to the tradition, sent out into the world to make a place for themselves or perish in the attempt. They were not to return home in any event. This swarming process relieved the pressure of numbers at home and enabled the remaining population to maintain its standard of living. This was obviously unfair, since some members of the community were thus enabled to profit by the misfortune of those whom chance selected for migration. It was an expedient only a little more humane than the still more primitive one of exposing surplus infants. Nevertheless it worked, — that is, it enabled the community to maintain its standard of civilization. It was undemocratic because accident rather than merit determined who should enjoy the fruits of their civilization. This is the essence of aristocracy.

A somewhat more advanced expedient for accomplishing the same purpose, though a distinctly aristocratic one, is the system of primogeniture. The fortuitous circumstance of being the eldest son determines in this case who shall enter most fully into the benefits of civilization. Though there is absolutely no reason why the eldest son, rather than the youngest, or a son rather than a daughter, should inherit the family estate, yet it is essential to the preservation of the family status that the estate should be held intact. By thus sacrificing the interests of all except one child, a standard of wealth and influence can be maintained, and it is considerably more humane than infant exposure, which is only another expedient for accomplishing the same purpose. Otherwise, in the course of time, estates tend through much subdivision to become microscopically small and the whole family to descend toward the equilibrium point, viz., the level of minimum subsistence. It is historically true that in those countries where the system of primogeniture prevails the rural land-owning classes have maintained a position of wealth and influence, whereas in those countries where the system of equal division of family estates has prevailed the tendency has been for these classes to sink in the course of time to the position of peasant proprietors — a position which is usually neither dignified nor on the whole desirable. Though this system is inherently more fair than that of primogeniture, it must nevertheless be admitted that it has usually failed to maintain as high a visible standard of comfort as that system. In fact the French custom of limiting offspring seems to be the only expedient under which any kind of a standard of wealth can be maintained in an old country under the system of the equal division of property. This seems to be the most civilized expedient yet effectively practiced. As was said of the civilizations of the ancient world of whose benefits only the fortunate few partook, a standard of wealth and dignity maintained by the few at the expense of the many may be better than no standard at all; but it is probably still better that only as many should be born as can maintain the standard.

In the same class of expedients for maintaining standards belongs the trade union policy of the closed shop. Recognizing that an indefinite increase in the number of laborers in any given employment means the inevitable lowering of the standard of wages, they adopt the most direct if not the most just method of preventing that result. Limiting employment to union men, and resorting to the primitive law of the club to effect their ends, they may succeed in maintaining a standard of wages in a few chosen occupations which would otherwise be impossible. The method is no more fair or just than the enforced migration of the Italian youth or the system of primogeniture; but it aims to accomplish the same results. The non-union man is placed in the same position as the migrating youth of the Italian village or the younger sons of the English nobility. He is sacrificed in order that a favored number may maintain a standard of life. Though neither fair nor just, the trade union policy has one supreme merit, viz., it *works*, — that is, in so far as the trade unions succeed in violating all our present sentiments of right and justice, as well as the law of the land, by enforcing their demand for the closed shop.

In this connection appears the only scientific basis for the doctrine of the minimum wage. It sounds well to say that no laborer ought to receive less than six hundred dollars a year. Certainly that sum is none too large. But this leaves unanswered the question what to do with those whose services are not worth six hundred dollars a year. Enforced colonization, the multiplication of almshouses, or a liberal administration of chloroform would be necessary to dispose of a considerable number of our population. It is easy to imagine the fine scorn with which some one will object to estimating the worth of a man in dollars and cents. But theologico-metaphysical disquisitions upon the supreme worth of a human being are entirely beside the present point. It is hardly a quibble to insist that it is not the worth of a man, but the value of his services, which we are discussing.

Now it is almost a truism to say that the value of a thing depends upon how much it is wanted in comparison with other things. It is obvious that if you want an apple more than you do a nut, the apple is worth more to you than the nut and you will give more for it. It is equally obvious that if you want some other things which six hundred dollars will buy more than you want my services, my services are not worth six hundred dollars to you. If every other member of the community feels the same way about it, it is obvious that I shall never be able to get six hundred dollars for my services, and therefore if that were established as the minimum wage I should not find employment at all. If my services are worth that amount at all, they must be worth it to some individual, either to you my friend, the advocate of the minimum wage, or to some other individual like yourself. Are you willing to say that my services, or the services of any other full-grown man of sound health whom I may select, are worth the minimum wage to you ? Or are you willing to take the responsibility of finding some other individual to whom they are worth it ?   If not, you have the problem on your hands of determining what to do with me or the other man for whom you cannot provide employment. Enforced colonization, the multiplication of almshouses, or the wholesale administration of chloroform may, after all, become your only practicable expedient, in which case you will be following the example, in a somewhat more drastic form, of the Italian villages and the English nobility.

Though it is evident that modern society will adopt none of these heroic measures, yet it is interesting to speculate, in a purely academic way, upon the results of the principle of the minimum wage thus severely enforced.   In the first place, it is apparent that such a policy would tend to weed out the less competent members of the community so that, in the course of time, there would be none left whose services were not worth at least the minimum wage.   In the second place, it can scarcely be doubted that after that was accomplished, the community would be vastly superior to the present one, for it would be peopled by a superior class of individuals, and the general quality of the population would not be deteriorated by the human dregs who now form the so-called submerged element.   Nevertheless it would be inherently inequitable because it would sacrifice one part of the population in the interest of the other, though it might not be more inequitable than nature herself, who ruthlessly sacrifices the weak in favor of the strong.

" From every one according to his ability, to every one according to his needs," is a formula which fairly well summarizes the older socialistic theory of distribution.   As a theory this has two distinct merits.   In the first place, if we could insure that every one would produce according to his ability, we should have the maximum of wealth to distribute. In the second place, any given amount of wealth would yield the maximum amount of utility to the consuming public if we could manage to distribute it according to needs. That is to say, with a given fund of wealth to be distributed and consumed, more satisfaction will be afforded, more wants gratified, by having it distributed and consumed in proportion to needs than when it is distributed according to any other possible plan. If, for example, A has so many apples that any one of them is a matter of trifling concern to him while B is hungry for apples, the sum total of the satisfaction of this community of two men would be increased by A dividing with B in such proportion that their needs would be equally well satisfied. The formula, " From every one according to his ability and to every one according to his needs " is therefore a perfectly sound one in so far as it relates to individual obligation. Each individual ought to produce according to his ability, for production means service to the community, and he can never fulfill his highest moral obligation until he has served his day and generation to the best of his ability. Again, he ought to *consume* only according to his needs. If he consumes more than this he fails to promote, in the highest degree within his power, the well-being of his community. If A, in the foregoing illustration, should insist on gluttonously devouring all his apples, he would prevent the attainment of the highest well-being of that community of two. It is important to note at this point that ownership and consumption are two different things.

But it is one thing to say that the individual ought to do thus and so, and quite another to say that the state ought to take the responsibility of making him do so. There are many things which the individual ought or ought not to do which it would be futile for the state to try to make him do or to leave undone. In such cases the question of the duty of the state must be discussed apart from the duty of the individual. This does not mean that there are two kinds of ethics, or two grounds of obligation, one for the individual and the other for the state. If it is the duty of the individual it is equally the duty of the state to promote the general well-being as far as its power will permit; but in many cases the state would defeat this very purpose if it undertook to make the individual live up to this standard in every particular. How can the state promote, in the highest degree within its power, the general well-being? The answer to this question is the answer to the question: What ought the state to do?

Now the problem of distribution is essentially a problem of public regulation and control, and not a problem of voluntary individual conduct. The question is not what the individual ought in conscience to do, but what the state ought, by its laws and institutions, to compel him to do; not whether the individual ought to increase his wealth beyond certain bounds, but whether the state ought to allow him to; not whether he ought to use his private possessions for his own gratification, but whether the state ought to allow him to have any private possessions at all. These two questions are logically so distinct that it is amazing how persistently they are confused by socialistic writers, especially by those known as Christian Socialists. The socialistic theory of distribution according to needs is not a mere preachment, a mere appeal to the individual to regard himself as a steward entrusted with the management of a portion of the wealth of the world; it is an appeal rather to the force of law; it proposes that men shall consume wealth according to their needs, not because they want to, but because the law allows it to them in that proportion.

An obvious difficulty with the plan to distribute wealth by force of legal authority in proportion to needs is the utter impossibility of comparing the relative needs of different individuals. If there were no other complications, the mere fact that needs are largely the product of historical conditions would make the problem hopelessly confusing. We are, for example, accustomed to assuming that the needs of the business and professional classes are larger than those of the laboring classes; but nothing could be more untrustworthy than this assumption. The mere fact that, under the present social arrangement, the business and professional classes have been accustomed to having more than the laboring classes, makes it seem necessary that they should continue to have more; but this seeming necessity would absolutely disappear in a single generation of equal distribution. Among all but the very poorest classes the cost of living is due not so much to the cost of things which are desired for their own sakes as to the things which are desired because they are possessed by others with whom one associates. If, then, one's associates, — those in the same social class with oneself, — consume largely, one feels under the absolute necessity of living up to the same standard. But a social arrangement under which all one's associates were reduced to a smaller average income would correspondingly reduce one's own wants, after one had become accustomed to the new condition. Another assumption of the same kind is that education and culture increase one's needs. The real fact is that education increases one's earning capacity and introduces one into a social class where consumption is more liberal because incomes are larger. This creates the appearance of larger needs. If we could divest the question of such complications and examine it apart from the presuppositions created by the existing system of distribution, we should probably find that the needs of the cultured man are less than those of the uncultured.   What is culture for if it does not give a man more resources within himself and render him less dependent upon artificial and therefore expensive means of gratifying the senses ?

Taken altogether the proposal to distribute wealth in proportion to needs would necessarily resolve itself into equality of distribution, on the assumption that all members of the community have equal needs.   This assumption, though obviously untrue, is much nearer the truth than any other workable assumption.   That is, it is much nearer the truth to say that all men have equal needs than it would be to say that the needs of one class are, in a definite proportion, greater than those of another class, for the chances would be exactly equal that the proportion would have to be reversed. Though it is extremely unlikely that A's needs are exactly equal to B's, yet it would be much safer to assume that than to assume that A's were fifty per cent greater than B's.   It would be quite as difficult to determine the relative wants of different individuals as it is to determine how long they will live.   The latter difficulty forces upon life insurance companies the necessity of constructing life tables.   Though it is extremely unlikely that two men, A and B, being of the same age, class, and state of health, will live exactly the same length of time, yet such an assumption is much safer than that either one will live longer than the other by a definite period.

Under the system of distribution according to needs, the only distinctions which could possibly be made would be certain obvious ones based upon age, sex, etc.; and even these would be arbitrary and of uncertain value.   Can we, for example, safely say that a child's needs are less than those of an adult ?   It seems doubtful.   Are a woman's needs less than a man's ?   The weight of the evidence seems to be to the contrary, though under present conditions men spend more on themselves than women do, mainly because they have the power to do so and choose to exercise it. The man who is cock-sure on all these questions is scarcely the man to whose judgment any of us would like to entrust a matter of such vital concern as the distribution of wealth.

Even more difficult than the determination of the relative needs of different individuals is that of determining their relative ability.   Physiological psychology has not yet discovered the method whereby the quality and capacity of a man can be tested, measured, and quantitatively expressed. Until that is done, we must depend upon the individual himself to demonstrate his own ability.   To this end we must give him an open field for the exercise of his talents and make the normal consequences of efficiency as agreeable as possible to him, at the same time making the normal consequences of his own inefficiency, uselessness, and harmfulness as disagreeable as possible to himself.   The individual who will not be spurred on to do his best by these conditions could scarcely be made to do any better except under the whip of a taskmaster.

In view of the utter futility of trying to determine by legal process either the relative needs or the relative abilities of different individuals, the formula " From every one according to his ability and to every one according to his needs " becomes a formula for the preacher of righteousness, whose appeal is to the individual conscience, rather than for the legislator, whose appeal must be to legal sanctions.   In strictness, the formula ought to be modified to, " Let every one produce according to his ability and consume according to his needs." The individual whose moral development will cause him to respond to such an appeal to his conscience, his sense of duty, or his desire for social esteem, can be reached as effectually under the present system of distribution as under any other, while he who will not respond to such an appeal could not be reached under any system except slavery. Those who, without compulsion but from a sense of duty or for the sake of the good opinion of their fellows, are willing to produce according to their ability and to consume according to their needs, furnish no problem in distributive justice for the legislator. But there is a class, large or small as the case may be, who need the stimulus of a prospective reward as an inducement to labor. Make their income independent of their exertions, and their exertions will cease or become less strenuous; but make their income to depend directly upon the value of their services to the consuming public, and they will be spurred on to their best endeavors. How to deal with this class is the problem in distributive justice which the legislator has to solve. It is the opinion of most men whose judgment carries weight that this class includes the vast majority of any community.

This does not deny that every man possesses generous impulses to which an appeal can be made.[1] Within the circle of the family practically every one is accustomed to render service without any hope of pecuniary reward. Did the same feelings prevail throughout the community at large which now prevail within the little family community, there would be no problem of the distribution of wealth, because every one would then be in the class which voluntarily produces according to its ability and consumes according to

[1] Cf. Chapter III, on Self-Interest.

its needs. But the mere fact that we have a problem to discuss is sufficient evidence that such feelings do not prevail. Again, nearly every one is accustomed to render certain services to his community, to his church, his club, his missionary society, or to some philanthropic enterprise for purely altruistic reasons. Frequently, however, these contributions of money or service come as the result of special appeals, and they often come hard, as every philanthropic worker can testify. Moreover, with the average man, such interests claim only a small part of his attention, his efforts being, for the most part, directed toward the well-being of himself and his immediate family, rather than toward that of mankind at large. Again, it is well-known that in times of national peril, or wide social danger, the whole citizenship of a nation will rise to considerable heights of self-sacrifice. It is also well-known that even in the midst of such manifestations the play of self-interest is not suspended, and that the watch-dogs of the public treasury have to be especially on their guard to thwart the designs of self-seeking men. Moreover, the mere fact that it takes a great occasion to arouse this general spirit of public service is enough to prove that the average man does not normally labor without an eye to some pretty definite advantage to himself.

Speaking of the family, it is sometimes customary to regard the condition within the family as that of communism. In one sense that is the truth, but in another it is the opposite of the truth. In the ideal case the family income and the family property are administered in the interest of all the members without regard to their individual capacity or usefulness. But even this is largely a voluntary communism such as might exist in society at large, without a change of law, if every one would regard himself as a steward or a trustee commissioned to administer a certain portion of the wealth of the world. In another sense, however, the family is the opposite of communistic since the family property is usually *owned* by one member, viz., the head of the family. When that one member is so inclined, he may administer the affairs of the family on an extremely inequitable basis. In reality the family is no more communistic than the United States would be if all its wealth belonged legally to one man, a plutocrat of unheard-of proportions, or to a hereditary despot. Were he thoroughly wise and benevolent, the wealth might be administered in the interest of all. Were he otherwise, it would be administered in his own interest.

This brings us to the exceedingly pertinent question, what difference does it make, after all, who owns the wealth, provided it is wisely and benevolently administered ? There are other examples than the family of an absolutely autocratic control of wealth, the very acme of concentration, which are yet so much like communism as to be easily mistaken for it. There could not possibly be a more acute case of the congestion of wealth than Zion City, near Chicago, where all the productive wealth is the private property of one man — the notorious Dowie.[1] Yet, according to all accounts, it is administered as though it belonged to the community, except for a few minor indulgences which Dowie allows himself. Sir Henry Main tells in his " Village Communities " of a functionary in the East Indian village whose duty it was to apportion the land to the cultivators and act as an umpire in boundary disputes and such matters. When the English came into possession they jumped to the conclusion that this functionary was the lord of the manor and they therefore vested him with the

[1] This was written in 1906.

legal title to the land. By this simple fact a state of communism was instantaneously changed into an extreme form of concentration of wealth, yet it was some time before the natives knew the difference. We may therefore ask: Was there any difference so long as the newly created landlord continued performing the same duties as before and taking for his own private consumption no more of the annual product than he did before ? Obviously there was not. But when the landlord discovered his new power and began to exercise it in his own interest, then it made a difference. It would likewise make a vast difference to the citizens of Zion City whether they owned a share of the wealth as individuals, or allowed it all to be owned by one autocrat, should that autocrat begin to exercise the power which the law undoubtedly confers upon him, viz., that of consuming, ostentatiously or otherwise, a large share of the annual income of the city.

We are now prepared to answer the question: What difference does it make who owns the wealth provided it is wisely administered ? The answer is, it makes no difference: but the proviso is too large to be safe. Under the extremest form of concentration imaginable, and under the widest possible dissemination of wealth, the average citizen would be equally well off *provided* the wealth of the community were equally well administered. It is quite the same with political authority. Despotism and democracy are equally good *provided* they are equally well administered.

If monarchs had been uniformly wise and benevolent there would never have been any reason for democracy. But the world has learned that monarchs are seldom either wise or benevolent, and therefore it has drifted toward democracy. It is not safe to entrust too much power to any individual, for the chances are that he will abuse it.

The world has learned that it is safer for the people to retain political power in their own hands, — that in spite of the weaknesses of democracy the chances of bad government are materially less under this form than under any form of concentrated political power. This is the one and only reason in favor of democracy, but it is quite sufficient. Similarly, there is only one reason in favor of a wide diffusion of wealth, and that is an entirely sufficient one, viz., that we cannot safely trust too much economic power in the hands of one individual. Though a wise and benevolent economic despot, in whom the law vested the ownership and control of a vast amount of wealth, *might* administer that wealth in such a way as to benefit the people as much as though they owned individual fractions of it themselves, yet the chances are that he will do nothing of the kind. Human nature being what it is, the chances are very much in favor of his appropriating a considerable share of the annual product of the community to his own particular uses and wasting it in riotous living, in ostentatious consumption, or, more disastrous still, in spoiling his family and unfitting them for usefulness by accustoming them to ease and luxury. It is therefore quite important that laws and institutions should be devised which will secure a wide diffusion of wealth — fully as important as it is that there should be a wide diffusion of political power.

Now there are two widely distinct notions as to what constitutes a wide diffusion of wealth. One is that the ownership of the productive property be concentrated in the hands of the state and administered by public officers, only the income or the consumable wealth being diffused among the individual citizens. This is the socialistic ideal. The other is that the ownership of the productive wealth itself should be widely diffused. This being the case, the income or consumable wealth would of necessity also be widely diffused. This is the democratic or liberalistic ideal. It is the opinion of the liberal school that this system gives greater plasticity and adaptability to the industrial institutions of the community than any form of public ownership and operation can possibly give. Socialistic writers have too hastily assumed that this ideal is unattainable, and that we are really shut up between the devil of plutocracy and the deep sea of socialism. Let us not thus despair of the republic. Once upon a time, according to an old fable, a man placed a heavy load upon the back of his camel and then asked the beast whether he preferred going up hill or down hill, to which the camel replied, " Is the level road across the plain closed ? " Possibly society is not, after all, confined to the two alternatives of plutocracy and socialism.

The democratic or liberalistic theory puts every one upon his merits. The worthless and the inefficient are mercilessly sacrificed, the efficient are proportionately rewarded. It frankly renounces, for the present, all hope of attaining equality of conditions and confines itself to the effort to secure as speedily as possible equality of opportunity. In fact, under the rigid application of this theory, there would be room for the greatest inequalities of wealth, because some would be forced, through incapacity or through moral delinquency, into a condition of extreme poverty. At the same time there would be no conceivable limit to the possibilities of wealth for men of great capacity and great industry. Millionaires and even billionaires would still be possible, *provided* there were men capable of producing such amounts, or of performing services for which the community would be willing to pay such sums.

By equality of opportunity is meant a free and equal chance for each and every one to employ whatever talents he may possess in the service of the community, and in seeking the rewards of his service, and a similarly free and equal chance for all other members of the community to accept or reject his service according as its quality and its price please or displease them.   This is about as different as anything could possibly be from equality of personal ability, or equality of wealth or economic conditions.   It simply means that such opportunities as exist for earning a living or acquiring wealth shall be open to all alike *so far as legal and social restraints* are concerned.   It does not mean that the individual is to be freed from the limitations of his own nature, physical or mental.   The lame, the halt, and the plethoric would have little chance of winning in a race where the prize was to the swift, yet there would be equality of opportunity provided the race was free to all and without handicap, and provided the course was broad and open. Similarly, the dull, the stupid, and the lazy would have little chance of winning in a contest where the prize was to the keen, the alert, and the strenuous, yet there would be equality of opportunity, provided the competition were open to all without legal discrimination or political favoritism.   Equality of opportunity requires that such avenues to wealth as are closed by law, shall be closed to all alike and such as are open shall be open to all alike.   To the individual whose genius fits him preëminently for the work of the burglar a law against burglary may seem like a discrimination, for he is thus forced into some other occupation for which he considers himself less fit.   For the same reason the confidence man, the trust promoter, the speculator, and every other individual who employs his wits in acquiring wealth in non-serviceable occupations would look upon necessary legal restrictions as discriminations; but in spite of these restrictions there would be equality of opportunity provided they were enforced upon all alike.

Equality of opportunity means liberty, it is true, but it means liberty in the performance of service and in seeking the rewards of service. It is not held, and it never has been held by the recognized expounders of the doctrine of liberty, that it meant absolute freedom from legal restraint. The very conditions of social life require that there should be restraints upon the non-serviceable and the injurious activities of individuals. The ideal of liberty is fully realized when every individual is absolutely free to seek his own interest or follow his own inclination in every possible way which is pleasing to himself and not harmful to the rest of society. Therefore, to say that a certain man's fortune is the reward of superior skill, shrewdness, or industry is no justification at all unless it is shown that that skill, shrewdness, or industry was usefully directed. If this condition is omitted, the wealth secured by the burglar, the counterfeiter, and the confidence man are all justified, for it takes skill, shrewdness, and industry to succeed at any of these callings. In short, the word *service*, and not intelligence or industry, is the touchstone by which to distinguish those opportunities which the principle of liberty requires should be open to all from those which should be closed to all. The principle of liberty is a part of the democratic or liberalistic theory of distributive justice.

An objection which does not argue much for the acumen of those who raise it is that this kind of liberty is sometimes simply the liberty to starve, — as if liberty could ever mean anything else. Freedom from restraint always involves the possibilities of disaster, and there is no other rational conception of liberty. The reason is that the concept of liberty is a political and not a physical concept. It means freedom from political or legal restraint, and not freedom from physical conditions. Therefore, freedom from such restraint sometimes means the freedom to fall into the water and drown, for liberty does not free us from physical laws. Freedom to travel too frequently means the freedom to get smashed in a railroad accident. In fact there are all sorts of harmful possibilities, both physical and social, necessarily involved in a state of liberty. Yet men choose liberty.

Liberty to pursue one's own interest in one's own way so long as the way is a useful one gives rise to what is known as competition, which can only be defined as rivalry in the performance of service. Production is service. Wherever two or more men are seeking their own interest in the same kind of service, or, more accurately, are seeking to obtain the reward for the same kind of service, there will normally be rivalry among them. This rivalry sometimes breeds ill-feeling, and generally breeds discontent on the part of those who are beaten. It also involves a certain amount of wasted effort, because producers frequently devote a part of their energies to the work of defeating their rivals by other methods than that of superior productiveness. In a few glaring cases, these predatory methods become the characteristic ones, and the effort to beat one's rivals by superior productiveness is almost lost sight of. But these are really the exceptional cases and do not actually characterize the competitive system as a whole. In the great fundamental industries like agriculture — which is the greatest industry in every country — and in well-established lines of manufacture like the textiles, efficiency in production is still the principal factor in success. It is only in the limited field of " high finance " that mere shrewdness without serviceableness becomes a relatively important factor. Such fields of business activity are trifling and insignificant in comparison with the great industries which occupy the bulk of our population. However, it is always the exceptional case, as it is the exceptional event, which arrests the attention. The fact that newspapers are full of accounts of the mal-administration of business is, in a very significant sense, a favorable sign. It shows that such cases are still *news*. When such cases become so normal, and cases of legitimate production so exceptional, that the latter become *news*, then may we indeed despair.

In spite of the glaring weaknesses of the competitive system, and its undoubted waste of effort, it is the belief of the liberal school that it is the most effective system yet devised — that it secures the greatest efficiency in the whole industrial machine. This belief rests upon a few well-known principles which only need to be restated. In the first place, every individual of mature age and sound mind knows his own interest better than any set of public officials are likely to know it. In the second place, such an individual will, if left to himself, pursue his own interest more systematically and successfully than he could if he were given his work and directed in it by any body of public officials. In the third place, if the public, through its legal enactments and its executive and judicial officers, effectively closes every opportunity by which such an individual could further his own interest in harmful or non-serviceable ways, he will then pursue his own interest in ways that are serviceable to the community. Finally, where every individual is left absolutely free to pursue his own interests in all ways that are serviceable, and where the degree of his well-being depends upon the amount of service which he performs, all will be spurred on by their own self-interest to render as much service as possible, and the whole community will then be served in the most effective manner possible, because all its members will be striving to serve one another in order to serve themselves.

In applying this argument there are two things which need to be observed, but which are frequently overlooked. In the first place, it is no argument in favor of *laissez faire*, or the let-alone policy of government. On the contrary, it requires governmental interference with every non-service-able line of activity which it is possible for the law to reach. In the second place, it is not a glorification of self-interest. It does not even involve in the slightest degree an approval of self-interest as a motive to action. In order to make this an argument for *laissez faire*, two additional assumptions are necessary: 1. Every individual is of mature age and sound mind. 2. All human interests are harmonious. No advocate of *laissez faire* has ever made the first assumption. Therefore allowance has always been made for the need of public direction in the care of children and persons of unsound mind, — in all cases, in fact, where it is evident that the individual does not know so well what is good for him as public officials do. But at the basis of the doctrine of *laissez faire* there has always been the assumption of a natural harmony of human interests. With this assumption the argument reaches the finality of a syllogism.

Major premise. Each individual of mature years and sound mind will pursue his own interests more energetically and intelligently when left to himself than when directed by any body of public officials.

Minor premise. The interests of each individual harmonize with those of the rest of society.

Conclusion. Each individual of mature years and sound mind will, if left to himself, work in harmony with the interests of the rest of society, and work more energetically and intelligently than he would if directed by any body of public officials.

This conclusion is contained in the premises and cannot possibly be questioned by any one who accepts them.   The first premise is not likely to be rejected by any one who seriously considers what it involves.   It may be pointed out that human judgment is weak and that the individual is therefore liable to error of judgment as to his own interests.   But if human judgment is weak, public officials are equally liable to error.   In addition to this, public officials are handicapped by the fact that they are not in possession of such intimate knowledge of the circumstances surrounding the individual as he himself is.   They are therefore even more liable to error than he.   If, however, we were to postulate something resembling omniscience on the part of public officials, at the same time acknowledging the weaknesses of other individuals, this premise might be rejected. And here lies the danger.   The natural egotism of men, and especially of those who thrust themselves forward as candidates for public office, as well as those who inherit power, leads them to assume something like omniscience in themselves.   With this belief in their own superior wisdom, those who hold power are under constant temptation to exercise it in the regulation of other people's affairs.   But the only safe assumption, and one which the public ought jealously to defend, is that the individual of mature years and sound mind is more likely to know what is good for him than any set of public functionaries are.   The government ought not, therefore, to be allowed to interfere with such an individual for his own good.

With the assumption that all human interests are harmonious, the case is different.   It was on this assumption that Adam Smith based his memorable dictum concerning the " invisible hand " which, in the absence of government interference, led the individual to promote the interest of society while trying to promote his own.   But all such dreams of a beneficent order of nature belong to an older system of philosophy.   One of the services of the evolutionary philosophy has been our disillusionment on the subject, and the opening of our eyes to the stern fact that, in spite of many harmonies, there is still a fundamental conflict of interests among the individuals of every species. The term " struggle for existence " means nothing unless it implies such a conflict.   In the light of this philosophy, the primary function of human government is to neutralize as far as possible this antagonism of interests and mitigate the severities of the struggle for existence.   The most enlightened governments of the present perform this function mainly by prohibiting those methods of struggling for one's own advantage which are harmful or non-serviceable in character.   This and this only is a sufficient reason for laws against robbing and swindling.   These are methods of pursuing one's own interests, or of struggling for existence, which all brutes practice and which man alone tries to prevent by conscious and systematic social control.   They are cases where a direct pursuit of individual interest leads one to do things which are harmful to the rest of society, in other words, where interests conflict.   Man has been defined as the animal which assumes the active rôle and adapts circumstances to his own needs, whereas other animals have to be passively adapted to their circumstances.   Lawmaking no less than tool-making is a means of active adaptation.   Perceiving the disadvantage of an unrestricted pursuit of individual interest, men consciously and intelligently frame laws to suppress such pursuits as harm the general interest, such as stealing, killing, swindling, etc.

There is precisely the same reason, and no other reason whatsoever, for laws suppressing every other method of promoting one's individual interest at the expense of the general interest.

We must conclude, therefore, that though there is no good reason why the state should interfere with a capable individual for his own good, there is yet an excellent reason why it should interfere with him for the good of others. Though he knows his own interest better than public officials can be expected to know them, and will, if left to himself, pursue those interests, yet because his interests sometimes conflict with those of the rest of society, he will, if left to himself, sometimes do things which are harmful to the general interest. Here only is the ground for public interference with the capable individual. It may as well be admitted that the old liberalism erred in assuming a general harmony of interests and in concluding that government control and regulation should be limited to mere protection from violence. The new liberalism must correct this error by recognizing the conflict of interests and extending the control of government to all cases where individual interests conflict. The new gospel of individualism must therefore proclaim three things: 1. The absolute necessity for the suppression of all harmful methods of pursuing one's self-interest. 2. The absolute freedom of the individual to pursue his self-interest in all serviceable ways. 3. The absolute responsibility of the individual for his own well-being, — allowing those to prosper who, on their own initiative, find ways of serving the community, and allowing those who cannot to endure the shame of poverty.

The effort of the state, if moderately successful to suppress all non-serviceable methods of pursuing one's self-interest, at the same time leaving all serviceable methods absolutely free and open, works such a transformation in the struggle for existence as to make that term a misnomer. Competition is the term which has been applied to this new phase of the struggle, and competition resembles the brutal struggle for existence very much less than a well-ordered athletic contest (not foot-ball) resembles a free-for-all shillalah fight. Even in a well-ordered athletic contest the prize winner performs a feat which is neither serviceable nor harmful — merely neutral, — whereas in genuine economic competition the winner must perform a feat which is more serviceable than his competitors can perform.

Instead of being a glorification of self-interest, this principle is merely a recognition of its existence at the present time, and an attempt to adapt legislation to it. The effort of the legislator to adapt his laws to the conditions of human nature, of which self-interest is one, is precisely like the effort of the mechanic to adapt his methods to the great forces of nature. He neither approves nor condemns them: he merely accepts the fact of their existence. If the original and conditioning forces either of human nature or of physical nature should change, the statesman or the mechanic of the future would then have to change his methods.

The principle of adaptation, which, according to the evolutionary philosophy, lies at the basis of all progress, cosmic, biological, and social, must determine our theory of distributive justice. As already pointed out, a theory of distributive justice is a rule for the guidance of the legislator rather than the individual conscience. A theory of consumption rather than of distribution is needed for the guidance of the individual conscience, because from the social point of view it does not matter so much how vast are the individual's possessions as how well he uses them. Since the ultimate purpose of the legislator is to facilitate the process of human adaptation, the question of distribution must be considered as a part of the general problem of adaptation rather than as a question of natural rights. This way of looking at it ought not to be considered revolutionary today, when the evolutionary philosophy is dominant, though in the eighteenth century, when the philosophy of nature and the doctrine of natural rights were dominant, it would have been incomprehensible.

There are two ways of approaching the question of distribution as a part of the general problem of adaptation, the analytical and the historical.   By the analytical method we may analyze the factors and forces at work in societies, present as well as past, which make for human progress. By the historical method we may find out what systems of distribution have proved most effective in promoting the progress of mankind.   Neither method has been worked out completely, and probably cannot be in the present state of knowledge.   Nevertheless, something may be learned from both methods.

It goes without saying that industry is the primary *active* factor in human adaptation.   It is the agency whereby the material environment is adapted to the needs of the race. That governmental policy which most effectively stimulates industry must, other things equal, be the most effective policy in the process of adaptation.   No method has yet been found which so effectively stimulates industry as that of leaving the individual free to pursue his own interests in his own way so long as his interests coincide with those of the community, at the same time blocking the way to the pursuit of his own interests when those interests, as he considers them, conflict with those of the rest of the community. This introduces into useful industry a degree of energy, spontaneity and originality which no system either of slavery or paternalism has yet achieved. The reason is that intelligence is applied more immediately and directly to those points in the industrial machinery where intelligence is needed when each worker has a chance to profit by the results of his intelligence than it can possibly be when the worker's advancement depends upon the good-will of a body of administrative officers who are not financially interested in the results of his intelligence.

It is the belief of all who accept the modern evolutionary philosophy that selection, natural or artificial, is the primary factor in passive adaptation. It is the factor by which the species is itself adapted to its conditions, — in other words, improved. Even they who reject Weismannism must admit that selection is, in the long run, more effective than training. No amount of training can improve the milk-giving qualities of a herd of cows generation after generation so effectively as careful selection and breeding. The same rule seems to apply to the working capacity, the intelligence, or the morality of the human species.

It must be granted, however, that artificial selection, where it can be intelligently applied, is vastly superior to natural selection. That is to say, a given result can be secured more speedily by intelligent breeding than it could possibly be by mere natural selection. The reason for this is mainly that the breeder can select more rigidly, rejecting all but a very few individuals for breeding purposes, whereas in a natural state there is likely to be a wholesale breeding, the superior individuals having only a slightly better chance of survival than the inferior. But it does not seem possible to adopt any scheme for the scientific propagation of the human species, nor is it even desirable that we should. All schemes of artificial selection tend to produce artificial results, however useful they may be in our highly specialized civilization. The highly-bred trotting horse answers a useful purpose, but a highly specialized one. While he is a triumph of artificial selection, it would be difficult to maintain, on general grounds, his superiority over the broncho. Any body of scientific experts on the breeding of the human species would be likely to aim at specialized results rather than general adaptability and usefulness. Besides, no democratic society is likely to consider for one moment the question of entrusting the control of such a matter to any body of scientific experts.

The rejection of any suggestion for scientific breeding does not commit us to the principle of natural selection and the survival of the fittest in the ultra-Darwinian sense. In the absence of some form of social control, this principle would work in the human species just as it does among animals and plants. Survival would depend simply upon the ability to survive and not upon fitness in any sense implying worth, merit, or usefulness. The adept murderer, thief, or confidence man would stand the same chance of survival as the efficient producer of wealth. The fact that animals do not commit crime is not because they do not do the things which men call crime; they do all of these things, that is, they kill, they steal, they practice deception, etc.; it is due to the fact that they have no accepted standard of fitness. Because the lower forms of life have no accepted standard of fitness and no social organization to make such a standard effective even if they had one, the individual animal or plant is quite as likely to survive by means of its destructive and harmful propensities as by means of its useful propensities. Thorns and briers, spurs and fangs, venom and evil odors are, under such circumstances, quite as likely to be means of survival, and, therefore, to be developed through natural selection, as any other faculties or qualities.

But when human society suppresses all harmful methods of pursuing self-interest, leaving open all useful methods, it deliberately sets up a standard of fitness for survival. If this standard is rigidly enforced, those individuals who are most useful to their fellows stand the best chance of survival, and those who are least useful or most harmful are selected for extermination — through poverty in the one case, and through criminal punishment in the other. This differs from artificial selection as practiced by the breeder in that it leaves the individual free, *within certain prescribed limits*, to shift for himself and survive if he can. It leaves him to demonstrate his own fitness for survival. Within these prescribed limits it works automatically like natural selection. It differs from natural selection in that, by virtue of these prescribed limits, a standard of fitness is set up. Under these conditions the term "survival of the fittest" means something more than the mere ability to survive; it means the ability to survive by means of useful powers and qualities. If this system were thoroughly established, the human counterpart of such adept rascals as Reineke Fuchs and Br'er Rabbit would stand no better chance of survival by virtue of their mere shrewdness than would the human counterparts of such stupid contestants as the hare in the fable of the hare and the tortoise, or the Br'er Fox of the Uncle Remus Stories.

A principle of human selection which exterminated the harmful and the useless and preserved the useful individuals would obviously tend to hasten the process of human adaptation. The useful individual is one who contributes to human well-being in some way, generally by manipulating the forces of nature or by teaching others how to do so.

This is adaptation.   The normal result of such a process of selection would eventually be the development of a race highly skilled in the work of adaptation.   A society formed by such a race would be a progressive and well-to-do society, because every individual in it would be capable of contributing largely to the well-being of the whole community, and would be spurred on to do so by his own self-interest *plus* whatever of altruism or public spirit he might possess.

Even they who believe that training rather than selection is the most effective means of race improvement ought to find much in this governmental policy to commend it.   The rarest, and at the present time the most valuable quality is the power of successful initiative.   It does not seem possible that any other system could train this power so efficiently as that under which the prizes go to those who exercise it.

Historically, the most significant social changes in the most progressive countries of the world during the last three hundred years — ever since the modern democratic or liberalistic movement began, in fact — conform to the principle of distribution according to worth.   These changes consist in the gradual suppression of predatory activities on the one hand, and the unshackling of useful work on the other.   In the early days of the liberalistic movement the artificial checks and hindrances upon useful enterprise, the legal discriminations and monopolies set up by most governments, seemed the greater evil.   Consequently, the early apostles of liberalism were led to emphasize the need of freer opportunity for enterprise rather than that of closer restriction upon harmful methods.   It remains for the apostles of the new liberalism to emphasize both needs equally.

This suggests the Scylla and Charybdis of economic reform.   Perceiving the obvious necessity of restrictions upon the free pursuit of self-interest, perceiving also that under the competitive system in its present defective form predatory methods of business still survive, some have been led to believe that liberalism is dead, that its conclusions were wrong, and that the competitive system must go.   Others perceiving the indisputable fact that self-interest is still a motive to be reckoned with by the legislator, perceiving also that some principle of selection which will work automatically is necessary for the improvement of the species, have been led to re-affirm the most extreme conclusions of the old *laissez faire* school.   Ignoring the ridiculous extreme of Nietzscheism, Mr. Benjamin Kidd may be taken as a fair representative of the latter tendency.   In one of the most significant passages in his " Social Evolution " he asserts (p. 150) that:

The political history of the centuries so far may be summed up in a single sentence: it is the story of the political and social enfranchisement of the masses of the people hitherto universally excluded from participation in the rivalry of existence on terms of equality. . . . The point at which the process tends to culminate is a condition of society in which the whole mass of the excluded people will be at last brought into the rivalry of existence on a footing of equality of opportunity.

Again (p. 152), he points out that the inherent tendency of modern social development " is not really to suspend the rivalry of life, but to raise it to the highest possible degree of efficiency as a cause of progress."   Still further, he argues (p. 155) that the superiority of Europeans over other races is the evolutionary product " of those strenuous conditions of life which have accompanied the free play of forces in the community, this latter being in its turn the direct product of the movement which is bringing the masses of the people into the rivalry of existence on conditions of equality."

There can be no doubt as to the superior selective efficiency of a condition of democratic freedom over a condition of aristocratic restraint.   It would be difficult to improve upon Napoleon's definition of democracy as an open road for talent; but an open road for talent necessarily implies an open road for incapacity to failure, poverty, and extermination.   Mr. Kidd's exposition is further to be commended because he sees with a perfectly clear and undistorted vision, as far as he sees at all, what is taking place in the modern world.   The progress from slavery, through serfdom and all that savors of caste, up to the modern system of individual freedom of movement, of contract, and of initiative, is proceeding directly toward a condition of still further freedom of movement, of contract, and of initiative, and not, as most of the socialistic writers since Rodbertus have acquired the habit of saying, toward a system of paternalism, where freedom of contract and of initiative will be denied the individual and industry be directed by the state.

But what Mr. Kidd does not see at all, so far as one can gather from his writings, is that while men are being admitted to the struggle on more and more equal terms, the field within which they are allowed to struggle at all is, at the same time, being more and more sharply defined, if not narrowed down.   While the advance of democracy is requiring the removal of political and legal discriminations as between persons, it is not requiring the removal of all discriminations as between deeds, business activities, or methods of getting a living.   On the other hand, legislators were never so busy as now, and legislative acts never so numerous.   Most of them, to be sure, prove ineffective;

but the net result of all of them is gradually to draw the meshes of legality closer, not against persons but against deeds. In so far as these affect the distribution of wealth, they aim to distinguish more and more sharply between the serviceable and the harmful methods of acquiring wealth, and they are measurably successful. The growing magnitude of businesss, however, and its growing complexity, are creating ever new demands upon the ingenuity of the legislator and the public prosecutor, because these conditions are creating new opportunities for cunning men to evade the law of service and acquire wealth without rendering an equivalent return. But this is a result inherent in any condition of change. It simply means that the reformer is now especially needed, and will be needed so long as human carnivores can find ways of preying upon their fellows. But an analysis of the factors of social progress, as well as a discriminating study of the direction which progress has actually taken, make it evident that the path of reform lies along the open road toward the further suppression of all parasitical and predatory methods of getting wealth, and toward greater freedom and equality in the struggle for wealth along serviceable lines, and not toward the overthrow of the competitive system, nor toward the setting up of any system where the individual of mature years and sound mind is in any sense relieved of the responsibility for his own welfare. Such expressive phrases as, " Root, hog, or die! " and " Every fellow for himself and the devil take the hindmost! " must still retain their meaning *within the field of service.*

The conclusion seems unavoidable that distribution according to worth, usefulness or service is the system which would most facilitate the process of human adaptation. It would, in the first place, stimulate each individual, by an appeal to his own self-interest, to make himself as useful as possible to his community. In the second place, it would leave him perfectly free to labor in the service of the community for altruistic reasons, if there was any altruism in his nature. In the third place it would exercise a beneficial selective influence upon the stock or race, because the useful members would survive and perpetuate their kind and the useless and criminal members would be exterminated. If this is the system which would most facilitate the process of adaptation, or stimulate social progress, the duty of the state is clear. The question, What ought the state to do ? is then answered so far as the theory of distribution is concerned. To answer this question is to establish a principle of social justice.

This question, however, is not completely answered until it is decided how service is to be estimated or measured. In principle this ought not to cause any difficulty. The utility or desirability of the service to those who receive it is the only possible test. It has been maintained, however, that service should be measured in terms of effort rather than in terms of utility; that if two men try equally hard they should be equally rewarded, regardless of their difference in ability. But this rule is hopelessly defective in two essential particulars. In the first place, the individual's value to society, or his effectiveness as an agent of well-being and progress, does not depend upon the amount of effort he puts forth. The bungling mechanic and the soulless artist may try as hard as the genius, but neither of them can be said to contribute as much to the satisfaction or the wealth of society. Neither is so valuable as an agent of progress. In the second place, this rule would fail to exercise the same beneficial selective influence upon the race. The mediocre and the genius would fare equally well; indeed the dull and the stupid would be put on the same footing with, and stand the same chance of survival as the capable and the talented. Worse still, he who goes into an occupation already overcrowded, and where an extra man is consequently not much wanted, would be rewarded equally with him who goes into an occupation which is under-crowded, and where an extra man is very much wanted, — provided only that he work equally hard. And yet the well-being of society would call for men to fill the gaps, to do the kind of work which is very much wanted because talent is scarce. The simple fact is that utility and not effort is what the community wants. There is no more merit in mere effort than in mere pain, and the attempt to apportion earthly rewards on the basis of efforts, irrespective of util-ity, would be no more rational than the belief that heavenly rewards are to be apportioned on the basis of pain, self-inflicted or otherwise, endured in this world.

It only remains to decide who shall determine the worth of the individual's service. Is it to be estimated by public officials who have no personal interest in the matter, or by those who receive the service and are therefore directly and immediately concerned ? As to the safer method there can be scarcely a moment's doubt. Granting all that may be said about the depravity of popular tastes and the whimsi-calities of fashion, of the maltreatment of genius and the cherishing of the time-server, much more may be said about the insolence of office, the arbitrariness and stupidity of public officials, elective as well as hereditary. Obviously no one is in so good a position to appraise the value of service as he who receives it. His judgment may be perverted, but so also may that of any functionary to whom the matter could be entrusted. The conclusion seems necessarily to follow that if the individual is to be left free to pursue his own interest in the way of performing service, he must also be left free to pursue his own interest in the way of securing the services of others. In other words, freedom of consumption is as essential as freedom of production, freedom to reject or accept a service as the freedom to perform service. There is only one way by which this result can be secured, and that is to allow the consumer and the producer to come together on the basis of freedom of contract. This may often involve hard bargaining, and may sometimes result in injustice, but it is much less likely to result in injustice than any system of paternalism, or any arrangement by which the value of a service is determined by some one else than the person who receives it, and rewards apportioned accordingly. Assuming that the parties are of mature age and sound mind, that neither party is allowed to use force or violence, or any form of compulsion, and (which is revolutionary) that liars, or all who practice deception by offering shoddy or adulterated goods, shall be put where they belong, in the same class with the counterfeiter and the gold-brick man, and that neither party is given a legal or political advantage over the other, this system is safer than any other. Under it the tendency is in the long run for each to get about what his service is worth.

The analysis of the actual results of the competitive process will show that where competition in the proper sense actually exists, substantial justice according to the democratic or liberalistic theory is secured. But that is another story. The purpose of this chapter has been to establish the principle itself, or to show that distribution according to worth, usefulness or service is the only sound principle for society to follow in its exercise of legal control over the process; in other words, that this is the principle of social justice. In what respects the present distribution of wealth conforms to this principle, and in what respects it violates it, is also another story. This latter question, however, is the real question for the social reformer. If distribution according to merit embodies the principle of justice, all rational schemes for economic reform, in so far as they relate to the question of distribution, must aim at the more perfect realization of this principle: in other words, must try to find in what particulars the present distribution of wealth departs from this principle, and must aim at their correction. The reformer who directs his efforts toward this end will be working in harmony with the principles of social progress, and his labors will be effective because he will be pushing the car of progress in the path which it has been following for the last three hundred years, and he will not be trying to turn it backward on its track or shunt it off on a sidetrack.

CHAPTER VII

HOW MUCH IS A MAN WORTH?

The value of a man is equal to his production minus his consumption.

His economic success is equal to his acquisition minus his consumption.

When his acquisition is equal to his production then his economic success is equal to his value.

It is the duty of the state to make each man's acquisition equal to his production. That is justice.

IF it is once agreed that, on the whole, the most satisfactory criterion of justice in distribution is distribution according to productivity, merit, or worth, we have next to consider the question as to how to determine the value of a man, or how much he is worth. This question, however, may mean several different things. It may mean moral worth, or the value of the man's moral example. This is a thing which can scarcely be measured in economic terms. Since the distribution of wealth is an economic problem, that is, since it relates to the distribution of economic goods for the reward of economic services, it hardly seems like a useful exercise to discuss even the possibility of adjusting economic rewards to moral virtues, especially those so-called virtues which do not materialize in the form of economic goods or services. This is all the more futile because it frequently happens that the meanest man proves to be a great moral asset to the community. The example of Benedict Arnold has been held up to the odium of successive generations of Americans, with the result that treason has become so odious and patriotism so attractive as greatly to strengthen the union of our people into a great state.   We have thus been able to turn to moral advantage that which was inherently immoral.   But we should not for that reason attempt to reward the Benedict Arnolds, because by so doing we should destroy every moral value which their example furnishes. Again, it is probable that the only kind of moral examples which deserve reward are those which either directly or indirectly contribute to economic productivity.   Where this is the case economic rewards are more than likely to follow.

Again, even the economic value of a man may be estimated on two distinct bases, one of which may be called his net value and the other his gross value.   By the net value of a man we mean the surplus of his production over his consumption.   Production may be either direct or indirect. It is direct in the case of the farmer or the mechanic. It is indirect in the case of the teacher, the policeman, the preacher, the doctor and possibly the lawyer.   When we are discussing the value of a man from the standpoint of vital statistics, that is, how much the country loses as the result of a higher death rate, or how much it gains by reducing the death rate, we are never on a sound basis of calculation unless we are figuring on the net value.   Let it be said, once for all, that this is not a proper basis for calculating the desirability of improved sanitation and a lower death rate.   But if one insists on discussing the commercial value of such things, he must base his estimates on the net rather than the gross value of men.

The man who produces nothing but consumes lavishly has a negative net value to the country as a whole, that is, the country is better off when he dies than when he lives.

He is adding nothing to the wealth of the country, but is consuming largely and therefore destroying good victuals. The only effect of his death is to stop his consumption, leaving for other people the wealth which he was consuming. Where there is a large leisure class having this negative value, they go a long way toward cancelling the positive value of the workers. Again, if an individual is actually working, but is consuming everything which he produces, the country neither gains nor loses with his death. Other people are neither better nor worse off after his death than they were before. But they only who produce more than they consume, that is, whose services are worth more than the cost of their keep, have any net value to the country as a whole. If these positive factors in the nation's wealth outnumber or outweigh in importance all those who have a negative value, then we have an economically progressive country, that is, a country in which wealth and well-being are increasing. If, on the other hand, they who have a negative value, that is, they who consume more than they produce, or whose cost of maintenance is greater than the value of their services, outnumber or outweigh in importance all those who have a positive value, then we have an economically decadent country, that is, a country in which wealth and well-being are diminishing.

Figuring on strict arithmetical averages, in a decadent country of this kind the *average* man is worth a little less than nothing; where the consumers and the producers just balance each other, the average man is worth exactly nothing; but where the producers outnumber or outweigh the consumers, then the average man is worth a positive quantity of greater or less magnitude.

It must be borne in mind here that we are speaking of actual rather than potential values. Potentially, even a member of the leisure class may have very great value, that is, he may have capabilities which, when developed, made active, and wisely directed would produce enormously; but if they are actually dormant or going to waste, their actual value is *nil*, and there is nothing to compensate for the large consuming capacity of the individual. It must also be borne in mind that we are speaking strictly of averages. The average man is not the common man necessarily. A man may be hopelessly commonplace and still be producing more than he is consuming, and he may be very brilliant and be consuming more than he is producing. By the average we mean strictly the arithmetical average. Add together the products of all the people of the country, subtract the consumption of all the people, and divide the remainder by the number of people, and you get the average net value. By way of illustration, if it should be found that a country of one hundred million inhabitants was adding one hundred million dollars to its wealth every year, that would signify that it was producing a hundred million dollars worth of wealth more than it was consuming every year. National production minus national consumption equals one hundred millions. Divide this by the number of people, namely, one hundred millions, and you would get the average net value of exactly one dollar per year for each person. This conception of the net value of a man is the only one to be considered in discussing the economic saving to the nation as a whole, of those sanitary measures which save life.

However, the author will go as far as anyone in contending that this is a wrong basis on which to consider sanitary improvements. The fact that improved sanitation will reduce the pain and discomfort of the living and prolong the life of the individual is certainly ample reason for laboring to improve sanitary conditions. Why weaken the argument by presenting fictitious figures to show the economic waste to the nation as a whole through the loss of its individuals ? This concept of the net value is also necessary for the appraisal of the merits of the competitive process.

But from the standpoint of distribution we are obviously not concerned so much with net value as with gross value. How much a man should get depends upon his gross value. Out of what he gets he must support himself. We are concerned, in the problem of distribution, with the question how much income a man ought to have, assuming that whatever income he has he may consume or not according to his choice. The principle of distribution according to product obviously, therefore, means distribution according to gross rather than net product, since we are discussing the gross rather than the net value of the man.

It has become a commonplace of economics that all industrial processes consist merely in moving materials, — moving things from one place to another. That is all that the eye can see in industry, it is all a moving-picture machine would reveal. Back of this physical process of moving things, however, there are mental processes, but even here mental processes are concerned primarily with moving materials, that is, thinking about how to move and where, etc. An analysis of these two processes, physical and mental, — namely, the moving of things and the thinking about moving them, — will reveal two or three great fundamental laws of the most elementary character. The first of these is the law of proportionality.

It will be found upon analysis that every movement of materials which takes place in the great play of industrial processes is governed by the law of proportionality. That is to say, each and every movement aims at getting things together in the right proportion. No matter what a man is doing industrially, it will be found that he is moving things from one place to another in order to get different things together in the right proportion, whether he be a chemist carrying out an experiment, or an engineer turning a river onto an arid plain. He is combining material things under the law of proportion, that is, he is trying to combine them in certain proportions in order that natural forces may then operate to produce the results which he desires.

But the very nature of this process implies that material things are not naturally in the right proportion to suit man's needs or purposes. In a swamp there is too much water to combine properly with the other elements of plant growth. The proportions are bad, and the simple way of improving them is to drain off the water. On a dry plain there is too little water to combine with the elements of soil fertility which may be there in abundance; therefore plants do not grow. The obvious solution is to bring water from other localities. In a non-commercialized society where each man is dealing directly with natural forces, there is never any confusion about this question. Under such conditions water does not command a price on the market, for there is no market; therefore the drainer of swamps and the irrigator of dry lands is never affected by market conditions. It would be very difficult to convince the owner of swamp land under these conditions that water was productive, at least from his point of view. He is quite certain that he does not need any more than he has, and anyone who offered to sell him water would meet with a cool reception. But the owner of dry land where there is too little water would have no great difficulty in convincing himself that water was highly productive. At least he is perfectly certain that the formula " More water more crop; less water less crop " is true so far as his land is concerned. But to attempt to carry that formula over to the owner of the swamp land would produce the opposite mental reaction. To the owner of the swamp land the formula would have to be reversed, so as to read " More water less crop; less water more crop."

But even if the right proportion between water and soil has been established either in the swamp or on the dry plain, there are still other factors which have to be combined in the right proportion. The three main elements in plant food, nitrogen, phosphorus, and potash, have to be combined, not according to the law of definite proportions as a chemist understands it; but according to a law of variable proportions as the economist understands it. Suppose in a given piece of soil there is an abundance of phosphorus and potash, but a dearth of nitrogen. You then have a situation which, economically, is the same as though you had proper soil but too little or too much water, that is, the essential elements are not combined in the right proportion. The capacity of the soil to produce is limited absolutely by the scarce factor, nitrogen. Under these conditions the formula " More nitrogen more crop; less nitrogen less crop " would be true and would convince the farmer if he understood the situation. But under the same conditions " More potash more crop; less potash less crop " would not be a true formula. Because of this situation the farmer would naturally be anxious to get more nitrogen; but would not be particularly anxious to get more potash. If this were a commercialized community with markets and prices, the farmer would obviously be willing to pay a higher price for nitrogen than for potash. It is very important that we remember that this market condition is not a mere social arrangement; it is a reflection of a physical fact. That is, the above formulae are physical and not social or psychological. Like many other economic laws, it is based on physical fact and is not, as some would have us believe, a mere way of looking at things.

Now these physical illustrations have been used in order to make it perfectly clear that economic values are sometimes based absolutely upon physical productivity, but productivity is always to be determined by the circumstances of time and place.   To some it may seem strange and unthinkable that water should be considered productive in one place and unproductive in another, but strange as this may seem it is precisely what the owner of dry land and of swamp land will say.   This means that a factor of production may under one set of circumstances be highly productive in a physical sense and in another set of circumstances unproductive in the same physical sense.

This is due to the law of proportionality which, as said above, is the most fundamental law in the whole field of economics.   But the same law of proportionality which applies to those purely physical factors applies universally to all factors which have to be combined, including the human factor, labor.   In your arid plain after it is brought under irrigation and after the elements of soil fertility are combined in the right proportion, still no product emerges unless there is labor to cultivate the soil.   Under those conditions the formula " More labor more crop; less labor less crop " is a true formula.   While this is true, it is also true that under other conditions it follows from the same law that where there may be an abundance of labor on a very little land, it ceases to be true.   More labor on a circumscribed area of land may add little or nothing to the crop, because the land is all so intensively cultivated that a few laborers more would add nothing to the crop, and a few laborers less would subtract nothing from the crop.   Since the land could not be moved it would then be necessary for the surplus laborers to move to a place where there was more land or fewer laborers. This is only another illustration of the universal necessity of moving the factors of production about in order to get them united in the right proportions. Since labor itself comes under the great law of proportionality it becomes as necessary that labor should be moved from one place to another as that physical materials should be moved. Too much labor in one place in proportion to the opportunities, too little in another place, is a situation which requires migration just as truly as too much water in one place and too little in another is a situation which requires drainage and irrigation.

In the application of labor in a non-commercialized state where markets and market values have not arisen to complicate the question, there would be very little confusion on this point. The productivity of labor would be seen to be a physical fact and not a social fact. If there was in one community more labor than could find employment on the land, whereas in some other part of the world there was more land than could be cultivated by the labor, the need of transporting men would be so obvious that no one would care to discuss it. However, if the communities had become commercialized and markets and market values had arisen, the fact that labor was cheap in one place and dear in another would strike many tender-hearted people as a great social injustice. They would blame the social system for the fact that in the one community men found it difficult to get work. They would probably forget that in other places there was land which could not be cultivated because of the scarcity of labor.

Such theories as that every man is entitled to an opportunity would not only gain headway, which is proper enough, but would be interpreted to mean that every man had a right to find employment at the exact spot at which he happened to be, which is quite a different proposition. These tender-hearted but unintelligent people would fail to see that the physical productivity was low at a point where there is too much of it in proportion to the other things which have to be combined with it. They would fail to appreciate that where there is an abundance of unskilled labor, but very little business knowledge or technical training to combine with it, or very little land and capital to combine with it, the formula " More unskilled labor more product " may be absolutely false even in a physical sense. Physically speaking, it might be true to say " More labor of this particular kind, *no* more product; less labor of this particular kind, *no* less product."

Such a physical fact may and frequently does exist in certain definite localities. To say that there is an abundance of land in Texas does not solve the problem of unemployment in New York City. Since the land in Texas obviously cannot be moved to New York City, it may be necessary to move the men to Texas. This is in harmony with the great law of proportionality which necessitates the moving of materials, and even of human beings. The claim, therefore, that every man has a right to find employment does not carry with it the claim that he has a right to find employment on the exact spot on the surface of the earth where he happens to be standing. He may at least have to move to the next block, possibly to the next town, sometimes to the next state, and sometimes half around the world in order to find a place where his labor is, or can be made physically productive. It is only where his labor is physically productive, that is, where the formula " More labor, more product " applies, that he can get a price for his labor.

Again, even though certain kinds of labor may be physically productive in this sense, that is, where you can say " More of this kind of labor, more product; less of it, less product " it does not carry with it the implication that all kinds of labor are then and there productive. The law of proportionality may apply to different kinds of labor as well as to the different elements of soil fertility, or to the ratio of soil to moisture, or to any other combination of factors in production. In order that a given number of spinners may work productively, there must be a fair proportion of weavers to combine with them. In order that both weavers and spinners may be employed productively, there must be a fair proportion of wool growers or cotton growers employed somewhere. If wool growers and cotton growers should be scarce so that textile materials were lacking, obviously a very limited number of spinners and weavers could be productively employed. If there were more than this limited number, then the formula " More spinners and weavers, more cloth " would not be true. Again, with an abundant supply of textile fibres and an abundant supply of spinners and weavers, if there should be a scarcity of men who knew how to run manufacturing establishments in a businesslike way, it might still happen that these workers were unproductive. If there were more of them than could be employed by the limited number of men who knew how to run business establishments, the formula " More spinners and weavers, more cloth " would be untrue as a physical fact, and where the physical fact of productivity in this especial sense is lacking, the market price will have to adjust itself to it. In a general way, in fact, the market values of all factors of production are ultimately determined by the physical fact of productivity as determined by the formula " More of the factor, how much more product ? " This physical fact of productivity is determined by the great law of proportionality.

The phase of the law of proportionality which has been most clearly understood and most frequently discussed in economics is the law of diminishing returns from land. The law of diminishing returns, however, is only one, and by no means the most important, phase of the larger law.

If we may begin with the rather obvious assumption that [1] the value of a transferable thing depends upon how much it is wanted in comparison with other transferable things, we have next to inquire what determines how much such a thing is wanted. Some of the more difficult phases of this question, so far as goods sold to consumers are concerned, have been satisfactorily answered by the marginal utility theory of value. To answer the same question concerning productive agents requires further analysis. It may be assumed, to begin with, that productive agents are wanted primarily because of their products. Doubtless there is also a certain element of consumers' satisfaction, coming directly to the owner or user of producers' goods, in addition to that which comes from their products. The farmer takes a certain amount of pride and satisfaction in the style and appearance of his horses and cattle, and the workman in the quality and finish of his tools. These qualities, therefore, increase somewhat the desirability of such goods and enhance their value. Nevertheless, it is safe to say that productive agents are wanted chiefly for the sake of their products rather than for their own sakes. Leaving out of consideration, for the present, all consumers' satisfactions which such goods may furnish, and assuming that they are wanted for productive purposes only, let us inquire into the

---

[1] From an article by the author on " Diminishing Returns and Value," in the *Rivista di Scienza*, 1907.

factors which determine the intensity with which they are wanted.

The answer to this question with respect to a given agent seems to depend upon two factors; first, how large a physical product it will produce; second, how much each unit of that product is wanted. If the physical product increases without any diminution in the desire for each unit, or if the physical product remains unchanged while the desire for each unit increases, the productive agent will be more wanted than it was before, and vice versa. These two factors may be reduced to one, and the problem therefore simplified, by regarding the product as a sum of value rather than as a physical quantity. With a given value per physical unit and a larger physical quantity produced, or with a given physical quantity and a higher value per unit, there is, of course, a large value-product; and vice versa. In a primitive economy where goods are produced for home consumption and not for a market, the assumption of a value-product would be a violent one. But in most modern communities, especially in the United States of America, production is normally for a market rather than for home consumption. The producers' purpose is therefore normally to produce as large a value as possible, and a productive agent is normally wanted in proportion to the value which it will produce. In other words, its value depends upon the value which it will produce. What determines how much value it will produce ?

The only real difficulty in this problem is that of defining sharply what is meant by the term productivity as applied to an agent which is used in conjunction with several other agents in a certain line of production. If that matter can be made perfectly clear, the problem becomes simple and there is little danger of confusion; but if it is not made absolutely clear, all further discussion is useless because nothing but confusion can result. Therefore it is important that this matter be cleared up at the very start, even at the risk of being tedious.

In almost every community there will be found certain parcels of land which are said to be unproductive, while others are said to be productive. What is the difference between them ? Even the unproductive land will usually be found to possess the same physical and chemical properties which make the better grades of land productive, though sometimes in lower degree. As a matter of fact, crops will usually grow on the unproductive land, and it may therefore be said to be physically productive, though economically unproductive: physically productive in the sense that it supplies the physical properties which enable crops to grow, but economically unproductive in the sense that it does not pay to try to grow crops upon it. As it appears to the individual farmer, it costs as much to grow the crops as they are worth, if not more. From the point of view of society, the use of this land adds nothing to the total product of the whole community. When this parcel of land is brought into cultivation, labor and capital have to be withdrawn from the cultivation of other lands, and this withdrawal will reduce somewhat the quantity produced upon these other lands. If this reduction in the product on these other lands is as great as the product from the land in question, the community gains nothing from its use and would lose nothing if it were again withdrawn from use. The piece of land in question is therefore unproductive in the sense that the community is as well off without it as with it. That is what it means for land to be economically unproductive. Anything which, under the circumstances of time and place, is of no advantage to society in production is, under those circumstances, unproductive in the economic sense, whatever its physical potentialities may be. It might as well not be as be so far as the productive work of the community is concerned.

With productive land, however, the case is different. If a piece of land of this grade is brought into use, the labor and capital necessary to its cultivation will, as in the former case, be withdrawn from the cultivation of other lands. This also will reduce the product of those other lands. But if this reduction is less than the quantity produced on the piece of land in question, there is a positive gain in the social product through the use of this land. That is what it means for land to be economically productive. Society has a larger product when it is in use than when it is out of use. If it were thrown out of use the labor and capital which had been employed in its cultivation would have to be employed elsewhere, either on poorer land which is now uncultivated (marginal land) or by cultivating more intensively the land already in cultivation — i. e., it would be employed on the *intensive margin* of cultivation. In either case it will produce less than it could produce on the piece of land in question. Find out accurately how much can be produced by the community when a given piece of land is in use over and above what can be produced when it is out of use and you will have an exact measure of the economic productivity of that piece of land.

It is only in this sense that any agent can be said to be productive. Whatever the laborer's capacity or energy may be, unless the community gains something through that capacity and energy which it would otherwise not have, his labor cannot be said to be productive. Find out accurately how much the community produces with his help over and above what it produces without his help and you have an exact measure of his productivity. However much intelligence and executive ability the business man may display in his machinations, he is productive only in the sense and to the extent that the community produces more by reason of those machinations than it would produce without them. If his machinations only result in levying tribute upon other lines of economic activity, or in causing two dollars to emerge from the pockets of others where one had emerged before, his machinations are unproductive, possibly destructive. But if they give the community a better and more efficient direction of its productive energy, they are productive in the highest degree. Find out with respect to the business man, as with respect to the other agent, how much the community produces by reason of his activities over and above what it could produce without them and you have a measure of his productivity.

This is a matter of great importance because it gives us the only possible clue to the problem of determining the productivity of each of a large number of factors when they are all combined in the same line of production. It is really nothing more nor less than the application of what logicians sometimes call the method of difference. This may be explained by means of the following formula. If A with B with C with D will produce 100; and A with B with C will also produce 100, then D contributes nothing to the result and is therefore economically unproductive. That is the exact situation with respect to the unproductive piece of land of the foregoing argument assuming that A, B, and C include all the other factors in use in the community. But if A with B with C with D produce 100 and A with B with C produce 90 then D contributes 10 to the joint product. This does not mean that D could produce 10 entirely apart from A, B, and C. D might not be able to produce anything at all if it worked alone. But in the combination, D is worth 10. That is, the combination produces 10 more when D is present than when D is absent. Economically speaking, 10 is the most that could be paid for D without loss. In these formulae, D may be assumed to represent either a piece of land, a laborer, or a business man. The logical test of productivity will be the same in each case.

It is obvious that this test becomes worthless if we try to let each of the terms A, B, C, and D represent, not a single individual factor, but a large group of factors. If, for example, D should represent, not a given piece of land, but all land, the method would be worthless. All land is never bought or rented, but only individual parcels of land. We have before us, therefore, the problem of evaluating, not all land, but individual parcels of land such as are bought and sold, leased and rented, in the actual business of the community. Similarly it would be purely academic to speculate upon the valuation of all labor. Labor in the abstract is never offered nor hired. Individual laborers offer themselves for hire, and their labor brings a price. We have, therefore, the problem of determining the value of the labor of individual laborers on the market.

In order to apply the method of difference and, at the same time, to avoid the danger of the foregoing error, let us use the following formula:

If 50 units of A with 30 units of B, with 20 units of C will produce 100 dollars, and 50 units of A with 30 units of B, with 21 units of C will produce 101 dollars, then one unit of C, under these conditions, produces one dollar, and one dollar is therefore the measure of its desirability. No one can say arbitrarily what a unit is. That must be determined in the actual market, a unit being whatever quantity is commonly used as the basis of price quotations. When conditions are such that one unit more or less of C will make a difference of one dollar in the product, that will fix the desirability and therefore the value of each and every unit of C, assuming that they are all alike.

It is an observed fact, however, that when the supply of one factor increases relatively to the others, its value falls. In the foregoing illustration, if the number of units of A and B should remain the same while the number of units of C should increase to 30, the value of each unit of C would fall. Why should this be ? If each unit of C should continue to have a productivity as determined by the preceding rule, of one dollar, i. e., if its productivity did not diminish as the result of the increasing number of units, there would obviously be no diminution in its desirability. If an indefinitely increasing number of units of C should continue to have each a productivity of one dollar as determined by the foregoing test, each and every unit would continue to be worth as much as ever to its purchaser (or employer). The fact that it is observed to be worth less and less would indicate that there must be something which makes a unit less desirable as the number of units increases. Since the desirability of a productive factor lies in its productivity, and since it is desired for the sake of its product alone, there must be a decline in its productivity. Such is found to be the case wherever a definite test can be applied.

Let us assume that in the above formula, A represents labor, B capital, and C land. Increasing the land by one acre will mean a slightly diminished product per acre. Since the same labor and capital must be spread over a larger number of acres and each one must therefore be cultivated a little less intensively, each acre will normally produce a little less. The more acres are added, the lower becomes the product of each acre for the same reason, and the less desirable it becomes.

Let us assume that the supply of land, labor and capital in the community is such that a certain fund of labor and capital has to be employed on every twenty acres of land of a certain grade, and this land, when cultivated by that fund of labor and capital produces an average crop of 30 bushels per acre. If, however, the same labor and capital could, by cultivating only 19 acres, make each acre produce 31 bushels, or by cultivating 21 acres could make each acre produce only 29 bushels, then one acre would be worth a rental of somewhere between 9 and 11 bushels. That would be its economic productivity. Such a quantity would be the amount produced by reason of the use of one acre over and above what could be produced without it. 20 acres at 30 bushels per acre would produce a total of 600 bushels; 21 acres at 29 bushels per acre would produce a total of 609 bushels. There is a gain of 9 bushels from having an extra acre. If 19 acres at 31 bushels produce a total of 589 bushels, there is a loss of 11 bushels due to the loss of one acre. But if the land should increase, or the other factors diminish until for such a fund of labor and capital there were 40 acres of land of the same grade, which, as now cultivated, would yield a crop of 20 bushels per acre, and if one acre more, i. e., 41 acres, would produce, with the same labor and capital, a crop of $19\frac{3}{5}$ bushels per acre, or 39 acres, a crop of $20\frac{2}{5}$ bushels per acre, then the rent of each acre would be something between $3\frac{2}{5}$ and $3\frac{3}{5}$ bushels. That would then be its economic productivity, though its physical quality would be the same as before. That is the amount by which the total crop would be increased or diminished by the use or disuse of one acre. Some such decline as this in the economic productivity of land is the only possible reason for a rise or fall in rent, in terms of bushels or units of physical product, with a change in the relative abundance or scarcity of land. As it is the decline in the *intensity of a desire* due to the increased consumption of a consumable article which explains the fact that its value falls when its supply increases relatively to that of other consumers' goods, so it is the decline in the *productivity* of an agent of production which accounts for the fact that its value falls when its supply increases relatively to that of other agents.

The law of diminishing returns from land, in its simplest form, is little better than a truism; but some of the less familiar variations of the same principle are far from being truisms, and very few economists as yet fully appreciate all the consequences which these variations involve.

In its simplest form it is merely one variation of the foregoing formulae, and may be stated as follows:

Units of labor and capital	Acres of land		Product	
If	X	with	Y	will produce	P	
then	aX	with	Y	will produce more than	P	but less than aP

(This assumes that a is a positive quantity greater than 1.)

It is, of course, theoretically possible, to assign so low a numerical value to X and so high a numerical value to Y that the addition of the increment $aX - X$ to the labor and capital would result in a product of more than aP. That would be a case of increasing returns. It would be equally possible to assign so high a numerical value to X and so low a numerical value to Y that the addition of an increment to the labor and capital would result in a product of less than P. But both of these assumptions would represent equally uneconomic and unprofitable combinations of the factors of production, and would be, except where land is valueless, equally abnormal and difficult to find in real life. Where land has any value whatever, a state of increasing, or even of constant returns from land can be found only where there is a farmer so deficient in judgment as to make his elimination by competition only a question of time.

The logical possibilities are exhausted by the five following cases. Assuming, as before, that X with Y will produce P, then aX with Y will produce:

(1) more than aP
(2) aP
(3) less than aP, but more than P
(4) P
(5) less than P

(1) aX with Y will produce more than aP. This is a case of increasing returns from labor and capital, but of negative returns from land. A larger total product would result if some of the land were abandoned if at the same time labor and capital were concentrated on the remainder. Assuming that one acre is as good as another, any acre in the whole combination might be abandoned with profit. It is worth less than nothing, and it could be cultivated only through a lack of judgment on the part of the farmer. To bring additional land under cultivation by the same labor and capital would result in a diminution of product. Under these conditions, X with aY will produce less than P.

(2) aX with Y will produce aP. This is a case of constant returns from labor and capital but of neutral returns from land. The total product would be neither increased nor diminished by the abandonment of a small fraction of the land, or by the addition of another small fraction. If the land costs nothing, it would be a matter of indifference to the farmer whether to use one acre more or one acre less; but if it costs him anything whatever, it would pay him to abandon any one acre of the combination, since, by so doing,

he would reduce his rent, but would not reduce his product at all. This being the case, any single acre of the combination is worth exactly nothing. Under these conditions also, X with aY will produce P.

(3) aX with Y will produce less than aP, but more than P. This is the case of diminishing returns from labor and capital, and also from land. Under these conditions, each and every unit of labor and capital and each and every acre of land is economically productive as determined by the test described in the earlier part of this paper. The addition of a small increment of labor and capital gives a small increase of product (the product being more than P). That shows that each and every unit of labor and capital in the combination adds something to the total product, and its abandonment would result in a diminution of the product, assuming that the units are all alike. Each unit is worth some positive amount. At the same time the product does not increase in as great a proportion as the labor and capital (the product being less than aP). That shows that each and every acre of land is a matter of some importance. The cultivation is carried beyond the point where returns begin to diminish, and the abandonment of a single acre would necessitate a still more intensive cultivation of the remaining acres, or a cultivation still further beyond the point of diminishing returns, and this would mean a somewhat smaller total product as the result of the abandonment of that acre. Each and every acre is therefore worth some positive amount. Under these conditions X with aY will produce less than aP but more than P.

(4) aX with Y will produce P. This is a case of neutral returns from labor and capital and of constant returns from land, being the exact reverse of (2). The addition of an increment of labor and capital to the combination adds noth-

ing to the product.   Where that is the case we must assume, as an approximation to the truth, that the subtraction of a small fraction of the labor and capital would subtract nothing from the product.   If the units are all alike, any one of them, taken separately, is worth exactly nothing to the combination, in the sense that the business would produce exactly as much without it as with it.   If any price whatever has to be paid for each unit, the only thing for the farmer to do is to reduce the number in his employ, though if they cost him nothing it would be a matter of indifference to him whether to employ them all or only a part.   On the other hand, a small increase in the number of acres of land in the combination would increase the product in exact proportion, assuming that the acres are all alike.   The labor and capital necessary for the cultivation of this increment would, of course, have to be withdrawn from the cultivation of the original amount.   But this withdrawal, as we have seen, would not reduce the total product from the original land, and the new increment would, under the same cultivation, produce as much per acre as the original;   therefore the total product would increase in exact proportion as the number of acres was increased.   This assumes, of course, that the increment of land is so small that the labor and capital required for its cultivation would not so reduce the amount left for the cultivation of the original amount as to bring its cultivation again under the law of diminishing returns.   Under these conditions X with aY will produce aP.

(5) aX with Y will produce less than P.   This is a case of negative returns from labor and capital and of increasing returns from land.   The added increment is worth less than nothing to the combination and a certain fraction of the existing supply could be dispensed with to advantage, even

if its use cost absolutely nothing.   Where this is the case, the addition of a small area of land to the combination would more than proportionally increase the product.   The labor and capital necessary for the cultivation of the new area would, as in the above cases, have to be withdrawn from the cultivation of the original area.   But this, as we have seen, would increase the total yield of the original area.   Since the new area would, under the same cultivation, yield as much per acre as the original, the total yield after the new area was added would be larger per acre than before.   In other words, the total product would increase more than in proportion to the increase in the number of acres.   Under these conditions, X with aY will produce more than aP.

Summing up the argument, we have found that:

(1) where aX with Y will produce more than aP, there X with aY will produce less than P; and

(2) where aX with Y will produce aP, there X with aY will produce P; and

(3) where aX with Y will produce less than aP but more than P, there X with aY will also produce less than aP but more than P; and

(4) where aX with Y will produce P, there X with aY will produce aP; and

(5) where aX with Y will produce less than P, there X with aX will produce more than aP

The main point to be learned from these formulae is that by varying the land, leaving the labor and capital unchanged, one gets the exact counterpart of the law of diminishing returns as it was originally expounded.   The objection may be raised that the conditions described under (4) and (5) would never be found in real life.   To this it may be replied that these conditions are logically as easily conceivable, and economically no more unprofitable, than those described under (1) and (2), assuming that land costs anything at all. Neither the conditions described under (1) nor those described under (5) can ever, under any possibility, be regarded as economic. Those described under (2) and (4) are economically possible only on condition that land costs nothing in the one case, and that labor and capital cost nothing in the other.

There is, however, considerable room for variation in the conditions described under (3). They may approximate to those described under (2) when land is very cheap and labor and capital very dear, or to those described under (4) when land is very dear and labor and capital very cheap. The conditions described under (2) are those which give the maximum product per unit of labor and capital, and if these were the only items of expense the farmer would find it most expedient to combine the factors in such proportion as would yield constant returns from these factors and neutral returns from the land. The more nearly this condition is approached, — that is, the dearer the labor and capital and the cheaper the land, — the more nearly he would need to approach these proportions in the combination of the factors of production. On the other hand, the conditions described under (4) are those which yield the maximum product per acre of land. If land were the only item of expense the farmer would find it expedient to combine the factors in such proportions as would yield constant returns from land and neutral returns from labor and capital. The more nearly the condition is approached in which land is the only item of expense, — that is, the dearer the land and the cheaper the labor and capital, — the more nearly he would need to approach these proportions. All this simply means that where land is cheap and labor and capital dear there will be extensive cultivation approaching, as a limit, the condition described under (2). Any other kind of cultivation would be uneconomic. But where land is dear and labor and capital cheap there will be intensive cultivation approaching as a limit the condition described under (4). Any other kind would be equally uneconomic. This discussion has been from the point of view of the individual farmer who finds the rent of land and the rate of wages and of interest fixed for him by the community at large.

When we come to discuss the question from the point of view of the community which must make its own rates of wages and interest and fix its own rent we find the corollary of the foregoing law. In a community where land is so abundant and labor and capital so scarce that, when it is all employed, so little labor and capital have to be employed on so much land as to approach the conditions described under (2), wages and interest will be high and rent low. But in a community where labor and capital are so abundant and land so scarce that, when all the factors are employed, so much labor and capital have to be concentrated on so little land as to approach the conditions described under (4), wages and interest will be low and rent high. The substantial reason for these results is that, in the former case, each unit of labor and capital has a high productivity as determined by the same test, whereas, in the latter case, the opposite conditions prevail.

As was stated above, the principle of diminishing returns as it was originally expounded is only one part of a general law relating to the varying productivity of a factor of production when used in combination with other factors. Another part of that general law has now been shown to exist in the form of the counterpart of the principle of diminishing returns, viz., the principle that varying quantities of land when cultivated by a fixed quantity of labor and capital are increasing, constant, diminishing, neutral, or negative, according to the quantity of land used in the combination.   But there are many other phases of the same general law.   With a fixed quantity of land and capital and varying quantities of labor, with varying quantities of land and capital and a fixed quantity of labor, with a fixed quantity of labor and land and varying quantities of capital, or with varying quantities of labor and land and a fixed quantity of capital, the results would always conform to the same general law.   Moreover, since there are many forms of labor (Cairnes' non-competing groups) the variation of the number of laborers in one group, all other factors remaining fixed in quantity, will give the same general result.   That is to say, beginning with an infinitesimal quantity of one kind of labor necessary to the combination, and gradually increasing the quantity leaving other factors the same, the resulting product would go through the stages of increasing, constant, diminishing, neutral and negative returns, just as would result from a similar increase in the quantity of labor on a fixed quantity of land.

This is the principle, — and this is the only known principle, — which furnishes any satisfactory explanation of the observed fact that the wages of a given class of laborers fall when their numbers increase relatively to other groups or classes.   Moreover this principle furnishes the most substantial possible reason why they ought to fall.   Though the laborers in the class in question may be subjectively as meritorious as they were before the increase in their numbers took place, and though they may put forth as much effort and skill as before, the fact remains that they become objectively less productive, man per man.   A mere increase of the number of men in proportion to the other factors with which they must work in combinations, results in diminished productivity, and each man becomes of less value, objectively considered. This does not in any way depend upon the form of the social organization. It lies much deeper than that. It is a matter of actual economic productivity as determined by a logical test.[1]

From the foregoing discussion of the law of proportionality in its varying and universal phases, we reach the conclusion that a factor of production is worth as much as it specifically produces, that is to say, — if you can find out in any given situation how much more you can produce with it than without it you will have a physical measurement of its productivity, and this determines its value. But it must be remembered that this applies to specific units of the factor. The law is the same whether it be a material factor or a human factor. On a piece of swamp land the question is one of more or less, not how much could he produce without any water, but how much difference in his product would be made by more or less water. So with the valuation of nitrogen as the element of soil fertility; not how much he could produce without nitrogen, for he could produce none, but how much more or less would he produce with one hundred pounds more or one hundred pounds less of nitrogen on his farm. That would determine for him the value of one hundred pounds of nitrogen. So in a given situation not how much could be produced without labor, for nothing could be produced, but how much more could be produced with one more laborer, or how much less could be produced with one less laborer; that would determine the value of one laborer of the kind in question at the spot where the valuation is made. If there should be too many of one kind of laborers at one particular spot, so that no more could be produced

[1] " Diminishing Returns and Value," by T. N. Carver. Published in *Rivista di Scienza*, 1907.

with one more of that kind, and no less with one less of that kind, the physical product of a man of that kind at that spot is exactly nothing, and therefore his value is exactly nothing. But if the number of a particular kind of laborers is so small and the other factors are so abundant that one more laborer of this particular kind would add greatly to the product of the combination, then it is not inaccurate to say that his physical product is very high. That being the case, his value is very high. This, therefore, is the principle which determines how much a man is worth, and consequently, according to our criterion of justice, how much he ought to have as a reward for his work. To pay him more than that would take something from other producers. If the total addition which a certain individual can make to the total product of the community is one dollar a day, or, which means the same thing, if the total reduction in the production of the community when he ceases to work, is one dollar a day, and if he is actually consuming two dollars a day, then there would be one dollar a day more for some one else if he should emigrate or die. The extra dollar which he receives, at the expense of some one else, is either given him for love or benevolence, according as the others look upon him. It is not given him for the sake of justice.

But, it may be asked, does not justice require that such readjustments be made as will enable every mature man in sound health, to earn at least two dollars a day? Much can be said for this point of view; but it is very important that we understand just what adjustments may have to be made. And first of all, it is one thing to bring about such readjustments as will enable every normal adult to *earn* a living wage, and it is quite a different thing to *decree* a living wage to every such person. If the individual who does not earn a living wage is given it, then some one else is given less than he earns, which would be unjust. In a general way, the necessary readjustments must be in accordance with the law of variable proportions, as previously stated. Men and materials must be moved about — that is all that is done in this world — until they are brought into such physical proportions as produce the best economic results. Men must be redistributed, first, territorially, that is, moved from places where they are too thick to places where their numbers are too thin; and second, occupationally, that is, from occupations which are overcrowded to occupations which are under-crowded. The first is a transportation, the second an educational problem. The latter is not only the more difficult, it is the infinitely more important problem.

CHAPTER VIII

INTEREST

ONE of the most progressive and beneficent movements of recent times is the organization of rural interests. One of the most important phases of this movement is the development of coöperative or mutual credit associations among farmers. Wherever there is marked progress in agriculture we find an enlarged use of credit, and in order to secure adequate credit facilities the farmers have generally been forced to create their own credit institutions.

The apparent reason for this movement is the enlarged use of capital in agriculture. Before the age of mechanical inventions, capital, that is, tools, machinery and equipment, played a minor part in agricultural development. Now it plays a very important part, — so important that no farmer can hope to succeed unless he is provided with an adequate supply of capital, that is, of farm equipment. This is expensive, and, when stated quantitatively in terms of money, makes a relatively large fund of capital.

A similar, but much larger increase in the demand for capital in manufacturing began in the middle of the eighteenth century, and in transportation in the first half of the nineteenth century. Taken altogether, this enormous increase in the use of expensive machinery, and the consequent increase in the importance of and demand for capital, is the largest economic fact of modern times.

A common rule, insisted upon by all the successful coöperative credit associations among European farmers, is that loans shall be made only for productive purposes. It is understood that the purpose of making loans is to promote better farming, to increase farm production. This is a clear and very practical recognition of the importance of capital in production. While urbane theorists, and even certain academicians, have been solemnly discussing the question as to whether capital is productive or not, these practical peasant farmers have shown, even in their coöperative work, that they recognize that capital is an aid to production, — that, under proper conditions, and up to a certain point, it is correct to say " more capital, more product; less capital, less product." The question as to the exact meaning of the word " productive " has not bothered them. Neither need it bother us. It is sufficient, for all practical purposes, that we recognize that tools are useful in production, which means that capital is a means of increasing production, or that one can produce more with than without capital. In order to economize ink and paper, the word production will be used in the discussion but it will be used in this sense and in no other sense whatever.

There is no mystery about capital. It consists of tools and equipment, though sometimes we speak of it as though it were the money necessary to buy the tools and equipment. Thus the large use of capital in industry has come because of the invention of machinery. When farming, for example, was done with a few very simple tools, most of which were made either by the farmer himself or by the local blacksmith, capital did not play a large part in agriculture. Another way of saying the same thing is that it did not take much money to buy all the equipment the farmer needed or knew how to use. The purchase of land was the only thing requiring much money, and that, in this country, was either free or very cheap. In other countries it was not a commodity to be bought and sold. Therefore, there was very little money required to start in agriculture. At the present time, not only is the price of land rising but the equipment of a farm is becoming more and more expensive because of the increased use of expensive machinery. This is likely to increase more and more as the years go by.

Capital is brought into existence in only one way, that is, by consuming less than is produced. If I have a dollar, I can spend it either for an article of consumption, say confectionery, or for an article of production, say a spade. If I buy a spade, I become a capitalist, to the amount of a dollar; that is, I become an owner of tools. The process is precisely the same whether the amount in question is a dollar or a million dollars. If I do not have the dollar, my only chance of getting the spade is either to borrow it, or borrow the money with which to buy it. That is, I must use credit. Again, the process is precisely the same, whether the amount be a dollar or a million dollars.

There are, therefore, only two ways of securing capital for the equipment of a farm or any other enterprise. One is to accumulate it oneself, by consuming less than one's income; the other is to borrow it. The advantage of borrowing is that one does not have to wait so long to get possession of the tools and equipment. One can get them at once and make them produce the means of paying for themselves. That is, one can produce more with them than without them. Without their help, the farmer's production might be so low as to make it difficult ever to accumulate enough with which to buy them. With their help he may be able to pay for them, that is, to pay off the debt, in a shorter time than it would take to accumulate the purchase price without their help. That is the only advantage to those who know how to use it. — From *Farmers' Bulletin* 593, U. S. Department of Agriculture. 1914.

But while capital is an aid in production, or productive in the sense in which we are using it, it is not inevitably and necessarily productive. Neither is labor. Either may be wasted, misapplied, or unintelligently directed, in which case it does not increase production. Shortsighted people, however, who do not realize how inexorably the time of payment arrives, who do not know how rapidly tools wear out and have to be replaced, or who do not keep accounts in order that they may tell exactly where they stand financially, will do well to avoid borrowing as they would avoid the plague. Debts have to be paid with deadly certainty, and they who do not have the wherewithal when the day of reckoning arrives, become bankrupt with equal certainty.

On the other hand, there is nothing disgraceful about borrowing for productive purposes. The feeling that it is not quite respectable to go into debt has grown out of the old habit of borrowing to pay living expenses. That was regarded, perhaps rightly, as a sign of incompetency. It was then natural that men should not like to have their neighbors know that they had to borrow money. But to borrow for a genuinely productive purpose, for a purpose which will bring you in more than enough to pay off your debt, principal and interest, is a profitable enterprise. It shows sagacity and courage and is not a thing to be ashamed of. But it cannot be too much emphasized that the would-be borrower must calculate very carefully and be sure that it *is* a productive enterprise before he goes into debt.

This distinction between borrowing for a productive purpose and borrowing to pay living expenses will help to explain why religious leaders in times past have been opposed to interest. It is undoubtedly a bad practice for men to borrow money with which to buy consumers' goods, except in the most extreme cases. When such an extreme case arises, the borrower is a proper subject for charity. Before the days of expensive machinery, when capital was not an important factor in production, such a thing as borrowing for productive purposes was practically unknown. The only borrowing that was done was for the purpose of buying non-productive goods. This, as stated above, is a bad practice, except in cases of extreme necessity, and even in these cases charity should offer relief.

The question may be asked, however, why did not the church forbid borrowing instead of forbidding the taking of interest? The reason was that so long as the usurers were permitted to offer loans, many shortsighted people would yield to the temptation to borrow. Since the purpose for which they borrowed added nothing to their earning capacity, they were in no better position to accumulate money after they borrowed than they had been before. If they had been able to accumulate anything before, they would not have needed money. The fact that they had not been able to accumulate anything before would then be pretty conclusive proof that they would not be able to accumulate enough afterward to pay the debt. Therefore, they put themselves in the clutches of the usurer.

A parallel case is found in the case of intoxicating liquor. It is regarded as bad practice for men to drink it, at least to excess. It has been found, however, that men *will* drink to excess so long as it is offered to them in excessive quantities. Therefore, the policy has grown up of forbidding the sale altogether, or of forbidding anyone to make a profit out of it, (under the dispensary system) instead of contenting ourselves with merely preaching and legislating against excessive drinking. Rightly or wrongly, this was the attitude of the religious and moral leaders on the subject of usury, or interest. Instead of contenting themselves with preaching against shortsighted borrowing, as all borrowing for purposes of consumption is, they went to the root of the matter, and attacked lending at interest. Since the use of productive machinery, that is, capital, has come to play such an important rôle, these considerations do not apply to borrowing for productive purposes. Therefore, all religious and moral leaders who have intelligence enough to discriminate, have withdrawn their opposition to the taking of interest. There is need, however, of a revival of the prohibition against lending for non-productive purposes, which was all that the old religious leaders opposed. They did not oppose lending for productive purposes because there was no lending for productive purposes.

In the payment of a debt, it is not the interest but the principal which gives the greatest trouble, except where interest rates are exorbitant.   If I borrow $100 for a year at 7 per cent, I have to pay, at the end of the year, $107.   If I borrow at 5 per cent, I have to pay $105.   The difference is $2.   Now, $2 is not to be despised.   Good business consists in large part in looking after just such items as this. Nevertheless, it is only a little harder to pay $107 than to pay $105.   The point is that the principal is the same in either case, and it is the principal which gives the greatest trouble.

The reason it has seemed necessary to emphasize this simple, elementary fact, is that many people seem to imagine that, if we can only find some way of reducing interest on loans from 7 per cent to 5 per cent, or from 6 per cent to 4 per cent, the way will be made easy for the borrowers. It is important that interest rates be lowered wherever it is economically possible, but it is vastly more important that the people who borrow should learn how to use the borrowed money in such a way as to enable them to pay back the principal easily.   The only way to do this is to use the money borrowed in such a way as to put one in possession of the means of repayment.   If the $100 which I borrow, is spent on fertilizer which adds $125 to the value of my crop, I should not find any great difficulty in repaying the loan, both principal and interest.   If I use it in such a way as to add only $75 to my crop, I shall have some difficulty in repaying the principal, saying nothing of the interest.   It is more important that I should be able to use the $100 so as to add $125 rather than $75 to my crop, than it is that I should be able to borrow at 5 per cent or even at 0 per cent, instead of 7 per cent. [1]

[1] The three preceding pages are adapted from *Farmer's Bulletin* 593, United States Department of Agriculture. 1914.

They who oppose the taking of interest usually agree that the investor or the lender should receive back the principal. That is, they agree that he should receive back 100 per cent of the sum which he invested or loaned, but deny that he should receive 105 per cent, or even 101 per cent. But why exactly 100 per cent instead of 99 or 101 per cent, or than 95 or 105 per cent? The answer usually is that the lender should receive back as much as he gives, and the borrower should pay back as much as he receives. But suppose that a dollar is worth more today than a year from today. Should the transaction close by returning the exact number of dollars regardless of their value, or the same value regardless of the exact number of dollars? Again, if the borrower was shortsighted enough to buy consumers' goods, he will almost as certainly become bankrupt in trying to pay back 100 as 105 per cent. Why should he be subjected to that hardship? Why not reduce his obligation to a point which would not subject him to hardship, since the loan was unproductive and did him no real good? Something may be said for this latter point of view, but it should be said in the name of charity and not in the name of justice.

Assuming that justice requires a *quid pro quo*, — that the interests of both the borrower and the lender should be safeguarded, let us consider the question raised above, whether the lender should pay back the exact number of dollars borrowed, or an equivalent value. The equivalence of value is apparently a more accurate expression of the equities of the case than the equivalence of monetary units. Neither the borrower nor the lender is likely to care anything for monetary units as such. They are prized solely for the value which they express. Since the interests of both borrower and lender are in the value of the money originally transferred, rather than in the number of units, it would seem that in the paying-off of the loan, the value rather than the number of units should also be considered.

Things present are, other things equal, more highly esteemed or evaluated than things to come. If one were given one's choice of a dollar today or a dollar a year hence, one would ordinarily choose the dollar today. One would not infrequently, if put to a practical test of this kind, choose a dollar today rather than a dollar and five cents a year hence, or than a dollar and ten cents two years hence. The way one reacts to a practical test of this kind is of vastly more economic significance than the way one reasons abstractly on the subject of interest.

If the lender evaluates a dollar today as equal to a dollar and five cents a year hence, he will certainly not lend a dollar today except on condition that he receive a year hence that which he now regards as equal to the dollar which he permits to go out of his possession. If the borrower evaluates a dollar today as highly as a dollar and ten cents a year hence, he will be willing to borrow and agree to pay back a year hence approximately a dollar and ten cents. When these two men come together, there is a probability that they will strike a bargain somewhere between these two limits. That is, a loan will be made at something between 5 and 10 per cent interest. As nearly as could be determined this constitutes an agreement that the borrower should repay and the lender receive, a year hence, that which they both unite in thinking equivalent in present value, or which they both esteem today as equal to the dollar which is today being transferred. Otherwise one of two things would happen. Either the lender would refuse to lend, preferring to keep his dollar in his own possession, or the borrower would refuse to borrow, preferring to give up the

chance of getting a dollar today rather than to obligate himself to repay a dollar and ten cents a year hence.

But why should men prefer present to future, or evaluate
a present dollar more highly than a future dollar ? This is
not a necessary part of the discussion. If it is once admitted
that they do, we have a satisfactory explanation of the fact
of interest. Under such conditions interest will exist in one
form or other wherever there is free exchange of services or
commodities. There are doubtless many reasons which
cannot be intelligently stated why men evaluate the present
more highly than the future. There are a few which can.
In the first place, whatever changes in fortune and circumstance may happen to either borrower or lender, one thing is
absolutely certain: both will be a year older a year hence
than they are today. Each will have one year less of life
in which to make use of the dollar or the results achieved by
its use. Each gains something by having its immediate use,
or loses something by postponing its use for a year. Therefore the borrower, who gains its immediate use, is willing
to pay something for this advantage, and the lender, who
gives up its immediate use, charges something for this
disadvantage.

Another and more cogent reason is found in the fact,
mentioned earlier in this chapter, that the dollar may be
spent for tools, which, in turn, are aids in production. This
enables the borrower, if he uses his tools wisely, to repay the
loan with interest, and make a profit for himself besides.
If he had to wait until he could produce enough without
sufficient tools to enable him to buy them, he would suffer
a greater disadvantage than if he could get them at once and
make them pay for themselves by increasing his production.

The borrowing and lending of capital for productive
purposes is a means of economizing the capital of the com-

munity or the nation. If A has a more productive use for capital than B, it is desirable that A should have the use of it rather than B. But it will sometimes happen that B possesses it and A does not. In that case, it is desirable that A should borrow from B. But if B has a slightly productive use for the capital in question, he can scarcely be expected to let A have it for nothing. He must be compensated for his loss. At the same time, the use to which A wishes to put the capital is so highly productive that he can well afford to pay B for the use of it. In that case both A and B are benefited, A getting the use of capital which is worth more to him than the interest which he has to pay, and B getting interest on his capital which is worth more to him than the use of the capital would be. In addition, which is more important, the particular fund of capital in question is made to produce more when in the hands of A than when in the hands of B.

If, however, B who has the capital, has a more productive use for it than A, it is improbable that there will be any borrowing or lending. In fact, it would be impossible except where one or both are ignorant of the true situation. Since B has a highly productive use for it, he could not afford to lend it unless he got a high rate of interest. Since A has a less productive use for it, he could not afford to pay so high a rate of interest. Consequently, if they are intelligent, there will be no transfer. This will be as it should be in the interest of the community or the nation, for the capital will remain where it is most productive.

In this respect, the economic use of capital comes under the same law as the economic use of any other factor of production which is so limited in quantity as not to be sufficient to meet all demands. On an irrigation project, for example, where there is more land than can be adequately watered by the limited supply of water, it is important that water be economized and made to produce as much as possible. If A has a more productive use for water than B, it is better that A should have it than B. If B happens to have it, or to have more than he can use to the best advantage, while A has less than he can use to good advantage, it would be better that B should sell his surplus to A. B, having a use for it, though an inferior one, or being in a position to make it produce something, though a small amount, must be paid for what he loses. A, having a superior use for it, or being in a position to make it produce a great deal, can well afford to pay B a reasonable price for it. In that case both gain. B gains because the price which he gets is greater than the product which he could expect from the use of the water; A gains because the product which he gets is greater than the price which he has to pay. And the community gains because the water is put to a more, rather than to a less productive use. The parallelism is, therefore, very close between the use of water and that of capital. Hundreds of other parallelisms could be cited.

However, all opponents of interest who have thought seriously about it, agree that if the private ownership of capital is to be permitted at all, there can be no sound objection to permitting it to be loaned at interest. They see clearly enough that if one is permitted to use capital to add to one's own income, there can be no objection to allowing one to lend it to some one else to be used in adding to his income; and if the borrower is permitted to profit by the use of capital, the lender must be permitted to charge him with interest for its use. The real question is, therefore, ought one to be permitted to own capital, or to profit by its use ?

In the discussion of this important question, much confusion has resulted from the different interpretations put upon the word productive. Some have seen fit to deny the productivity of capital, and have thought that this denial constituted a denial of the proposition that any individual ought to derive any benefit from its ownership. Others have defended the productivity of capital, and have thought that, by so doing, they were defending the justice or expediency of interest. A little careful analysis will show that the two sides are using the word productive in two different senses. Since they are not discussing the same question, it is impossible for them ever to reach the same conclusion. If by the productivity of capital it is meant that capital has some original and inherent power of producing wealth when entirely separated from labor and land, obviously capital is not productive. But if it is meant that it is a useful factor in production when used in combination with labor and lands, or that a given fund of labor and land can produce more when supplied with capital than when not supplied, or with an adequate supply than with an inadequate supply of capital, then it is equally obvious that capital is productive. Let us no longer waste time quarrelling over the meaning of words. Capital is either useful in production or it is not. It is either an advantage to the community to have an adequate supply of capital or it is not. If it is neither useful nor advantageous, it would be difficult to find a satisfactory reason why the state or the public should own it. If there is any reason why the state or the public should own it, it must be because it is of some use, or of some advantage to have it. It may or it may not be better that the public rather than private individuals should own it, but no logical person with a sense of humor could maintain, in one breath, that capital is unproductive, in the sense of being of

no use, and, in the next, that the public should own that
which he had declared to be useless.

When confronted with the categorical question, is capital
or is it not, an aid in production, there are few who are so
ignorant or so unfair as to answer in the negative. However, something will depend upon the meaning attached to
the word capital. So long as it is clearly understood that
capital is tools, machinery and equipment, the answer is
perfectly clear. With this understanding of the meaning
of the word, to deny that capital is an aid in production
would be to deny that tools are useful. But some confusion
is occasionally introduced into the problem sometimes even
by academic economists, when capital is defined, not as
tools, but as an abstract fund of value. When one allows
the concept of a lot of tools to pass out of his mind, and is
unable to think except in terms of an abstract fund of
value, he may easily become puzzled. How, it may be
asked, can an abstract fund of value aid in the production of
material goods ? What does an abstract fund of value do
to help the farmer to grow wheat, or the shoemaker to make
shoes ?

The answer is that the abstract fund of value is no help
to the producer, — it is the tools that help. The value
embodied in the tools is not a cause, but a result or a symptom of their usefulness or productivity. If they were not
useful, they would have no value, and there would therefore
be no abstract fund of value to consider, though the tools
might still have a very concrete and material existence. The
presence of value in tools is a symptom not a cause of their
usefulness, it is a final demonstration of the fact of their
usefulness in production, it is therefore the final argument in
refutation of the doctrine that capital is unproductive; but
this fund of value is, in itself, neither productive nor a cause

of productivity. The distinction is precisely that between a cause and a symptom. The tools are a contributing cause of an increased product. Their value is a symptom of this fact.

Capital may, however, be quantitatively expressed in terms of value, just as coal may be quantitatively expressed in terms of weight. But the fact that we express the quantity of a lot of coal in terms of tons, as we express the quantity of a lot of tools in terms of dollars, does not lead us to define coal as an abstract fund of weight, nor does it lead to learned discussions as to whether an abstract fund of weight will heat a furnace or not. Ask any practical man how much capital he has, and he will probably answer in terms of dollars. But if you then ask him in what his capital consists, he will answer you in terms of buildings, tools, equipment, etc. When put to this kind of a test, his ideas are perfectly clear, though he might not be so clear if you were to ask him for a definition of capital.

If we can once agree that capital is tools, though quantitatively expressed in terms of dollars, and that tools are useful in production, the way is then prepared for an intelligent consideration of the question of interest. The essential part of the question is: should the owner of tools receive any income from them? Whether he handles them with his own hands, or hires others to handle them, is not the fundamental question, though that will come in for discussion later. If it be admitted that the farmer who owns tools and uses them himself should be permitted to enjoy an additional income because of his ownership over and above what he could produce without them, it could not very well be argued that, if he chooses to lend them to another farmer, who in turn secures an additional income by reason of their use, he, the owner, should not be allowed any compensation from the borrower.   Again, if the farmer who owns the tools should, instead of lending them to another farmer, hire that other farmer to work for him, guaranteeing him fixed wages, it could hardly be contended that he should pay the entire product in the form of wages, reserving nothing for himself to compensate him for the use of the tools.   He could use them himself and gain some advantage thereby.   If he were not allowed at least an equal advantage when he hired some one else to work with them, he could hardly be expected to hire anyone.   Under these conditions, no one would have an opportunity to work unless he owned his own tools. Again, therefore, let it be said, the real question is, should the farmer who owns tools, be permitted to enjoy any additional income by reason of his ownership.   If so, that additional income is interest, and no good reason can be found why he should not receive the same interest if he allows some one else to use them.

Why should tools, in any case, return an income to their owner ?   If they add anything to production, is not the maker of the tools the real producer of that which is attributed to the tools, and should he not have been paid that amount for making them ?   If a plow, for example, will enable the farming community to produce fifty dollars worth of produce over and above what it could produce without it, or with one less plow, should not the plow maker have been paid fifty dollars for making it ?   If he had been, the owner would merely get back his principal, that is, the amount invested in the plow, and there would be no interest. But if the owner pays only forty dollars for the plow, and eventually realizes a gain of fifty dollars from its use, he has received ten dollars over and above his original investment. That is interest.   Why should he not pay fifty rather than forty dollars ?

If men did not mind waiting he would have to pay fifty dollars for it. That is, if the blacksmith who made the plow would just as lief have fifty dollars in ten annual instalments of five dollars each as to have fifty dollars cash down, he would probably not be willing to sell the plow for less than fifty dollars in cash. Assuming that the plow in question lasts ten years, the farmer who buys it gets whatever advantage there is in it in the form of ten annual additions to his income of, say, five dollars each. If he did not mind waiting, but would just as lief have his fifty dollars in that form as to have it in present cash, he might be willing to pay fifty dollars for the plow. If both he and the plow maker were of that mind, the price of the plow would be approximately fifty dollars, the man who made the plow would receive the whole of its surplus product, the owner would merely get back his principal, and there would be no such thing as interest. But if, on the other hand, the plow maker would rather have forty dollars in cash than fifty in ten annual instalments of five dollars each, and if the purchaser would likewise, it is certain that the plow would never sell for fifty dollars. The fact that it does sell for less makes interest inevitable.

This disinclination to wait, which results in a higher valuation upon present than upon future goods, may, in a certain sense be said to be the source of interest. Of course this does not conflict with the theory that capital is productive or useful in production. Both ideas are essential to a proper understanding of the subject. If tools were not productive, in the sense in which we are using the word productive, they would not be worth anything. They would earn a man nothing, not even enough to pay their cost of production. It is the fact of their productivity which gives them any value whatever; but it is the disinclination to wait which prevents their present value or selling price from equalling the sum of their future earnings. Being productive they therefore have a value; but the difference between their present value and the sum of their future earning power is due to the fact that men prefer present to future. Their present value is man's present estimate of their future earning power.

This disinclination to wait is closely related to the doctrine of abstinence. One cause of confusion in many discussions of the doctrine of abstinence is the failure to analyze the meaning of that word. It does not mean that there is a positive sacrifice involved in the saving or investing of every dollar that is saved or invested. Many a dollar would be saved and invested even if no gain resulted therefrom. In fact, if there were no other opportunities, a certain amount would be saved even if the savers had to pay storage instead of receiving interest on their savings. But this case resembles many others.

There are, for example, a few poultry fanciers who would keep poultry even if they could never sell an egg or gain any income from it. There are many who would go fishing even if they could never eat or sell a pound of fish. If the demand for eggs or fish were so low, and the number of poultry and piscatorial enthusiasts so large, as to supply the whole demand, neither eggs, poultry nor fish would command any price. And yet production would go on. Let us confine our attention, for the moment, to the possibility of egg production and illustrate the principle by means of the diagram on the next page.

Let the quantity of eggs produced be measured along the line OX, their cost as well as their price along the line OY, and their negative cost along the line OF. A certain number of eggs would be produced at a negative cost, that is, they would be produced for the pleasure of keeping poultry, even if they could not be used or sold. There is no disinclination, or mental resistance which has to be overcome by the hope of a pecuniary reward. This quantity that would be produced anyway, let us represent by the line *OE*. The cost, in terms of disinclination or mental resistance, is represented by the curved line *FEA*.

Now if there were a very small demand for eggs which could be easily satisfied, it might be possible to satisfy it completely by the quantity *OE*. Such a small demand is

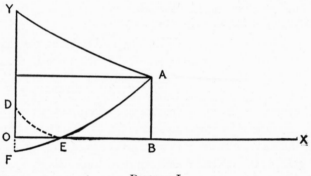

DIAGRAM I

represented by the curve *DE*. There would thus be an equilibrium of demand and supply at no price. That is, as many would be produced as consumers were willing to take at no price. But if the demand were very much greater, another equilibrium would have to be found. Let us assume that the demand is represented by the curve *YA*. The small quantity *OE* would fall short of satisfying it. If only so many were produced, they would be so scarce and the consumers would so bid for them as to give them a high price. But this high price would serve as an inducement for other and less enthusiastic poultry men to enter the business. For them, the lure of profit or wages is necessary. The supply would increase, and be measured along this line *OX* until an equilibrium was reached, at *B*. When a quantity represented by *OB* is produced, the cost of the last few units has risen, as indicated by the cost curve *FEA*, until it is measured by the line *BA*, and assuming that *YA* represents the demand curve, *AB* will also represent the price. There will now be an equilibrium because, at that price, consumers are willing to buy as much as, and no more than, producers are willing to sell. But the price *AB* is uniform for all, as indicated by the line *CA*. Even those poultry enthusiasts who would produce eggs at no price, will be able to sell their eggs at the same price which others get.

The same diagram will serve to illustrate the case of interest, or the price received for the use of capital, since the principle is the same. Let the amount of capital accumulated by saving be measured along the line *OX*, and the cost of saving, or the disinclination or mental resistance, as well as the rate of interest, along the line *OY*. The cost curve, in this case as in the case of eggs, is represented by the line *FEA*. *OE* represents the amount that would be saved without cost, that is, with no disinclination or mental resistance to be overcome. If that small amount were sufficient to supply the demand for capital, the demand being represented by the curve *DE*, there would be no interest rate. Since this represents the limited number of cases where there is no disinclination to wait, no preference for present over future, no real abstinence, tools would be evaluated at the sum of all their future earnings, and the makers would sell them at a price which their entire future earnings would just replace. The owners would, in other words, merely get back their principal or their original investment, with no surplus which could be called interest.

But if the demand for capital were much greater, as represented by the curve YA, the small supply OE would fall far short. Under such conditions of scarcity, the price offered, i. e., the rate of interest, would be very high. This would serve as an inducement to other people to save or invest. There are the men for whom the lure of gain in the form of interest is necessary. They also must be induced to save if there is to be enough capital. Men who would be unwilling to forego present consumption unless they could gain something by it, would now begin to respond to the offer of a surplus in the future to repay them for present abstinence. The supply of capital would increase along the line OX until a new equilibrium was reached, at B. At this equilibrium, the rate of interest would be represented by the line AB, at which rate the inducement would be sufficient to persuade savers to save as much as, and no more than, borrowers and purchasers of present goods were willing to take.

This should dispose of the question so frequently raised by the opponents of interest, as to whether there is any real sacrifice involved in saving. They can easily point out instances or illustrations where there is no sacrifice such as requires an interest rate as compensation. An equal number of instances could be shown to prove (?) that it costs nothing to produce eggs, fish, and many other commodities which bring a price. But in the case of the saver as in these other cases, the man who saves at no cost gets the same rate of interest as those who save at considerable sacrifice. This gives rise to what Dr. C. W. Mixter has called the principle of " saver's rent." [1] But, as we have tried to show, this principle is not confined to saving; it applies equally well to various kinds of productive work.

[1] *Quarterly Journal of Economics*, vol. xiii, p. 245.

That capital originates in saving can scarcely be doubted
by anyone who will give it careful consideration.   Saving,
however, must not be too narrowly defined.   In the first
place, it is not to be confused with hoarding.   The man who
received a talent, which, by the way, was a piece of money
and not a spiritual quality, and hid it away in a napkin, was
hoarding money, but the other men who put the talents, in
money, entrusted to them, to use, were also savers.   They
did not spend the money for articles of consumption, which
every man would be tempted more or less strongly to do,
but they used it in a way which brought increase.

To save in the ordinary modern sense is virtually to buy
producers' goods rather than consumers' goods.   One may,
it is true, deposit his savings in a savings bank.   In that case
he entrusts some one else with the work of investing it, so
that he invests it, that is buys producers' goods with it,
indirectly instead of directly.   When I decide to buy producers' goods rather than consumers' goods with a part of
my income, I direct, to the extent of my purchase, the productive energy of the community toward the making of
producers' goods rather than toward the making of consumers' goods.   The result is that the community is thereafter better supplied with producers' goods, that is, tools,
than it would otherwise have been.   The more people there
are making this choice, that is, buying producers' rather than
consumers' goods, the better the community will thereafter
be supplied with producers' goods, that is, the greater its
productive power will be.

Not only will its productive power increase, but the share
which goes to capital will diminish, leaving a larger proportion of the larger product for other shares in distribution.

Tools and other instruments of production will become so
abundant that their owners will have increasing difficulty in

getting enough from them to more than pay their original cost of production. As shown already, when the owner of tools cannot get any more on the average from them than will pay their original cost of production, he gets no interest. The nearer we can approximate to that point, the lower the rate of interest becomes. In proportion as thrift and foresight increase, in that proportion will men spend increasing shares of their income for producers' goods, in that proportion again will capital increase, and in that proportion will interest tend to disappear.

This brings us, by another route, to the conclusion reached before, viz., that if men did not prefer present to future consumption there would be no such thing as interest. When one buys producers' rather than consumers' goods, one virtually defers the possession of consumers' goods. If no one were disinclined to this deferment, so many would be willing to buy producers' goods as to make them so abundant as to cause interest to disappear. That is, they would become so abundant that the owner could not get enough out of them on the average to more than pay the original cost.[1] The remedy for a high rate of interest, therefore, is to encourage rather than to discourage thrift.

One effect of the lack of thrift, the preference for present over future consumption, or the disinclination to save, as it may be variously called, is to reduce the amount spent for producers' goods as compared with the amount spent for consumers' goods. This directs more of the productive energy of the community into the production of the latter and less into the production of the former. This results in a reduction in the stock of producers' goods or capital

---

[1] For a fuller and more complete discussion of the problem of interest, see the author's *Distribution of Wealth*, New York, 1905, Chapter VI; also his article on " The Place of Abstinence in the Theory of Interest," *Quarterly Journal of Economics*, August, 1893.

available at any given time, and this, in turn, enables the owner of a given set of tools or stock of capital, to get more income from them.   The effect of this disinclination is to limit the supply of capital and enable the owner of each unit to get a higher return from it.   This may be illustrated by the following diagram:

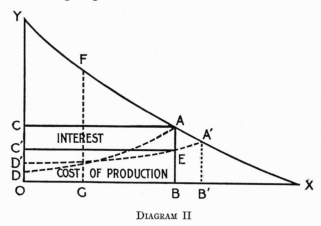

DIAGRAM II

Let us assume that the amount of a certain kind of capital is measured along the line OX and the productivity of various increments of that amount along the line OY, and that the curve $YFAA'X$ is formed by a succession of points measuring the productivity of these successive increments. That is to say, if the supply were measured by the line OG, the opportunities for the use of this kind of capital would be so great that each unit would have a productivity measured by the dotted line FG.   If, however, the supply were much larger, represented, let us say, by the line OB, the difficulty of finding suitable opportunities for the employment of this kind of capital would be so great, and each unit would have to be employed with so few other things in combination with it as to give it a low productivity, represented, let us say, by the line $A'B'$. That is to say, this line $A'B'$ measures the quantity of product which depends for its existence upon a single unit of the supply of capital. One unit more of this kind of capital put into industry would add a product approximately equal to the line $A'B'$, or one unit subtracted from this supply of capital would subtract from the total product the quantity represented by this line. The first question is, therefore, what determines the supply of this kind of capital? Why should the supply be OG, OB, or OB', rather than OX?

Here we must consider the motives which lead to the production of this kind of capital or tools. The motive is the desire for the product which results from its possession. If the product which results from the possession and use of a given unit is represented by the line FG, there is a powerful motive to the production and accumulation of more of this kind of capital. But, if the product is represented by the line $A'B'$, the motive is much less. Again, we must consider the motives which check or limit production as well as those which encourage production. If there were no adverse motive, there would be no reason why production of this particular kind of capital should not increase until the supply was represented by the line OX, in which case there would be so many units as to make the question of more or less a matter of indifference. That is to say, one more unit of this kind of capital would add nothing to the product, and one less unit would subtract nothing. Why does not this kind of capital increase until the supply becomes thus abundant?

In the first place, we have to consider the cost of producing it. Remembering that capital is tools and that it costs something to produce each tool, we have a sufficient explanation for the limitation of the supply. Let us assume that the cost of producing the different units of the supply is represented by the dotted curve $D'A'$. In that case, the tendency would be to check production at a point where the supply would be measured by the line OB', that is to say, at this point the cost of production would be equal to the product, the line $A'B'$, measuring both cost and product. Since the price of the tool or unit of capital would have to be sufficient to cover the cost of production, it would then happen that the price would also equal its product. The owner of such a tool would get from it just enough to cover the price which he paid for it. In other words, he would get back his principal, but no interest. Moreover, he would have to pay the price in present cash and wait during the effective life-time of the tool to get back his principal in the form of product.

If he has a disinclination to wait, it is clear that he will never be willing to pay such a price as this. But the tool-maker must have this price or he will stop producing. Evidently, therefore, this price is impossible. Buyers will not be willing to pay a price which would induce tool-makers to make tools. In short, the disinclination to wait is a further factor in the limitation of the supply of tools. It operates in the same way as an additional item in the cost of producing tools. Let us represent this additional cost or disinclination by the dotted curve DA. The fact that some waiting is not burdensome is represented by the fact that the curve DA is, in part, below the curve $D'A'$. As stated earlier in this chapter, some waiting does not involve sacrifice, but other waiting does involve sacrifice. This fact is shown by drawing the curve DA in its later projection above the curve $D'A'$. The effect of the disinclination to wait, when added to the disinclination to undergo the ordinary cost of producing the tool in question, is to check the making of the tool and to limit the supply. In other words, another equilibrium point must be found where the desirable product of a unit of capital is sufficiently great to overcome both forms of disinclination. Let us assume that this point is reached when the supply of the kind of capital in question is measured by the line *OB*. In this case the product per unit of capital will be represented by the line *AB*. This would allow sufficient to pay the cost of making the tool, represented by the line *BE* and a surplus besides, represented by the line *AE* to induce the purchaser of the tool to buy it and use it. In short, he would then have to pay for the tool or unit of capital a price *BE*. By keeping it during its effective life-time he would secure a total product represented by *AB* and receive in the form of interest during the whole of that period, a sum equal to *AE*.

We have thus far labored to show that interest is due to four large factors: first, that tools are useful and capital, in that sense, productive; second, that buying tools instead of consumers' goods with a part of one's income is deferring consumption; third, that so long as men prefer present to future, they are disinclined to defer consumption beyond a certain point; and finally, that because of this disinclination they will not defer consumption beyond the point where by buying tools they can gain something by it. The question remains, however, ought they to be allowed to make anything by deferring consumption in this way?

Let us not make the mistake of assuming that there is something inherently meritorious in deferring consumption, or in abstinence. Nothing is inherently meritorious, not even labor. Like everything else, it is meritorious only when it results in a definite addition to social utility. Mere waiting, or deferring consumption, unless it is done in such a way as to add to the productive power of the community has

no merit in it.   But when it does so result, it is of value.
The question resolves itself, therefore, first, into the question
is it better for a given community at a given time that more
should be spent on producers' goods, or is it not ?   That, in
turn, depends on whether the community at that time can
use productively more producers' goods than it has.   If so,
it would be desirable to have an increase.   So long as that
is true, they who spend a part of their income for producers'
goods are performing a service.   They add to the productive
power of the community.   When the time comes that the
community has no need for more producers' goods, it ceases
to be a service to save and invest.   Up to that point, they
who buy producers' goods will, on the average, get a return
from them, which is a payment for a service rendered. When
it ceases to be a service, there is no longer any interest.

The measure of a service is not its cost but its usefulness.
It may be a positive joy to one man to work, and a pain to
another.   But if the two perform work of equal utility and
quality, their services are equal and they have earned equal
amounts.   Similarly, it may be no sacrifice whatever for
one man to save and invest in producers' goods, whereas
it may cost another severe self-repression.   Yet if they save
equal amounts, and invest them with equal wisdom, their
services to the rest of the world are the same.   They have
earned equal amounts.   To hold the contrary is to hold that
there is something inherently meritorious in sacrifice.
Nothing should be paid for except service.   So long as more
tools are needed, so long is the saver and investor performing
a service, and so long as he is performing a service so long is
he earning a reward.   That reward is interest.

While it is thus made clear that the individual who increases the community's stock of tools, that is, capital, by
his own frugality and foresight, has performed a definite ser-

vice and, therefore, earned a definite reward, it does not follow that he who receives interest on capital which he has not thus created has earned his interest. There are other methods of acquiring capital. It may be inherited, it may result from a speculative rise in land values, or it may result from monopolistic control of business.

The inheritor may secure interest upon the capital which has come to him by inheritance as well as upon that which he has himself created by his own frugality and foresight. This problem, however, must be dealt with under the head of inheritance rather than under the head of interest. To attempt to deal with it under the head of interest would result in the worst kind of confusion. To prohibit interest as a means of preventing anyone from receiving interest on inherited wealth would strike also at the individual who had created his own capital and deprive him of the reward of his service. This would be unjust, and it would react disadvantageously to society in general. If it is desired to prevent individuals from receiving interest on inherited capital, the logical and direct method is to abolish inheritance. This question will be the theme of another chapter.

The same principle will apply to the question of an accumulation of capital which results from a rise in land values or from monopolistic exploitation. Whether the income from which capital was accumulated was earned or not is one question. It is another question whether a man having been permitted to receive an income, or an increment of wealth, should then be permitted to receive interest on that part of it which he invests in tools. Even granting that a man should not have been permitted to receive a certain fund of wealth, still, if he has actually been permitted to receive it, it is better for the community that he should invest it productively than that he should consume it luxuriously or use it unproductively. If not allowed any return from a productive investment he would be more inclined to consume it, and less inclined to invest it, than he would be if he were allowed interest on it. Society would only injure itself therefore if it permitted the wrong to take place and then tried to punish the innocent with the guilty in order to reduce slightly the advantage which the guilty might obtain from his guilt. He could still consume his unearned income and derive that much advantage from it. That would be like allowing thieves to steal and then, in order to prevent thieves from profiting too much by their crimes, providing that no one, whether he be producer or thief, should have the advantage of ownership. Here, as in the case of inherited wealth, the logical and direct method is to attack unearned wealth at its source instead of allowing it to be acquired and then trying to correct it afterward by punishing the innocent with the guilty, the producer with the exploiter, the one who serves with the one who injures.

It is a sad commentary upon the intelligence of many of our ardent reformers that they are unable to see this important point. The reader is hereby challenged to find an opponent of interest who can talk on the subject to a popular audience without using as illustrations cases of inherited wealth, wealth resulting from a rise in land values, or wealth resulting from monopolistic exploitation. If he were excluded from using illustrations from these three sources, but compelled to choose them from other sources, he could neither talk convincingly to a popular audience, nor could he avoid a shamefaced appearance while he was talking. Since these are the three conspicuous forms of wealth to which real objections are raised, attention should be focused upon them to see what can be done to correct them. This will promote progress more effectively than indulging in indiscriminating diatribes against the whole social system.

CHAPTER IX

SOCIALISM AND THE PRESENT UNREST

" Where there is no vision the people perish. "   They like-wise perish where there is a vision.   It has not yet been statistically determined whether they perish faster in the one case or in the other.

No movement is trying so hard or so successfully to attract the busy world's attention away from its work, as socialism. The " conspiracy of silence " with which the world is always accused whenever it is too busy, or taking its work too seriously, to stop and listen to some new thing, is being broken in this case; and we are likely to give a good deal of attention to socialism for a generation or two at least.   The only real danger in the situation, aside from the waste of time and energy, is that the world may get the impression that no one but the socialist has any " plan."   It is so much easier to see the " plan " in an invented language like Volapük or Esperanto than in one which has grown natur-ally by a long process of adaptation that they who persist in using an existing language are likely to be called reaction-aries, or, at best, " planless progressives."   This puts them at a tactical disadvantage, and it sometimes looks as if the devotees of a new cult, either linguistic or economic, after they once get the world's attention, would hold it to the exclusion of the advocates of rational improvement of existing plans.

This rising tide of socialist sentiment is no accident.   It is the natural result of conditions for which no one in particular can be held responsible, and over which no one in particular has exercised any control. This is a period of vast and inarticulate discontent in all parts of the world where mechanical inventions have played an important rôle, and even other parts of the world are catching the spirit of unrest in these latter days. Socialism, rather better than any other system of thought, has succeeded in voicing and making articulate this discontent in the mechanically advanced countries. Its language may be illogical and incoherent, but this discontent has at least found a voice with which to bellow its protest against the courses of the stars. This discontent is a perfectly natural and almost inevitable result of the readjustment forced upon us by the mechanical inventions of the last century and a half. Periods of readjustment are always periods of irritation and protest, because of the simple fact that the strain is very unequally distributed throughout the social structure. More literally, the gains and the losses which result from economic readjustment are unequally distributed. So rapid and fundamental are the readjustments of the present period that certain large classes are literally buoyed on the waves of fortune while others are sucked down by the undertow. These results cannot often be ascribed to any special fault or special merit on the part of any class.

One conspicuous phase of the readjustment through which we are now going is seen in the unprecedented growth of cities in those parts of the world where machine production has reached a high state of development. Though mechanical inventions have contributed much to the productivity of agriculture, they have contributed more to that of manufacturing. The reason may be that the productivity of agriculture is limited by the productive forces at work in and on the soil, whereas that of manufacturing is freed from such limitations, and, given markets, knows no limits except those fixed by the principles of mechanics. Whatever may be the reasons, the fact seems to be clear. If these inventions have increased the productivity of agriculture by 100 per cent and that of manufacturing by 200 per cent, the effect is very much the same, so far as the distribution of wealth and population between country and city is concerned, as though they had not increased the productivity of agriculture at all and had increased that of manufacturing by 100 per cent. Either result would have given the advantage to the urban as compared with the rural industries, and would have caused a growth of urban out of all proportion to rural populations.

This vast development of the indoor industries and of urban populations in any country depends, however, upon outside markets. It is only another form of the international division of labor. The mechanically advanced nations find it more profitable to bring the products of rural industry from outside regions and send out to them the products of the mechanical industries, so long as there are outside regions to supply the raw materials and buy back the finished products, than to produce their own raw materials and thus preserve within their own areas a balance between the rural and the urban industries. But this balance has to be preserved in the world at large, whatever may happen within the narrow confines of a single nation or group of nations. This simply means that the world at large must be fully and completely self-supporting, though an urbanized nation may specialize just as a city may. When a few more nations become urbanized and dependent upon outside areas for the products of the soil, and when these outside areas begin to develop their own mechanical industries, then we may expect a partial ruin of our overgrown cities and a partial redistribution of our congested city populations. Then will come another period of irritation and protest, but the fortunate owners of agricultural land, instead of urban capitalists, will then be the objects of class envy and covetousness, especially if they put on the airs and indulge in the ostentatious luxury now assumed by certain fortunate urban classes.

The tremendous growth of city populations in our day has, among other results, the effect of enormously inflating urban land values. They who are fortunate enough to possess urban land, or shrewd enough to acquire it at the favorable moment, find themselves carried on to fortune by forces over which they exercise little or no control. This is simply one of those ' tides in the affairs of men which, taken at the flood, lead on to fortune.' But there are also tides which lead on to misfortune in any period of rapid change. It is not always easy to see any superior merit on the part of the fortunate over the unfortunate classes. But if the fortunate begin to assume an air of supernal wisdom or merit, to domineer over the rest of the community, or to act as though they thought that their fortunes entitled them to live idly and luxuriously, their attitude is certain to provoke resentment and hostility on the part of the less fortunate classes.

Another change, even more profound than the shift of population and wealth from country to city, is the increasing rôle played by capital in modern industry. This also is a direct and necessary result of mechanical inventions of our age. The leading result of all these mechanical inventions is to substitute capital for labor in production, to use common forms of expression. Somewhat more technically and accurately expressed, these mechanical inventions require the coördination of a larger quantity of past labor with a given unit of present labor than was possible before. Under a regime of simple tools, a very little past labor — that which made the tools — is combined or coördinated with a given unit of present labor — that which uses the tools. But under a regime of powerful and complicated machinery, a large quantity of past labor — that which made the machinery — is combined or coördinated with a given unit of present labor — that which uses the machinery.

Of course, if we change our point of view, we could speak of the coördination of present with future labor, meaning precisely the same thing as when we speak, from the present point of view, of the coördination of past with present labor. From this changed point of view we might paraphrase the above statement as follows. Under a regime of simple tools, a very little present labor — that which is making tools — is to be coördinated with a given unit of future labor — that which is to use the tools after they are made; whereas, under a regime of machinery, a larger quantity of present labor — that which is making the machinery, is to be coördinated with a given unit of future labor — that which is to use the machinery. But whether we use the words past and present, or present and future, the principle is the same. The enlarged use of machinery calls for more coördination of labor expended at different times.

With this explanation, let us for convenience hold to the use of the terms past labor and present labor, and proceed with the discussion. After the past labor has once produced the tools and machinery, it ceases to be called labor and comes to be called capital. More accurately, the things which that labor has produced constitute capital. Capital is merely a collective name for an accumulation of tools, machinery, and other instruments and material of production, that is, of those products of past labor which have to be

portunities, this taking of the necessary steps in advance, becomes a more and more important function as mechanical inventions increase. The necessary result of this is that they who perform this function come to fill a more and more important place in society.

This is another way of saying that the increase of mechanical inventions, by increasing the quantity of past labor which has to be combined with a given quantity of present labor, has the effect of vastly increasing the function of capital and augmenting the rôle and the power of the capitalist. It may be all summed up in the statement that it has increased the demand for capital out of all proportion to the demand for everything else. The great demand is for capital. Everything is dependent upon that, and the capitalist, or he who can supply the thing which is now demanded in such enormous quantities, can dictate his own terms and dominate the whole situation. Here is another of those tides in the affairs of men, which, taken at the flood, lead on to fortune. The economic world has called for capital more loudly than it has called for anything else, and it has offered glory and honor and power and dominion to any one who would supply the one thing so urgently demanded by the new situation.

This is in no way the fault of the capitalists, and nothing is to be gained by denouncing them, though they may sometimes have abused the power which has thus been thrust upon them, and they are in special danger of yielding to the temptation to indulge in irritating ostentation. Nor is it the fault of the social system, for the demand for capital lies deeper than the social system. It is the fault, if fault it can be called, of the inventors who have given us a system of mechanical production which demands increasing supplies of capital, that is, which requires the coördination of increasing quantities of past labor with given quantities of present labor.

While this is not the fault of the capitalists, it is, on the other hand, no sign of great merit upon their part that fortune has thus been poured out to them so lavishly. While individual capitalists have undoubtedly achieved greatness by supplying the great needs of society, and others have been born great by merely inheriting large funds of capital for which there is now a demand but which would have been of little use to them in a simpler and less mechanical age, yet the capitalist class as a whole may not inappropriately be said to have had greatness thrust upon them. This good fortune is neither the result of exploitation, as the socialists maintain, nor is it the result of any transcendent merit on the part of the capitalist class. It is simply the result of a fortunate turn of events which creates a hitherto unknown demand for the service which they are able to render. The case is similar to what might happen if the world should develop a hitherto unheard of desire to hear music. They who were in a position to satisfy that demand would find themselves in a very prosperous condition, and also in a position of great power and influence. If they were over-conceited, they might put on airs and claim for themselves more credit than really belonged to them. If, meanwhile, the demand for books had subsided while the demand for music was rising, the producers of books would find themselves, through no fault of their own, in a very unfortunate position. If they were covetous or resentful, they would probably dislike the musicians, and demand a share of the good fortune which they saw going to the latter class, particularly if this latter class were putting on airs. Any such necessary readjustment as this is almost certain to breed that kind of resentment and covetousness, especially if it is provoked by the airs and ostentation of the fortunate class.

It may be laid down as a general and invariable law that any desirable thing, the demand for which is increasing more rapidly than the supply, will increase in value, and that those who are in a position to supply it will be not only prosperous, but in a position of power and influence as well, in any normal, rationally organized, or ethically conducted community. Suppose, by way of illustration, that the world were to become vegetarian and decide to live mainly on potatoes. The enormous increase in the demand for that tuber would bring prosperity to the potato growers, and a corresponding loss to the growers of beef, pork, and mutton. If these producers of meat stupidly persisted in their old occupations, or if their situations made it impossible for them to turn to potato growing, they would doubtless feel very much aggrieved. If they were covetous, or jealous of the prosperity of others, they would doubtless lay the blame upon the potato growers, reasoning, as is now done in the matter of capital and labor, that the riches of the potato growers were in some way the cause of the poverty of the meat producers, instead of both being the joint result of another cause.

It is not inconceivable that they might charge potato growers with being a parasitic class, fattening on the needs of the world. It is probably too much to expect of them that they should see that any one who earns anything in this world does so by contributing to the satisfaction of human wants or needs, and is, to that extent, fattening on human needs. The greater the need which he satisfies the more useful he is, and the more he earns. Accordingly, if the need for potatoes were greater than for beef, pork, and mutton, the potato growers would be more useful and would be earning more than the producers of meat. Instead of being parasites upon society, the potato growers would be, under the circumstances, the most useful members of society. And the meat producers, instead of being the real producers, would be the least useful members. However, they would not enjoy being told such plain economic truths; and, if they were in a majority, they would doubtless solemnly vote themselves to be the real producers of the world's wealth, imagining that a majority vote could alter an economic truth.

Few economic principles, by the way, lend themselves more easily to the glib sophistry of the demagogue than this interrelation of needs and services. It is so obvious that service consists in supplying needs that there ought to be no difficulty in seeing that earnings, being the reward for services, are commensurate with the needs which are supplied. The general common sense of mankind is sound enough upon that subject, but the demagogical sophist finds here an opportunity for the exercise of his gifts. Seeing that some one is in receipt of a large income because he is supplying a great need, it is easy to assail him on the ground that he is fattening on the needs of his fellow men. Since they who supply small needs, or perform small or mediocre service, greatly outnumber those who supply great needs or render great service, the demagogue, with an unerring instinct for his own advantage, invariably appeals to the latent jealousy of the masses by attacking conspicuous success. The fact that the masses have not been utterly spoiled by the social and economic nonsense which has been so persistently and stridently preached to them during the last decade or so, is a striking proof of the essential soundness and hard common sense of our people. If economic sense had been preached half as effectively as economic nonsense, we should be very near a practical and rational solution of our difficulties.

There is, however, an opprobrious sense in which certain individuals may be said to fatten on the needs of mankind. It is when they gain not by supplying those needs but by withholding supplies of goods or services through monopolistic power. Perhaps it is too much to expect of sporadic reformers that they should distinguish between the supplying of a need and the withholding of supplies. At any rate, no socialist does, as a matter of fact, distinguish between the man who supplies the need for capital and the man who so manipulates capital as to prevent others from supplying the same need. Until they learn to see so broad a difference as this, they must continue to be classified as blind guides. When they do learn to see it, they will cease attacking capitalism as such, and will begin to attack some of the perversions of the capitalistic function.

In a most fundamental sense, the prosperity which comes to those who supply great and growing needs, and the poverty which comes to those who supply small or lessening needs, is a necessary feature of any rational or ethically arranged social system. The problem of human adjustment, which is the basic problem of both economics and ethics, is more satisfactorily worked out under this kind of an arrangement than under any other. Where needs are great, it is highly important that services should be increased. By offering larger inducements for this kind of service, more of it can normally be obtained. But where needs are small, or where they are or are tending to be oversupplied, it is a waste of human energy to have so much of it devoted to supplying them in proportion to the quantity which is devoted to the greater needs, or the needs which are undersupplied. It would be a better adjustment to have some of the oversupply (the meat producers of the fore-going illustration) diverted from the relatively overcrowded occupation into the relatively undercrowded occupation — (potato growing of the same illustration). By automatically reducing the rewards in the one occupation and raising them in the other, labor power tends automatically to be redistributed. When it is redistributed, and the ratio of supply to demand is approximately equal in both occupations, the rewards will also be approximately equal. Where there are hindrances to this automatic redistribution of human energy, they must be removed, otherwise this equalization will be defeated. The removal of these hindrances is the great task of the constructive statesman.

Normally, these readjustments take place automatically and without the special intervention of the state. Similar readjustments are continually taking place, and, in the great majority of cases, we are unaware of their occurrence, and hence we do not consider them as social problems. In some cases, however, the readjustment is interfered with by monopolistic control. This monopolistic control is sometimes deliberately granted by the public for what is believed, rightly or wrongly, to be a public purpose, as in the case of a patent or a franchise or a protective tariff. Such control interferes with the speedy readjustment of supply to demand and gives a temporary surplus profit to the possessors of the privilege. Whether such interferences with the automatic redistribution of human energy are justifiable or not would have to be argued out separately in each individual case. But there are other hindrances which are not intentionally granted by the public, and exist in opposition to every public interest. The monopolistic control of limited natural resources which cannot be reproduced or duplicated, may put the serving of certain needs into the hands of a special group of men. Since others cannot, for lack of natural opportunities, enter the same business, there is no reason to expect such a redistribution of human energy, or such a readjustment of supply to demand as to bring the remunerations of this business down to a level with those of other, non-monopolized industries. Again, monopolistic control is sometimes achieved through financial manipulation, with the same results, for a time at least, as are secured through the ownership of a limited natural resource. These problems, however, though they do not tend to solve themselves automatically, are relatively simple and easy of solution if we only have the courage to go seriously about it.

A much more serious problem arises when one class of society becomes so impoverished through the oversupply of the service which they are trying to render, and the undersupply of the services which other classes are rendering, as to make it difficult or impossible for them to respond to the demands of the situation, and change their occupation. Their very poverty, though it may be the result of oversupply of the kind of service which they are offering, and may therefore obviously call for a redistribution of the labor supply, that is, may palpably demand that some of them should abandon the overcrowded and seek the undercrowded occupations, may itself be the obstacle which prevents their doing so. It is as though the meat producers of the foregoing illustration were so impoverished as to make it impossible to migrate to a potato-growing region, or to procure the seed, the fertilizer and the tools necessary to grow potatoes. Something very much like this has taken place with respect to the oversupply of the general class of unskilled labor in modern industrial society. Here is a complication of the evil which creates a social problem of the first magnitude. Before such a problem as this, the common type of politician, who has been described as " claptrap made flesh and dwelling among us," is as helpless as he would be in the presence of the bubonic plague.   The demagogic socialist, who is, after all, only an extreme development of the common garden variety of politician with his unerring instinct for the wrong method, has never shown the slightest capacity for understanding causes, but has insistently demanded a drastic treatment of the symptoms of this disease.   Instead of attacking abnormal interest, he has attacked interest as such, being unable to see that interest is the symptom of a scarcity of capital, and that if capital could be made sufficiently abundant, interest would disappear, or fall to a minimum.   He would decree higher wages, overlooking the fact that low wages in any occupation are a symptom of an oversupply of labor in that occupation, and that if it could be made sufficiently scarce wages would rise automatically. Instead of attacking monopoly profits, or income secured by chicanery, he has attacked business profits as such, overlooking the fact that large profits are a symptom of the scarcity of business talent, and that if it could be made sufficiently abundant, profits would fall automatically.   On practically every point in his analysis, and in every one of his specific proposals, the socialist manages to be wrong, to mistake symptoms for causes, and to apply his remedies at the wrong place, making it morally certain that his remedies would produce evils worse than those they were intended to cure.

On the other hand, if we go about it intelligently, patiently, and courageously, applying our remedies to causes rather than to symptoms, we can secure something infinitely better than socialism without any of its evil consequences. That is to say, we can secure equality *with* liberty.   By equality is meant not only equality of opportunity, which, of course, we must have at any cost; but something approximating to equality of income as well. And we can have this approximation to equality of income without infringing upon the liberty of the individual in any essential particular, and without surrendering any of the social institutions which every civilized nation has learned, through ages of experience, to prize, such as private ownership of instruments of production, freedom of contract, freedom of initiative and enterprise, freedom of competition.

By equality of income is meant not equality as between individuals, but equality as between occupations. If one bricklayer can lay twice as many bricks as another, he is worth twice as much and ought to have it. Equality as between those two individuals is neither just nor desirable. But as between such an occupation as that of the bricklayer and some other, such as the bank clerk, the lawyer, or the railway president, there is no reason why there should not be something approximating to equality, if the conditions of demand and supply could be made to bring it about automatically. That is to say, if the supply of various kinds of human talent could be so readjusted as to make the skill of the railway president as abundant relatively to the demand for it as is the skill of the bricklayer, the average incomes of the two occupations would automatically equalize themselves, though within the same occupation there would be considerable differences, due to measurable differences in ability. Again, if one occupation requires a longer period of training by way of preparation than another, the average annual income in the one should be enough higher to compensate for the expense and the loss of time involved in the course of training. Otherwise there would be inequality in favor of the occupation requiring little preparatory training.

The possibility of equality as thus conceived *with* freedom of initiative, freedom of contract, freedom of competition, liberty to own tools, machinery and other forms of capital, is so much better than anything which the socialist has to offer as to make his scheme look like a pitiful makeshift in comparison. In order that this possibility may be fairly considered, it is necessary to consider certain objections which may be raised against it by the *a priori* reasoner.

As a by-product of the historical determinism which has impregnated all socialistic thought since Karl Marx, we have certain formulae regarding economic development which are not only false but which obscure the real issue by begging the whole question. One is that the labor system necessarily goes through the stages of slavery, serfdom, and wage slavery, before reaching the final stage, socialism. In the first place, the wage system is not only earlier, but more universal than either slavery or serfdom. These grow out of peculiar and abnormal conditions, and are exceptional rather than universal, whereas the wage system is earlier, more permanent and more universal than either. In the second place, the term wage slavery begs the question. The large modern fact which this term probably implies is that large numbers of laborers are in a position of dependence upon others for a job. But that this is a necessary result of the wage system is absolutely false and will not bear a moment's examination. There are also large numbers of wage earners who are in a position to dictate terms to their employers, and whom the employers must placate by means of almost obsequious treatment. During the wheat harvest of 1914 this was the case in many parts of the West. It is pretty generally the case in the

matter of domestic service in America. It is true of laborers possessing a high degree of technical skill. In short, it is
always true where labor is scarce and hard to find. Whenever employers have to go out and look for men to work for
them, laborers are well treated and in a position of great
independence. If you were to call one of them a slave, he
would either laugh at you or knock you down. But when
laborers are so abundant and jobs so few that employers do
not have to look for men, but men are continually looking
for jobs, when the employer can hang out a shingle saying
" Men Wanted," and find a hundred men applying for every
job, then laborers are in a position of dependence. The
mistake of the socialist, and of some other emotional sym-
pathizers with laborers, is in assuming that there is some
magic about capital and the wage system which makes this
a necessary state of affairs. There is no magic about it, nor
is there anything occult; it is simply a case of maladjust-
ment of supply and demand. A rational analysis of the
situation would lead to some such reasoning as follows.
Wherever labor is scarce, relatively to the need for it, laborers are independent, well paid, and well treated. Where-
ever labor is abundant relatively to the need for it, laborers
are dependent, poorly paid, and badly treated. Therefore
the obvious thing to do is to make labor scarce relatively to
the need for it; that is, to increase the need for it, or to reduce the supply of it.

But the question arises, is there not always need for
labor ? Does not the very fact of human wants signify a
need for labor to satisfy those wants ? The difficulty with
this question is that it assumes that the demand for labor is
the demand for " human labor in the abstract." There is
no such thing as human labor in the abstract. There are
various kinds of labor in the concrete. One does not hire

labor in the abstract any more than one buys bread in the abstract.   One buys concrete loaves of bread.   One hires individual men to do specific kinds of work.   The prevalence of human want may call for certain kinds of labor, but not necessarily the kinds of labor which are overabundant or unemployed.   In fact, it is almost certain to be not the kind that is overabundant and unemployed, or it would not be overabundant and unemployed.   Where several different kinds of labor have to be combined in order to get a given product, it is quite possible that one kind may exist in greater abundance than will combine satisfactorily with the existing supply of other kinds.   The case is exactly the same whether several different kinds of labor have to be combined, or several different material things have to be combined in the making of a given product.

Take, for example, such a mixture as gunpowder, requiring for its manufacture charcoal, sulphur, and saltpetre.   It is quite possible that there may be more charcoal on the market than would combine with the existing supply of saltpetre.   In that case, no matter how great the demand for gunpowder, some of the charcoal would be unemployed or unused.   Moreover, under the natural laws of valuation it would be very cheap, unless there are other uses to which it can be put.   It would be cheap because it would have a low productivity in a most important and logical sense. Under the conditions assumed, an increase or decrease in the supply of charcoal would have very little effect upon the amount of gunpowder produced.   If more charcoal were brought to the market, it would not enable more gunpowder to be produced, therefore the makers of gunpowder would pay very little for that ingredient.   On the other hand, saltpetre, being the scarce factor, limits production.   A little more saltpetre brought to the market would enable more gunpowder to be produced. It is in that sense highly productive.

Or, take the case of the fertility of land, depending upon a number of factors, including sunlight, moisture, and chemical fertility, which in turn consists of phosphorus, nitrogen, and potash. Suppose the soil to contain an abundance of nitrogen and phosphorus, but to be deficient in potash. A fertilizer man comes along and tries to sell nitrates to the farmers. If the farmers are wise, they will refuse to buy them, or will consent to pay a very low price for them, because a little more nitrogen is of very little use and will contribute practically nothing to the crop. But potash, being the scarce factor, a little more of that constituent would add considerably to the crop. Under such conditions, what the farmer wants is potash and not nitrogen. Potash in a very important sense is more productive than nitrogen under these circumstances. More potash, more crop, under those peculiar conditions. More nitrogen, no more crop. The logic of the situation is not likely to be mistaken by the practical farmer. It would be useless to tell him that nitrogen is the producer of crops, therefore he ought to pay as much for nitrogen as for potash. Reverse the conditions of course, and let nitrogen be the scarce and potash the abundant factor, and the valuations would be reversed.

Identically the same principle applies to the valuation of different kinds of labor. If there is a kind of labor which seems to be undervalued and poorly paid, the student who really and seriously wants a scientific solution of the problem must ask himself this question — Under the circumstances of time and place, is that labor highly productive, or is it relatively unproductive, in the sense that charcoal and nitrogen were in the foregoing illustrations ? Would more of that particular kind of labor add to the productivity of the community ?   If not, then it is unproductive, though it may be perfectly good labor, just as nitrogen and charcoal were unproductive in the foregoing illustrations; but the sheer oversupply of it with respect to other factors will make the question of more or less a question of very little concern. Some of it might leave the city or the nation and make practically no difference in the total product.   More of it might come and make practically no addition to the total product. If that be the situation, it is utterly useless to argue that labor produces all wealth.   An additional unit of this particular kind of labor does not produce any, just as truly as that an additional unit of charcoal would not produce any gunpowder, or of nitrogen any crop in the foregoing illustrations.   The obvious thing to do, in the case of the charcoal, would be either to reduce the supply of charcoal or increase the supply of saltpetre.   The obvious thing to do in the case of the oversupply of labor is to reduce its supply or increase the supply of the other factors which happen to be scarce.

It is quite as important to increase the supply of the scarce factor as it is to reduce the supply of the overabundant factor.   An additional supply of saltpetre would enable more gunpowder to be produced, and that would use more charcoal, thus reducing the oversupply by raising the demand.   So in the case of labor, an additional supply of all kinds of talent which are scarce would enlarge industries and increase production, and this would call for more of the unskilled and overabundant kinds of labor, thus reducing the oversupply by increasing the demand.

Another of those misleading formulae which permeate socialistic thought is that as the eighteenth and nineteenth centuries had achieved political democracy, it remains for the twentieth century to achieve industrial democracy.   To

this I reply, as I have already said in chapter V, that as
a matter of fact, the world had industrial democracy before
it had political democracy. Moreover industrial democracy is today farther advanced than is political democracy,
in any country. In fact there is no government on the face
of the earth today so democratic as industry is here and
now. The trouble with those who make use of this formula
is that they are not able to see beyond the ballot, or to
understand that democracy means anything more than
voting. There are two and only two essentials of democracy. The first is, that there shall be an open road to
talent; and the second is, that those who are in authority
shall be made very sensitive to the desires of the people
whom they serve or govern. Because of the principle of
territorial sovereignty, it would be very difficult, if not impossible, to secure these two essentials without the ballot.
Since there is no such thing as territorial sovereignty in industry, the ballot is unnecessary. It is a clumsy and inefficient method, but in government it is the *only* method there
is of making those in authority sensitive to the desires and
interests of the governed. In industry much better and
more efficient methods than the ballot are already in use.

Owing to this principle of territorial sovereignty, the
citizen is not on a contractual basis with the government.
He cannot accept or reject the service which the government offers him. He must pay his taxes whether he approves of the purpose for which they are expended or not.
He must sometimes join the army, whether he approves the
purpose of the war or not. In this situation, the ballot is
the only means he has of expressing effectively his assent or
dissent. This is a clumsy method, because if he happens to
belong to the minority he still has no choice. In industrial
relations he may be a minority of one, and yet can reject the

service of the producer. He does not need to pay for the service unless he likes it, nor to deal with the business man unless he thinks he is getting *quid pro quo*.

The second worst form of idolatry in the modern world is the worship of the almighty dollar. The worst form is the worship of the almighty ballot. Both are bad enough, but the latter is several degrees worse than the former. In the first place, the world realizes pretty generally, though it does not act accordingly, that the worship of the almighty dollar is idolatry. It has not even begun to realize that the worship of the almighty ballot is idolatry. Therefore, it is in the way of being cured of the former kind of idolatry, but has not yet awakened to the fact that it needs to be cured of the latter. It is already convicted of sin in the case of the former, and is therefore a candidate for conversion. But it is not even conscious of guilt in the latter case. We realize that the getting of a large number of dollars is not invariably a test of merit, and yet it is a very much better test than the getting of a large number of ballots. This follows from the simple fact that if I am an average man I know more accurately and definitely what I am getting for my dollar than I know what I am getting for my ballot. I will more frequently, therefore, get a genuine service when I spend my dollar than when I deposit my ballot. The man who gets my dollar more frequently, therefore, renders a genuine service and earns what he gets than the man who gets my vote.

In both respects industry is more democratic than government. That is to say, merit will more frequently win in industry than in politics. Industry comes more nearly being the open road to talent than politics in any part of the world today. Again, except in the case of extreme monopoly, the business man is more sensitive to the whims, desires, and notions of his customers than the politician is to those of his constituents. The customers have a more effective way of making the business man sensitive to their wishes than the voters have of making the ruler sensitive. They do not have to wait until his term expires. They can instantly reject his service and put him out of business.

In cases of monopoly the condition approximates but does not equal the case of government. Though it would be a hardship, still we could if we wanted to do so, refuse to buy Standard Oil products. We could not refuse to pay taxes no matter how strongly we disapprove them. However, in cases of monopoly, the ballot will have to be used as a method of increasing the sensitiveness of the monopolist. Here, again, it is a clumsy method but the best there is.

Another formula which has been used with considerable effect among religious people toward the obscuring of the problem is that by doing away with industrial competition socialism would be setting up a system of coöperation and human brotherhood. As a matter of fact, it would not decrease competition in the least, for in proportion as industrial competition was diminished by the socialist's program, political competition, or the struggle for votes and advancement in the civil service, would increase. There are a great many forms of competition in the world besides a purely industrial form. Of these forms political competition or rivalry, or the struggle for place and power in government, is one of the greatest and probably the worst. By enlargement of the functions of government and the narrowing down of the field for private enterprise, more and more of the population would find it necessary to seek advancement in the government service. One does not need to look very far into the methods of political campaigns, or the methods in vogue in the civil service, to realize that there is just as bitter rivalry here as you can possibly find in industry. Moreover, it is a vastly more wasteful kind of competition. When two farmers compete with one another in growing corn, the result is more corn; and the world is better off. When two politicians run against one another for office, the result is that one gets it and the other does not; and all the time and energy that were spent in campaigning were absolutely wasted. So far as human brotherhood is concerned, it would be a distinct step backward to close the door of economic competition by enlarging the field for political competition.

Again, there is no greater mistake than to assume that competition and rivalry are incompatible with human brotherhood. One would find it very difficult even to amuse oneself without some form of competition. The man who tries to beat me in a tennis game is not my enemy, but my friend. I should not consider it as a favor if he were to reverse his policy and try to help me to win. If we two could bring ourselves to the point of trying to play the game so as to make the other win, it would be another kind of game and another kind of competition. Neither is the man who tries to beat me growing corn or making shoes my enemy. There are conditions, however, or states of mind, which do make enemies of competitors. The fault, however, is not with competition, but with the state of mind. If a tennis game is played for a prize, and that prize is the one and only object of my soul's desire, for which I care more than I care for anything else in the world, and if my antagonist feels the same way about it, there is danger that the tennis game may be incompatible with the ideals of human brotherhood. As a matter of fact, that is what spoils a good many sports. When the players care more for the prize of victory than for the game, sport degenerates and produces ill feelings and hatred, together with evil practices. It sometimes happens, of course, that money does become the one object of desire. In that case business degenerates, just as sport does under similar conditions. The fault is not with business, nor with competition, it is with the state of mind with which the competitors enter the game. Instead of inveighing against competition as such, therefore, the apostles of human brotherhood should concentrate their attention upon the motives and the desires which dominate the competition. There is nothing any more incompatible between business competition and Christianity than there is between a tennis game or a baseball game and Christianity. There may be games played, and there may be forms of business competition carried on in a spirit which is incompatible with the spirit of religion, but it would be a poor kind of religion which would condemn games or business competition as such. The older Christian idea that riches are not the chief thing in life, if preached effectually, would take the sting out of business as effectively as the doctrine that the prize or the victory is not the chief thing in sport has removed the reproach from sport.

Thus far we have been considering the general theory of socialism.[1] Socialism, however, as a movement is quite distinct from socialism as a theory of industrial organization, and it is also to be distinguished from socialism as a program. Socialism as a movement is merely a development of class spirit among propertyless workers, and of class antagonism against the owners of capital. This movement does not depend in the least upon justice or injustice, or upon economic soundness or unsoundness. It is wholly a matter of class consciousness and class antagonism. It will succeed,

[1] The remainder of this chapter is a reprint from *The Independent*, vol. 75, no. 3374, July 31, 1913.

whether its views be just or not, whenever its class consciousness becomes strong enough, and its class antagonism bitter enough to sweep away the present social order. It will fail, whether its views be sound or unsound, if this class consciousness fails to include the majority of the people, or if their class hatred does not become bitter enough to make them revolutionists.

More specifically, the day when fifty-one per cent of the voters find themselves in the condition of the propertyless wage workers, with no reasonable hope of ever becoming anything else, will be the last day of the present social order, and the next day will be the first day of socialism. Let us not imagine that we can avoid this cataclysm by arguments, however sound, to show that the proposed new social order is economically unsound or impracticable. It does not need to be either practicable, sound or just. It will come anyway whenever fifty-one per cent of the voters see that they have nothing to gain by preserving the present system. It may be that the change will send us all to perdition; to perdition we shall go whenever the conditions described above are reached.

There are two classes of people working to bring about these conditions, and both are equally to be regarded as enemies of the laboring classes. There are, first, leaders of socialism who see that there is no hope for their schemes until they can put fifty-one per cent of the voters in the position of propertyless wage earners, with no hope or prospect of ever becoming anything else. Consistently with this view, they openly advise laboring men to avoid improving their condition by acquiring property of their own. " Beware of thrift, it is the workingman's enemy; let him spend what he gets and demand more." According to Hyndman, the most intellectual of the English socialists, " To put money in the savings bank is to accumulate orders on other people's labor and is no benefit to those who save." According to Bax, one of the most distinguished of the disciples of Marx, " The socialists are radically at variance with thrift. A man who works at his trade more than his necessity compels him, or who accumulates more than he can enjoy, is not a hero but a fool from the socialist's point of view." Hobson has written a widely-read book on *The Fallacy of Saving.*

These are not sporadic views of individual socialists; they are a logical part of the socialist movement. These ideas must spread, otherwise socialism will never have the ghost of a show. They are, of course, at variance with the general common sense of mankind. The destinies of civilization are safer when entrusted to the general common sense of the people, — which is a kind of empiric wisdom, based upon ages of accumulated experience — than when placed in the hands of half-baked economists, who have studied just enough to lose their common sense and not enough to get it back again. A wide reading of Benjamin Franklin's *Poor Richard's Almanack* would do the laboring classes infinitely more good than the most careful study of all the socialist books in existence. All large masses of people who have really progressed industrially, and improved their economic conditions, have done so by practicing the economic virtues of industry, thrift, forethought, economy, and mutual helpfulness. This is the economic gospel taught by Franklin and all genuine friends of the poor, including Mr. Booker T. Washington, and Sir Horace Plunkett. They who are striving to combat the wholesome influence of these men, in order to increase the number who live from hand to mouth, and who must therefore live in perpetual poverty, merely in order to make a certain kind of propagandism acceptable, must therefore be put down as enemies of the laboring classes.

Moreover, many of these false guides are deliberately profiting by the misery which they are trying to increase. By discouraging thrift and enterprise, and thus increasing the number who must expect to remain propertyless wage workers, discontent is increased and as a result of this discontent these leaders find a more ready sale for their speeches, books, articles, and journals.

Another class which must be put alongside of the socialist leader as an enemy of the laboring classes includes all those who advocate a large supply of cheap labor as a means to industrial expansion. A certain narrow-minded, short-sighted type of capitalist who confuses the public interest with his own immediate and temporary profit, says that we must have large numbers of low-wage laborers in order that his particular enterprises may succeed and flourish. He does not seem to realize that large numbers of low-wage laborers mean large numbers of people living on very small incomes, and that this means widespread poverty. Few of these men are so crude as to discourage the laboring classes from trying to rise through thrift, economy, and foresight; and they are, therefore, perhaps, less venomous enemies of the laboring classes than are the socialists. But they strenuously oppose any measure or policy which will otherwise reduce the number of laborers who are looking for jobs. If the socialists' effort to keep the laborers down can be defeated, and laborers and the children of laborers can be encouraged by sound teaching to rise into the property-owning and employing classes, this tendency alone would thin out the ranks of unskilled labor and make it scarcer and harder to find, were it not counteracted by a rapid increase of the labor supply from new sources. But no matter how rapidly men rise from the ranks of unskilled into the ranks of skilled labor, and from skilled labor to business positions, if the supplies of unskilled labor from new sources increase rapidly enough we shall have a continuous mass of poverty — that is, a continuously large mass of low-wage labor.

One source from which we draw the fresh supplies of unskilled labor in order to counteract the influence of our democratic institutions and our system of popular education, is immigration. If we could shut out immigration, and allow these institutions to do their work uncounteracted, it would not take very long, probably not more than a decade, so to thin out the ranks of unskilled labor and so fill the ranks of property owners and employers as materially to raise wages on the one hand, and reduce interest and profits, the income of the employing classes, on the other. They who oppose the restriction of immigration are really working in harmony with the socialists in trying to increase the number of propertyless wage workers. The socialists try to prevent laborers from rising, thus keeping them down in the ranks of labor; while this narrow-minded type of capitalist is trying to prevent the checking of the inflow of unskilled labor from other countries. If both should have their way, they would facilitate the socialist movement and make socialism inevitable.

But immigration from heaven produces very much the same results as immigration from Europe. If the ranks of unskilled labor are kept full by large families and the rapid rate of multiplication among them, that also would go a long way toward counteracting the influence of our democratic institutions and our educational system. That is, it will tend to perpetuate our large supplies of unskilled labor, making it difficult for them to secure good jobs at high wages and compelling them in consequence to accept poor jobs at low wages.

One way of checking the increase of unskilled labor from this source is to raise the standard of living among the unskilled laborers. If no man would marry until he had a good job with two dollars a day, the result would be so to retard the marriage rate and the birth rate among unskilled laborers and so to thin out the ranks of unskilled labor that, barring immigration, in about one generation every man could find a job that would pay him at least two dollars a day. If the standard marrying income were put at five dollars a day, even that standard wage could eventually be achieved, though so high a standard as this is distinctly *not* to be advocated at the present time. As a mere statement of cause and effect, one may assert that such a standard income for marriage would produce, as an effect, a similar standard wage. But this does not commit one to the statement that such an effect would be desirable. However, it does not seem like an extreme statement to say that two dollars a day is the minimum upon which a man can bring up a family properly in any of our large cities.

Foxes approve large families among rabbits. A certain type of military adventurer approves large families among the poor, for that means plenty of cheap food for gunpowder. A certain type of priest approves them because they provide plenty of submissive parishioners. A certain type of employer approves them because they provide an abundant supply of cheap labor. They also mean low wages and widespread poverty. They mean an increase in the number of propertyless workers. That means a ready market for the wares of the socialist leader. It also means a nearer approach to the point where fifty-one per cent of the voters have no interest in the laws for protection of property, nor in the state which enforces those laws. That means a complete change in the character of the state, of society, and of civilization.

It is easy to show that the program which the socialist proposes to carry out after he has gained control of the state is unsound, and that the economic theories upon which he bases his program and his propaganda are absurd. But these are not the most important questions. The important question is whether he will be able to create conditions which favor the socialist movement, and which therefore, tend to make socialism inevitable.

CHAPTER X

CONSTRUCTIVE DEMOCRACY

How to secure equality of wealth with liberty, without sacrificing anything that we now prize, such as private property, freedom of contract, freedom of initiative, and economic competition. (Parts of the program are arranged in the inverse order of their importance.)

I. LEGISLATIVE PROGRAM

A. For the redistribution of unearned wealth.
   1. Increased taxation of land values.
   2. Graduated inheritance tax.
   3. Control of monopoly prices.

B. For the redistribution of human talent.
   1. Increasing the supply of the higher or scarcer forms of talent.
      (*a*) Vocational education, especially for the training of business men.
      (*b*) Cutting off incomes which support capable men in idleness, thus increasing the supply of active talent, cf., 1, 2, and 3, under *A*.
   2. Decreasing the supply of the lower or more abundant forms of labor power.
      (*a*) Restriction of immigration.
      (*b*) Restriction of marriage.
         (1) Elimination of defectives.
         (2) Requirement of minimum standard income.
      (*c*) Minimum wage law.
      (*d*) Fixing building standards for dwellings.

C. For the increase of material equipment.
   1. Increasing the available supply of land.
   2. Increasing the supply of capital.
      (*a*) Thrift *versus* luxury.
      (*b*) Savings institutions.
      (*c*) Safety of investments.
      (*d*) " Blue sky " laws.

II. Non-Legislative Program

A. Raising the standard of living among the laboring classes.
   (*a*) The function of the advertiser.
   (*b*) The educator as the rationalizer of standards.
   (*c*) Thrift and the standard of living.
   (*d*) Industrial coöperation as a means of business and social education.

B. Creating sound public opinion and moral standards among the capable, e. g.
   1. The ambition of the family builder.
   2. The idea
      (*a*) That leisure is disgraceful;
      (*b*) That the productive life is the religious and moral life;
      (*c*) That wealth is a tool rather than a means of gratification;
      (*d*) That the possession of wealth confers no license for luxury or leisure;
      (*e*) That government is a means not an end.
   3. Professional standards among business men.

C. The discouraging of vicious and demoralizing developments of public opinion, such as:
   1. The cult of incompetence and self-pity.
   2. The gospel of covetousness, or the jealousy of success.
   3. The emphasizing of rights rather than obligations.
   4. The worship of the almighty ballot and the almighty dollar.
   5. The idea that a college education should aim to give one a " gentlemanly appreciation " of the ornamental things of life, such as literature, art, golf, and whiskey, rather than to strengthen one for the serious work of life.
   6. The idea that the capitalization of verbosity is constructive business.

HAVING cleared away in the last chapter the misconceptions fostered by socialism, let us now proceed to the consideration of a constructive program in harmony with the general laws of economics. This program must be based upon the universal law of proportionality, which is the basis of all sound valuation. Let it be understood with the utmost clearness once and for all, that we can have any degree of equality we want and in the strictest harmony with economic laws *if* we are willing to pay the price and to pursue a constructive program in harmony with economic laws. Economic laws are not opposed to equality. They do, however, interfere with certain ideas of equality. Gravitation does not prevent aviation; it does, however, make certain systems of aviation impossible, as Darius Green found to his sorrow. Economic laws interfere only with the plans of the Darius Greens of social reform.

It is not only inevitable, but justice requires that any factor of production which is over-supplied in proportion to the other factors which have to be combined with it, shall be poorly paid, whereas any other factor which is under-supplied in proportion to those which have to be combined with it, shall be well paid. There is only one possible way to bring about equality of pay without violating the principle of justice, and that is so to adjust the quantities of the different factors to the need for them that a unit of one factor is just as much needed and just as productive as the unit of any other factor. So long as a man of one kind of training or ability is more needed than another, owing to the scarcity of the ability or training of the one and the abundance of the ability or training of the other, it must follow that the one will be better paid than the other. But if things can be so readjusted as to make a man of one kind of training and ability just as essential as another, *so that the community will gain as much by the accession of an additional man of one kind as of another, or lose as much through the secession of one as of another*, then, under the automatic operation of economic law, one man will get as much as another in return for his work or his services. A constructive program of social democracy must, therefore, aim finally and ultimately at such a redistribution of human talent as will make it as desirable that one kind should be increased as another, or as undesirable that one kind should be reduced as another.

A program of distributive justice may be divided, however, into two main divisions, the legislative and the non-legislative. Of the two, it is probable that the non-legislative is the more important, but it may be well to consider the legislative program first, because people are at the present time looking to legislation for the relief of their economic wants. The legislative program may be again subdivided into three parts, the first of which is aimed at the elimination of unearned wealth or the securing of actual justice. The second part, more important than the first, is aimed not so much at injustice as at inequality, that is to say, the first part aims to secure for each individual exactly what he earns or what he is worth, but this would not eliminate poverty so long as there were men possessing talents or ability so over-supplied as to make the accession or loss of a man a matter of indifference, whereas others possessed talents or ability so scarce as to make the accession or the loss of a man a matter of the greatest concern. In order to secure equality under justice, we must have a redistribution of human talent. And finally, in order that labor power of all kinds may be effectively applied, there must be an abundance of land on which to work and of tools or capital with which to work. This represents the third part of our legislative program.

A legislative program for the elimination of unearned wealth must be aimed at the three largest and most characteristic forms of unearned wealth, namely, wealth which has accrued through a rise in land values, inherited wealth, and wealth resulting from monopoly profits. There are, of course, a great many pilferings and stealings going on in modern society, ranging all the way from the petty pilfering of gardens and orchards in our suburbs up to the looting of corporations by inside cliques. But while these may call for new legislation at times, in the main they call merely for the administration of existing laws, and therefore will not be considered here. The three forms of unearned wealth mentioned, however, are not only in complete harmony with existing governmental policies, but public opinion is generally favorable to them, at least it is not sufficiently condemnatory to make effective legislation immediately possible. This will require, therefore, considerable popular education, as well as legislation, and is not a merely administrative problem. So nearly do these three forms of wealth exhaust the category of unearned wealth that even the socialist never uses an illustration drawn from any other source. While he may attack capitalism as such, he never in any popular discourse selects an illustration of the evils of capitalism except from one of these three forms of wealth, which are not essential to capitalism at all. That is to say, in his actual illustrations of the evils of the capitalistic system he will invariably refer to some fortune which has been built up by a rise in land values, which has been inherited, or which has been gained through monopolistic methods. So nearly universal is this practice among socialists that the author hereby challenges any socialist to talk fifteen minutes on the evils of capitalism without making use of an illustration from one of these three sources.

A very little discrimination at this point will help amazingly in clearing up the problem. If we object to that form of individual wealth which comes to a private owner through a rise in the site value of his land, the obvious course is to attack the evil directly and not to attack the private ownership of all productive wealth, which includes many other things besides land. If we object to the private ownership of a fortune which has come to the present owner through inheritance, the obvious remedy is to modify our laws of inheritance and not attack, at the same time, the ownership of capital which has not been inherited but accumulated by the present owner. If we object to wealth which has been accumulated by monopolizing industry and securing abnormal profits, the obvious remedy is to attack monopoly and not, at the same time, attack accumulations that have been the result of productive, as distinguished from acquisitive, efficiency, and by the exercise of the useful economic virtues of frugality, thrift and forethought. It is certainly not unreasonable to ask students of this problem to make use of this very moderate degree of discrimination, and the writer hopes that he will not seem to be setting up an impossible standard if he suggests that no speaker or writer is worth attention who refuses to observe these rather wide distinctions.

As already intimated, the non-legislative part of our program is more important than the legislative. This includes all those subtle but mighty forces which determine and direct the sentiments and opinions of the people. One of the most tangible economic results of social sentiment is found in what economists have come to call the standard of comfort. By this is simply meant, the amount of income or the degree of comfort which is commonly regarded, in any class of society, as essential to the support of a family. To be effective, this opinion or sentiment must be so strong as to lead men to defer marriage until they are assured of an income sufficient to maintain that standard of comfort.

In such cases it operates on wages very much as the cost of production operates on prices. In the last analysis, cost of production is only the price which is necessary in order to persuade producers to keep on producing. When the price of a certain commodity is so low that men will, in considerable numbers, stop producing it, the supply of the commodity decreases. This tends to check the fall in price, or to cause the price to rise. A similar principle operates in the supply of labor and the price of it. If wages were so low that men in considerable numbers would stop marrying and producing families, labor would, barring immigration, eventually become scarce and hard to find. This would check the fall in wages or cause them to rise.

It makes a great deal of difference in the case of a material product, how much is necessary to induce the producers to keep on producing. If they are satisfied with very little, they will keep on producing even when the price falls to a very low level. Under these conditions, there is no counteracting tendency to cause the price to rise again. It is similar in the case of labor. It makes a great deal of difference how much is necessary in order to induce men to reproduce their kind. If they will marry on a very low wage, it operates to keep up the supply of labor, and to keep wages low. If they will not marry except on a high wage, it tends, barring immigration, to make labor so scarce as to raise wages to that level. The parallelism is very close, in all these respects, between the cost of producing a material commodity and the standard of comfort of the laboring classes.

But the same principle applies as well to the employing classes as to the laboring classes. If the employing classes were willing to marry and raise families on smaller incomes than they now consider sufficient, there would be more people in the employing classes. This would make competition more severe among them. This competition would take on various forms. They would, among other things, compete for the labor of the laboring classes, bidding against one another to get it. This would tend to raise wages.

If, therefore, the laboring classes would develop a higher standard of comfort, and refuse to marry until they had attained it, and if the employing classes would develop a lower standard of comfort, and be willing to marry when they had attained it, we should have a better balanced population and a better distribution of human talent. This would reduce the incomes of the employing classes and raise those of the laboring classes.

There cannot be the slightest doubt in the mind of any reasonable person that both these changes ought to take place. The standard of comfort among the business and professional classes is altogether too high, and that among the laboring classes, especially the unskilled classes, is altogether too low. Education and democratic freedom tend to raise that of the laboring classes, but it is kept down by the immigration of millions of people with a low standard. If this factor could be eliminated, the low standard of comfort among laborers would soon take care of itself. But there is nothing except a wholesome religion or sound moral ideals which will correct the tendency of the standard among the employing classes to become too high. This is one of the most important questions now before the world, and legislation is powerless to affect it. No one but the moral leader and the preacher of righteousness can reach the difficulty.

Another tangible result of public sentiment on economic conditions is found in the matter of our attitude toward productive work. If the chief desire of every one is to avoid useful work and to pursue the arts of elegant leisure, or indulge in graceful consumption, it will cause much excellent talent to go to waste.   Men who ought to be draining swamps, irrigating dry land, building factories, roads and bridges will fritter away their time in self-amusement, ' loafing and inviting their souls,' or dilettantism.   But if the chief ambition of every capable man is to achieve something for the building up of the nation, this talent will be kept from going to waste.   Being turned into productive channels it will help the laboring classes in two ways. First, it will increase the comforts and conveniences and place more of them within the reach of those classes. Second, it will give employment to increasing numbers of those classes.   As pointed out in a preceding chapter it takes several different kinds of talent or labor power, to do effective work in any kind of production.   If one necessary kind is lacking, or very scarce, it limits the amount of the other kind which can be employed.   The effective supply of business talent is made scarce by the tendency among business men to retire, and among their sons to cultivate the arts of elegant leisure instead of training themselves for the hard work of the world.   If they would do the latter, there would be more productive enterprises started in which laborers might find remunerative employment.

In a similar way, the attitude of the popular mind toward saving has a most powerful effect upon economic conditions. As shown in the chapter on interest, saving increases capital, and capital requires labor to work it.   If there is less capital (that is, tools) than is needed by the existing number of laborers, either some of them will be poorly equipped with tools, or some must remain unemployed.   If men would save more, that is, invest more of their incomes in tools instead of consumers' goods, there would be tools enough to equip every laborer adequately.   There might be even more than the laborers could use.   In that case, capital would be cheap, interest low, and the laborers would get a larger share of the total product of industry.   Besides, there would be a larger total product.   Thus the laborers would gain in two ways.   Luxury tends to produce poverty whereas frugality and simplicity, especially among the rich, tend to produce high wages and prosperity.

The government can, it is true, provide savings institutions and other encouragements to savings, but the general spirit and mental attitude of the people is what will determine whether they will make use of them or not.   This attitude of mind is probably of greater importance than anything which the government can do, unless, indeed, the government becomes the means of creating that attitude.

Aside from these direct and tangible ways in which economic conditions are determined by the spiritual attitude of the people, there are a vast number of indirect and intangible but none the less powerful results springing from this fruitful source.   A robust and virile morality, stimulated by a sound but fervid religion, may create an intense activity in nation-building among all the people.   When every man, woman and child feels a direct and personal responsibility for the nation's welfare, and an eager desire to have a part in the building of its prosperity, you have conditions of growth which nothing but a geological cataclysm or an international war can counteract.   This, more than anything else, according to the best students of the problem, accounts for the prodigious growth and prosperity of Germany from 1871 to 1914.

A really vigorous church, whose preachers were burdened with a sense of responsibility to their country, and endowed with the powers of leadership, could become, next to the government itself, the most powerful agency for the creation of this type of national prosperity. It would have to preach hard and honest work at one's regular job, rather than a vague kind of " social service." It would have to rise to the conception of religion as a means of stimulating the productive virtues rather than of providing passive spiritual enjoyment to its communicants. In short, it would have to preach the gospel of the productive life, and itself become a fellowship of the productive life if it would accomplish these results.

Suppose that every time a doctor got religion he began to give himself to the study of medical science with a new zeal and to the practice of the healing art with a new devotion. The more doctors there were who got this kind of religion the more rapidly medical science would advance, the better medical practice we should have, and the lower the death rate would be. Spreading this kind of religion would be a very good way of reducing the death rate. The man who would not try to spread such a religion would have something wrong with his mental and moral make-up, and would be a candidate for the madhouse or the jail.

Suppose that every time a farmer got religion he began to give himself to the study of agricultural science with a new zeal, and to the practice of his productive art with a new enthusiasm. The more farmers there were who got this kind of religion, the better agriculture we should have. The effective preaching of such a religion as this would be one of the very best ways of reducing the cost of living.

Suppose that every time a business man got religion he began to give himself with a new enthusiasm to the study of the science of business management, and with a new devotion to the art of business administration. The more business men there were who got such a religion as this the better business conditions we should have, the more pro-

ductive enterprises would be started and the larger the
demand for labor would be.   Spreading such a religion as
this would do more than anything now being done by any
organization for the improving of industrial conditions and
the elimination of poverty.

And suppose that every time a mechanic got religion he
began to give himself with a new devotion to the study of the
sciences underlying his trade, and with a new zeal to the
application of his skill.   The more mechanics there were
who got this kind of religion the more rapid would be the
advancement in the mechanic arts.   Spreading such a religion as this would be one of the most effective means of
promoting general mechanical improvement.   And so on
through all the other occupations, trades, and professions
including that of the statesman, — suppose that the spread
of this type of religion made every one who came under its
spell a better worker in his own field of useful endeavor, not
only stimulating him to greater expenditures of energy, but
leading him to conserve and utilize his energy in the most
useful and productive ways, avoiding waste and dissipation,
lavish consumption and ostentatious display, and all the
other uneconomic vices.   You would then be able to detect
the spread of this religion in the vital statistics of the
country, in the statistics of production, of the increase of
capital and the rise in the rate of wages.

This type of religion could base itself upon a very definite
doctrine of salvation, which always implies a doctrine of
damnation as its counterpart.   This doctrine of salvation
would be quite as clear cut as the old doctrine, but would
differ from it in some particulars.   Having a clear cut
doctrine of individual salvation, instead of a vague doctrine
of social service, the church could preach to individuals with
all of the old fervor and would need no longer to make a

spectacle of itself by running around in a circle trying to find something in the way of social service or political reform to espouse in order to justify its own existence.

A thing may be said to be saved when it is prevented from going to waste. If a man's life is going to waste, he is lost. If it can be prevented from going to waste and put to some use, he is saved. The old Hebrew word for sin meant an arrow that has missed the mark. It is wasted, — ineffective, — thrown away, — lost. The only rational definition of immorality is the waste of human energy. That, and that only is sin which results in the waste or dissipation of human energy. When a man's energy is being wasted or dissipated in sloth, in vice, in needless conflict with his fellows, or in misdirected effort, the man is to that extent going to waste, his life is to that extent lost, and he stands in need of salvation. Perhaps it would be better to say that the community needs his salvation. The most precious resource of any community is its fund of human energy. If that resource is wasted the community will be impoverished. If it is saved, the community will be enriched. Here is a doctrine of salvation in which the whole community is vitally interested. This kind of a program of salvation is the greatest conservation program ever conceived. Where is the man with the least spark of patriotism who would not support such a gospel of salvation as this ?

Possibly we may conclude that we have been talking prose all our lives without knowing it. As a by-product of the old gospel of salvation men were taught such economic virtues as industry, sobriety, thrift, forethought, and mutual helpfulness. These are virtues because they are ways of economizing human energy. That is what a virtue is. Men have been taught to avoid such uneconomic vices as sloth, drunkenness, riotous living, frivolity, and quarrelsomeness. These are vices because they are ways of wasting human energy. That is what a vice is. In so far as the churches have been means of promoting those virtues and discouraging these vices, of conserving human energy and turning it into useful channels, they have been performing the greatest possible social service. Compared with this kind of conservation all other programs of social service are trivial.

This by-product of the old gospel of salvation, which some of our more ardent religionists have affected to despise, must become the chief end and aim of all preaching. " The stone which the builders rejected the same is become the head of the corner." The wild, untamed energy of human nature, which tends too much to run riot, to waste itself in the pursuit of whims, to dissipate itself in vice and luxury, to consume itself in fruitless conflict, needs to be tamed, harnessed, and put to work. This is a task of even greater importance than that of taming and harnessing the winds, the tides, and the waterfalls.

In many respects the moral leader, provided he is genuine, and the engineer are performing parallel functions, the one conserving and utilizing human or social energy, and the other physical forces. Viewed from this standpoint, the real moral leader or the preacher of genuine righteousness need not apologize for his existence in the presence of either the engineer or the lawmaker, for his work is more constructive than theirs. Much less does he need to apologize in the presence of those self-styled political reformers whose chief task is that of trying to invent a fool-proof government. This assumes, of course, that we have a rational idea as to what righteousness is, namely, that it is the economizing and utilizing of human energy, the application of it to the building of a strong, prosperous society; that it is " that which keeps the tribe alive " to use the words of an old Indian chief; that it is the kind of conduct which strengthens the pack and enables it to prevail against the hostile forces of the surrounding universe; that it is that which enables the human pack to subdue the earth " and have dominion over the fish of the sea, and over the fowl of the air and over every living thing that moveth upon the earth."

All this becomes perfectly clear to one who has grasped the full meaning of the two fundamental and antagonistic philosophies of life, the " work-bench " philosophy and the " pig-trough " philosophy.   By the work-bench philosophy is meant that philosophy of life which regards the world as an opportunity for work, or for the active joy of productive achievement.   By the pig-trough philosophy is meant that philosophy of life which regards the world as an opportunity for consumption, for the passive pleasures of absorbing the good things which the world supplies.   Under the former, we consume in order that we may produce, under the latter we produce in order that we may consume.   Under the former wealth is regarded as tools to be used in further production or usefulness, under the latter it is regarded as means of self-gratification; under the former as wealth accumulates it is invested and put to work, under the latter it is gathered into barns in order that its possessor may say, " Soul, thou hast much goods laid up for many years, take thine ease, eat, drink, and be merry."

He who has adopted the work-bench philosophy of life will obviously avoid idleness, vice, and luxury.   Since he is intent upon production rather than consumption, on seeing how much he can put into the world rather than how much he can take out, he will naturally avoid destructive conflict as he will idleness, vice or luxury.   Competition among such people becomes rivalry in well-doing, in productive achievement. Since the faculties, impulses, and propensities of each are harnessed to productive purposes, each is also freed from the distractions which would waste human energy. But precisely the opposite happens to him who has adopted the pig-trough philosophy of life. He continually tries to avoid work, and seeks idleness as soon as he is able to live without work. From his point of view, since there is no special reason why he should discipline himself and conserve his energies, vice is cultivated as a means of immediate and obvious pleasure. And, from the same point of view, if one is able to afford luxuries why should one deny oneself merely in order to be more useful, or to use one's wealth more productively? Again, if one's purpose in life is to get as much out of it as possible, rather than to put as much in it as possible, the manners and the morals of the pig-trough prevail. It is only under this attitude toward life that destructive conflict prevails. And finally, the distractions of life have a peculiar hold upon people who are not anchored to a purpose outside themselves.

One of the most wasteful and destructive of all vices is that of covetousness or jealousy of success. Wherever the tendency is strong to regard with hostility the man who has achieved conspicuous success either in business, politics, scholarship, or art, you have one of the most effective means of repressing useful endeavor. Such a community can never prosper. But on the other hand, where in addition to such pecuniary rewards as may be won, conspicuous success in productive work of any kind whether it be in business, in politics, in scholarship or in art, receives the reward of a high degree of social esteem and popularity, we have the greatest possible stimulus to high endeavor in these productive fields. This consideration has peculiar value in the field of productive business where accumulation of capital, that is, tools, is such an important element in business success and social service. In a community in which the man who consumes lavishly and even ostentatiously or wastefully is well thought of, while the man who lives simply, preferring to spend his surplus wealth for more tools rather than for the means of luxurious consumption, is despised, we have the greatest possible encouragement to wastefulness, and the greatest discouragement to productive accumulation. Such a community will remain poor and unprosperous, and the people who display such vicious sentiments will be the ones to suffer most, but they will have the poor consolation of having inflicted the suffering upon themselves. In proportion as a community has acquired the radically different spirit which makes it condemn wasteful and ostentatious luxury and approve the simple but strenuous life of productive business, the investment of surplus income in tools of production rather than in articles of self-gratification, in that proportion will the community prosper and the poor be benefited. In this and many other ways a wholesome moral sentiment throughout the community will promote its prosperity, even more effectively, if that be possible, than sound legislation under wise administration of law.

CHAPTER XI

THE SINGLE TAX

Forms of income
{
1. Earnings
{
Wages paid for productive labor
Interest on one's own accumulation
Profits on the business which one manages honestly
}

2. Stealings
{
Income from burglary, swindling, deception, chicanery, mendacity, monopoly
}

3. Findings
{
Mineral wealth discovered by a prospector
Rise in the site value of land
Inherited wealth
Etc., etc.
}
}

As to wealth which accrues from a rise in the site value of land, there can scarcely be any two opinions. From Adam Smith down, economists have recognized the fact that the fortunate owner of a piece of land whose mere site value, irrespective of all improvements, has increased on his hands, is simply a recipient of good fortune, and that this part of his wealth does not represent his own earnings in any way, shape, or manner. There may be a good deal of difference of opinion as to the proper inference to draw from this fact. The single taxers certainly go too far, first in assuming that the wealth which goes to one individual in this way is necessarily taken from somebody else, or that it in some way deprives somebody else of what he has earned, and in the belief that by taxing away land values we should eliminate poverty and many other social ills. If my neighbor's land has increased in value on his hands, it would doubtless be a fine thing for me if I could share in that good fortune; but I could not with a straight face claim that his increment of wealth had in any way impoverished me or deprived me of what I had earned. My earnings are entirely independent of the value of his land. His income as a landowner (not as an improver of land) may not be due in any proper sense to his own contribution to the product of the community. It is, however, a measure of the contribution which that piece of land makes to the productivity of the community, and is not due in any sense to the contribution which I make.

The assertion that the owner of land who profits through a rise in the value of his land has necessarily subtracted something from the earnings of others is based on the assumption that all wealth has been " earned " by some one. If the owner has not earned it he must necessarily have robbed some one else, either in a legal or an illegal manner. But this assumption is incorrect. Some wealth is found. If I stumble upon a gold nugget, or a rich vein of valuable mineral, I cannot truly say that I have earned it, nor can any one else. Until some one could be found who could prove that he had produced or otherwise earned it, I could not be accused of depriving any one else of his earnings.

In the opinion of the present writer, the site value of land belongs in the class of findings, rather than in that of earnings or stealings. Even in the case of the gold nugget, a pretty good argument could be made in favor of my dividing it with my fellows, but that argument could scarcely be based on the ground that they had earned it. Unless some one wished to resort to cheap political claptrap he would have to base his argument on two propositions. 1. The others need it. 2. I can't show a very good or positive reason why I should be allowed to keep all of it.

There is a disposition on the part of certain reformers to deny that land is productive. This follows as a corollary of the proposition that all wealth is produced by labor. If that were true, it would follow, as a matter of course, that none of it is produced by land. Whatever may be one's opinion on that subject, no one is likely to deny that land is useful. When asked, for what is it useful ? he would be compelled to say, at least so far as it concerns land which is used in production, that it is useful in production. To say that a piece of land is useful in production can only mean that when it is used the community gets more product than when it is not. If that cannot be said of a given piece of land, that piece of land is not useful, and will not as a matter of fact be used in production. If we can agree upon this, we need not stop to quarrel over the meanings of the word " productive," that is, whether that is the proper word to describe the land which is useful in production.

One of the arguments by which the single taxer supports his contention that land is unproductive is to the effect that if it were not for the community around it, together with the roads, police protection, churches, schools,—in short if it were not for civilization in general, the piece of land in question would not be worth anything. Since its productive value is due to the presence of the community, it follows, they say, that the community and not the land is the producer. In the first place, this proves too much. All that is said respecting land could be said of any other factor of production. If it were not for the community round about, neither the buildings on the land nor the labor of the lawyer, the doctor, the merchant and the manufacturer would be of any great value. In the second place, if we begin at another link in the chain and follow the same method of reasoning, we could prove that land produces everything. If it were not for the land there would be no productivity, or any community either; therefore, since all productivity is due to land — would be impossible without land — land produces everything.

But this method of reasoning is so palpably fallacious that it is useless to pursue it further. The fault with it is that it fails to distinguish between the community in general and the individuals of whom it is composed, or between land in general and the particular parcels of land which are being rented, bought and sold.

Since it is not labor in the abstract but individual laborers who are hired, the test of the productivity of labor is to find out how much more the community could produce with than without the individual in question. The difference is the measure of his value or worth as a productive agent. The same method is applicable to a given piece of land. Find out how much more the community can produce when that piece of land is in use than it could if it were not in use. The difference gives you the measure of its value or worth as a productive agent. From this point of view, land is as clearly an agent of production as is labor, and the productive value of each is to be tested by precisely the same method. Assume a given piece of land to be withdrawn from use. The labor and capital now employed in cultivating that land would have to be employed elsewhere. Being employed elsewhere would mean that it would have to be added to the labor and capital employed on other land. This would require somewhat more intensive cultivation of the other land, which would increase somewhat its total product, but would not increase it sufficiently to balance the amount formerly produced on the piece of land in question. Or to put it another way, suppose that the piece of land is now being held out of use for speculative purposes. Its potential rent is the amount which its use would add to the total productivity. If it were brought into use, labor and capital would have to be expended upon it. This labor and capital does not come out of air. It would have to be withdrawn from other land. Being withdrawn from other land, the product from that other land is diminished. But if the piece of land is of any value, this diminution of the amount produced on other land would not be equal to the amount which could be produced on this particular piece of land. The difference between the diminution in the amount produced on the other land and the increase of the amount produced on this land is the measure of the productive value of this land.

There are two distinct dangers, however, lurking in this argument. While land is undoubtedly a productive agent, as productivity is thus defined, it does not follow by any means that the landowner is a productive agent. In one important respect he differs from the owner of a productive agent which has been made by human labor and ingenuity. The owner of the latter either made it himself or bought it from some one who did. If he made it himself he may be said to be the real producer of the apparent product of the material agent. If he bought it he may be assumed to have paid the producer what it was worth. The producer having transferred his rights to the buyer, the latter may be assumed to be standing in the place of the producer. In the case of land, however, since no one made it, no one can be called the real producer of the apparent product of the land. The land is, in other words, an original or primary factor of production, and no person can claim to be the producer of land as he can in the case of a machine. The landowner's rent, therefore, while payment for the productive value of land, cannot be said to be payment for the productive value of the landlord himself — it being understood that we are now speaking of the land itself and not the improvements which the owner may have placed upon the land.

On the other hand, it is not to be assumed that the land-owner is a parasite, or a useless member of society. While he is not in any sense the producer of the land, he is, in a very important sense, the conserver of its productive powers and other valuable qualities. Property in land there must be, either private or public. Throwing land open to use is so unthinkable that not even a single taxer in his sane moments would advocate it. Its effective use requires definite control, fencing the public off, and devoting it to specific purposes which require the exclusion of trespassers. Either under public ownership or under private ownership subject to the single tax, this would be precisely as necessary as under the present form of private ownership. If the land is worked by private individuals who either do not own it, or nominally own it under the obligation to pay its full rental value to the public in the form of a single tax, it is worked by men who are actually or virtually tenants. Under the single tax the nominal owner is virtually a tenant of the public because he pays economic rent to the public, and does not gain or lose by a future increase or decrease in the value of the land — (as distinct from improvements). His rent will go up or down accordingly. Every one knows what a tenant does to land if he is not controlled by the owner. Having no interest in the future increase or decrease in its value, his interest is concentrated in the present. If he is not prevented by the control of the landowner, he will speedily exhaust the soil and leave it when he is through with it. In its own interest as the virtual owner of the land, the state would be compelled to safeguard its future value by very close and detailed regulation and inspection. This would require an army of officials who would have to be paid salaries. It would not be pretended that these officials were not earning their salaries if they were doing their work reasonably well. That precise work is now done by land-owners, the only difference being that they receive rent instead of salaries. It may be that they are not doing it as well as they ought, and it may be that they receive more in the way of rent than that body of officials would receive in the form of salaries; but in any event, it could not be denied that they are earning *something*, whether they are earning all they are getting or not. Possibly a refined form of the single tax could be devised which would tax only site value and not soil or anything else which could possibly be exhausted or destroyed. In that case the public would be the virtual owner of the site alone, and the private owner would be the real as well as the nominal owner of everything else, including the soil. He would then have the same motive as now for conserving the value of everything which might be exhausted and which therefore needs conserving, leaving to the state the virtual ownership of the site, the only thing which cannot be exhausted and therefore needs no conservation.

There is another and far broader aspect of the question of landownership than any we have yet considered, an aspect, by the way, which is almost universally ignored in modern discussions of this important subject. It is obvious that this becomes a social problem only where there is a considerable landless class, on the one hand, and where, on the other hand, land has become very scarce and valuable. These two conditions necessarily go together. Land becomes very valuable only when there is a dense population. A dense population means a large landless class. In other words, without a large landless class, no land would be very valuable, and no landowner would be able to get a large rent. We may well ask the question in all seriousness why there should be a dense population and a large landless class at any particular spot. We too frequently assume that the density of Boston Neck or Manhattan Island is a part of the providential ordering of the universe, that it must be taken for granted as divinely ordained, and, being so, it is very wrong that so many should own no land while the little land that there is in such places should be owned by so few. To a person who looks at the matter in this way, it is useless to point out that there is plenty of land elsewhere where all those people might become landowners. To him it is so unnatural that men should spread out and live on the land, and so natural that they should flock together in these vast rookeries called cities, that he simply cannot take you seriously. The writer's hope is that there may be a few readers who have enough of the scientific imagination to see that there is no necessity why men should herd together in this way, that it is quite conceivable that they might continue to spread out, as every colonizing race has spread, and that they may have enough historical knowledge to realize that every great race has been a colonizing race. To such a reader it may be worth while to present the following argument.

The fact that men congregate in cities instead of going on the land is because they prefer the pleasures and hardships of the cities to the hardships and pleasures of landownership where land may be had. The reason that men prefer to work in the employ of landowners is because they prefer the wages and the lack of responsibility, to the hard work, the danger, and the other hardships of pioneering. This condition is made easy for them because an older and sturdier race of pioneers has preceded them, has subdued the land

and brought it under control. If you compare the hired man, as thus understood, with the pioneer, it would be so difficult to determine where to bestow the term " parasite," that we should do well to omit it altogether from our economic vocabulary. When we come to compare not the hired man with the pioneer for whom he works, but the later hired man with the descendants of the pioneer, the question becomes mixed up with the question of inherited wealth and is not a question of landownership pure and simple.

The cry for a share in the value of the land which a certain aggressive type of single taxer is so busily engaged in stirring up, is quite different from the desire to own and use land. They who desire land know where they can get it; what the aggressive single taxer wants is not *land*, but a share in the value of the land which somebody else has. He can get land in Canada, but he prefers it in New York, Boston, or some other large city where it is very scarce and valuable. The single tax movement, therefore, differs fundamentally from the agrarian laws for which the Gracchi sacrificed their lives. They proposed to give the people land — to make them owners of land — where it was to be found; the modern movement is to give them, through taxation and public expenditure, a share in the value of the land already occupied by other people. Moreover, it must be said, this modern movement is promoted, not by appealing to the pioneering, colonizing, spirit of a sturdy, conquering race, but too often by appealing to jealousy, covetousness, and other of the less commendable motives which actuate mankind. However, no pity need be wasted upon the land-owners in our large cities. They find it profitable to encourage the coming of masses of mankind who prefer to sweat and stew in cities rather than to pioneer the way for civilization.   If this mass of people should vote to confiscate the value of the land on which they are now living, the landowners need not complain of being badly treated. They have gambled with economic and political forces, and must stand to lose.

However, while no sympathy need be wasted either upon landless men who refuse to go where there is land to be had, or upon the landowner if the landless masses should decide to take his land, or its value, away from him, still, this is not a matter of sympathy.   It is a matter of constructive statesmanship.   From this point of view we must consider fairly and patiently whether priority of occupation is or is not a sufficient ground upon which to base a legal right to land, and if so, what are the reasonable limitations of that right.   It is so universally agreed, in civilized societies, that the man who first occupies a piece of land has a somewhat better right to it than they who come later, that it would seem that the burden of proof should lie upon those who deny it.   In actual practice, however, there are several recognized qualifications to this agreement.   In the first place, it is customary to give a preference to the members of our own civilization, over others.   These considerations are sometimes allowed to take precedence over mere priority of occupation, as illustrated by our treatment of the American Indian.   Nevertheless, as between citizens of our own state, we allow some precedence to the first occupier.   In the second place, for the proper recording of titles, and the proper safeguarding of the public interest, the occupier is generally required to go through certain legal formalities. If he neglects these, his mere priority of occupation may not avail to secure his superior right to the land.   With these and a few minor qualifications, there is no doubt that civilized nations do, as a matter of practice, allow priority

of occupation to count as a factor in giving a legal right to
landownership.   Couple with this factor the right of transfer, under which the original occupier may transfer the rights
which he has acquired to others, either to his heirs by
bequest, or to others by bargain and sale, and you have
every essential feature of the modern right of property in
land.

But it is not necessary to rest the case in favor of priority
of occupation as a basis of property rights on the mere fact
of the universality of the practice, or upon the fact that the
burden of proof is thrown, by this universality, upon those
who attack it.   It is even less necessary to base the argument upon any absurd or metaphysical doctrine of human
rights in general.   An excellent example of this class of
argument is as follows:

1. Every man must be assumed to have a right to himself.   2. When a man has worked upon a thing he has put a
part of himself into it.   Therefore he has a right to that
upon which he has worked.   If the premises were true,
the conclusion would follow as a matter of course.   Unfor-
tunately neither premise is necessary.   The first may or
may not be true, it does not matter.   The second is absurd
and meaningless, and that is sufficient to spoil the argument.
What does it mean to say that one puts a part of oneself
into anything ?   When one has worked upon a thing, has
he diminished himself — i. e., the part of himself which is
left outside the thing — or has he not ?   If, after he has
parted with the thing he has as much of himself left as he
had before, can he be said to have put a part of himself
into it ?

But such arguments are as unnecessary as they are futile.
All sound and genuine rights are based upon social utility.
Is it useful in the long run, i. e., does it work well, to allow

the first occupant of a piece of land some rights in it which we deny to those who come later and want a part of it or of its value ? Of two communities otherwise equally favored, one of which recognizes this right while the other does not, which is likely to become the more comfortable, prosperous, and powerful ? These are the considerations which must guide the law-maker or the nation-builder in his quest for social justice, rather than the mere sentimental notions of equality and fair play. These notions are important factors, to be sure, and when they are not too short-sighted, are fairly safe guides. But when short-sighted they are the most destructive factors in any civilization. Justice is mercy writ large. It is benevolence with a long look ahead, a look which takes in the most distant generations of the future and places them on an exact equality with the present generations; which has as much regard for an as yet voiceless individual to be born a thousand years hence as for any individual now alive and clamoring for his rights.

As an illustration of the way in which a sentiment of fair play and justice may prove to be short-sighted, let us take the law of primogeniture under which only the eldest son can inherit land, as compared with the modern system under which all the children share equally in the inheritance. Primogeniture seems obviously unfair to the younger children, and therefore unjust, while the other system seems obviously fair to all, and therefore just. But if it should happen that, under primogeniture, the younger sons, realizing that there is nothing to be gained by staying on the ancestral estate, should go out into the world to conquer little kingdoms for themselves, by pioneering and bringing new lands under cultivation, by starting new business enterprises and expanding the nation's productivity, or by exploring in the fields of science, that would produce a growing, expanding and prospering civilization. If, on the other hand, under the other system, the sons should decide to hang around home waiting for the old folks to die in order that each might get his little share of the estate, that would tend to produce a narrow, contracting, decaying civilization. Of two nations, the one reacting in the former and the other in the latter manner, there is not much doubt as to which would grow more prosperous and powerful, and play the larger rôle in the civilization of the future. This is a large consideration which should make us pause before we decide to follow a sentiment of fair play and justice which does not look beyond the present generation and its immediate successor.

This should lead us to give careful consideration to several questions. First, to what extent is pioneering stimulated by the desire to get the future " unearned increment " of land value ? Second, to what extent would a sharing in the enormously inflated value of land in overcrowded urban centers induce the landless classes to stay in these centers rather than to spread out where land is more abundant and cheaper?

If the later comers to a growing community are made to feel, like the younger sons of the English nobility, that the land is all taken and they are to have no share in its rent, they are then thrown upon their own resources and are forced to make good in some other way, that is, to find some other source of income, or to go somewhere else where there is land to be had. If, added to this, they are given to understand that if they do face the hardships of pioneer life and take up vacant land they shall be allowed to profit by it, not only in the present, but in the distant future when that land increases in value, you will have a double stimulus to pioneering and a double discouragement to hanging around old and overcrowded centers in the hope of sharing in the prosperity of the earlier comers. You may not think it desirable to encourage pioneering, you may think that it is better not to pioneer, but to encourage men to stay in the older centers and get a share of the land values accruing there, but here again is a situation in which it is difficult to know where to bestow the word parasite.

This difference in the point of view of the old timer and the new comer is one of the oldest and most persistent causes of class antagonism. Fundamentally there are only two kinds of aristocracy in the world. One is a military aristocracy, under which a race of military conquerors set themselves over a more or less subject population. The other is the aristocracy of old timers, or old families who have attached themselves to the soil, built up the community, and attracted new comers. At first the new comers are the plebeians and accept a distinctly lower social position than that of the patricians. But as their numbers increase, and their sense of power and solidarity grows, they resent the exclusiveness of the upper classes, that is, of the old timers, and gain greater and greater control over the affairs of the city and state. Naturally the old timers resent this, and much bitterness ensues. This kind of social distinction and its attendant bitterness of feeling will probably persist as long as populations shift, and as long as, through this shifting, they can be divided into the two classes, the ins and the outs, the attached and the unattached, those in established positions of economic independence, and those new arrivals who are as yet unestablished. In the case of a military conquest, of course, it is the new comers who form the aristocratic class. In other cases, they form the plebeian class.

If we are at all to consider pioneering, and the conditions of industry which prevail in a pioneering community, there will not appear to be so very much difference between property in land and property in other things. But if we ignore the possibility of pioneering several distinctions occur. One is that land is a free gift of nature. Another is that other products are made by human labor.

To the first distinction it may be objected that other goods are, in their original form, free gifts of nature as truly as land. The only basis of a man's claim to them is that he appropriated them and changed their form to suit his own or some one else's purpose, — that is, he put them into a form which was valuable. The same is true of land, and it is this aspect of the case which would naturally appeal, and did as a matter of fact appeal, to the first settlers in a new community. If one settler saw a tree which seemed to contain possibilities, and chopped it down and made it into a table, it would be in accordance with social utility that the table should be his. If another settler saw a piece of land which seemed to contain possibilities, and cleared it and ploughed it and reduced it to cultivation, on the same reasoning the land would be his. Each settler would have found a free gift of nature, each would have worked upon it, each would have changed its form from the raw state in which he found it to a form which would serve his purpose. The mere fact that the result of one's labor happened to be a farm, and that of the other's labor a table, would not have appeared at the time to be a real difference. This aspect of the case is recommended to the consideration of those who believe that the private ownership of land is forbidden by a moral law ordained from the foundation of the world.

If, however, the community should grow in population, a real difference between the table and the land would begin to appear. In the first place, it would be found that the owners of the land held control of the original raw material for the manufacture of tables and all other produced goods. When the maker of the first table wished to make a new one to replace the old one when it was worn out, he would have to pay the landowner for the privilege of cutting a tree from which to make it. In the second place, the value of the land would increase in proportion to the number of persons wishing to make use of its products either for purposes of consumption or for the purpose of producing other goods. The fortunate owners of the limited supply of land would find themselves in possession of a growing income far in excess of anything which the land might have cost them, whereas the owners of the tables and other such goods would find themselves always compelled to expend approximately as much in the making of them as they were worth.   As time goes on this difference increases, especially in a growing city, until small areas of land come to have fabulous prices, while the value of tables continues to bear a fairly close relation to their cost of production.

To the second distinction it may be objected that land is sometimes " made " in the sense of being reclaimed from the sea or the desert, whereas there are other goods, such as antique furniture and rare works of art, which cannot now be reproduced.   But the fact remains that by far the greater part of the present land supply is not " made." In fact, there is not enough " made " to have any appreciable effect on the value of land in general, and it certainly does not prevent certain choice situations from rising to stupendous prices.   On the other hand, with few exceptions, other goods are capable of reproduction, and are actually reproduced so long as they have a value high enough to repay the cost of production.   Whereas non-reproducible land is the rule and reproducible land the exception, reproducible goods of other kinds than land are the rule and non-reproducible ones the exception.   This may be called a difference of degree only, but the difference of degree is so great as to constitute, for scientific and practical purposes, a difference of kind.   As a matter of fact, nearly all scientific differences are differences of degree.   It is not denied, however, that there are many resemblances between land and other goods. There are also certain resemblances between a man and a clothes-pin, but the differences are sufficiently important to warrant our placing them in different classes.[1]

In view of all these considerations it will be difficult for any reasonable man to lash himself into a state of moral indignation against the private ownership of land.   If a pioneer settler were brought face to face with a certain type of radical single taxer who makes a moral issue of the ownership of land values, and makes free use of certain formulae, such as the equal right of all to access to God's earth, the moral indignation would not all be on the side of the single taxer.   To the demand for access to God's earth, the pioneer would reply, " You do not seem to want access to the earth,

[1] T. N. Carver, *Distribution of Wealth*, pp. 108–111.

you want access *at this particular spot,* which is mine. You may have all the access you want elsewhere, but I have access here and shall defend my position." He would naturally feel that his priority of possession gave him a right superior to that of the later comer.

However, the single taxer disclaims any desire to dislodge the prior possessor from his possession. All he proposes is to require the possessor to pay for the privilege. After the first possessor has settled himself, others come and say to him, " We outnumber you, we can therefore outvote you. We shall, therefore, vote that you pay for the privilege of holding this land. It is we who create the value of your land anyway." The matter might, of course, be presented to him in a more reasonable way. They might say to him, " We will come to your community and live on your land provided you will make an inducement. Our coming will add to the value of your land and, therefore, you can well afford to pay considerable sums for public improvements in order to attract more people. It will really be money in your pocket to do so." This might or might not appeal to him, but it would scarcely stir up moral indignation. However, the single taxer who makes a moral issue of his doctrine would disdain to temporize in this way.

Pioneer conditions, however, have long passed away in those centers where the single tax propaganda is active. The first generation of settlers and their immediate descendants having passed away, this argument, it may be said, no longer applies. But we grant the right of transfer, either by sale, gift, devise, or inheritance, then we grant that each later owner has acquired the rights of the original settler. If we grant the right of the original settler, we cannot deny the rights of any of these later owners without attacking the right of transfer. As a matter of fact, the problem of landownership has, in all old communities, become so mixed up with the problem of inheritance that it is difficult to discuss them separately.   It will be found, upon analysis, that every real objection to the laws of property in land is as much an objection to inheritance of land as to property in land as such.   In no case can the question, by any process of mental contortion, be made a moral question.   It is wholly a question of expediency.   The question is, how does landownership work ?   Are there any modifications of the right of inheritance, which may reasonably be expected to improve economic or social conditions, to stimulate the productive energies of the community, or secure such a distribution of wealth as to develop the productive virtues of the people ?

There are, as a matter of fact, three specific advantages which would result to modern society through an increase in the taxation of land values.   The first is that under such a system it would become less common than it now is to hold valuable land out of use for speculative purposes. When the owner sees that the taxes on the site value of his land are eating up all possible profits through the annual increase in that site value, and that his only way of making anything out of his land is by using it rather than by holding it to sell at a higher price, he will either begin to use it himself or hastily sell it to some one else who will use it.   Thus there would result a certain increase in the amount of land in actual use, or a diminution in the amount held out of use, which amounts to the same thing.

Under the laws of value already outlined, this increase in the available supply of the factor called land would result in an increased demand for the other factors which have to be combined with land in production.   In order to use this land which is now held out of use, there must be labor and capital. Where, as in thickly populated parts of the country, land has become a scarce factor, it occupies very much the same position in actual production that saltpetre did in the illustration used above.[1] Bring more land into use, and it will have very much the same effect upon the demand for labor and capital as an increase in the supply of saltpetre had upon the demand for charcoal in the illustration.

A second beneficial effect which may be expected from an increase in the taxation of the site value of land would be the reduction in the taxation on active industry. Assuming that a certain revenue has to be secured for public purposes, it must be secured either by taxation on land or on industry, or on both combined. In proportion as the burden is placed upon the site value of land, it is taken off active industry. The result of reducing taxes on active business, that is on the products of industry, must invariably be to encourage business and industrial activity. If the farmer knows that his land must bear all the taxes, and his buildings, crops, improvements, and live-stock none, that is to say, if his taxes will be as high when his land is unimproved or half improved as when it is highly improved, he will have every encouragement to improvement. But if he knows that every time he adds to the value of his estate by putting improvements on his land his taxes must go up, that must operate, to a certain degree at least, to discourage improvement. And if the owner of a vacant city lot knows that his tax will be as high as it would be if a valuable building stood upon the lot, in other words, that he will not be taxed at all upon the building, that would be, to some degree at least, an encouragement to building. All these improvements upon farm land and buildings upon city lots not only require labor in the first place, but they continue adding to the total

[1] See Chapter IX, p. 250.

productivity of the community thereafter, making goods more abundant for all members of the community, including the laborers.

A third beneficial result of this process, more important perhaps than all the others, is that it would tend to eliminate a certain kind of waste labor. The most serious waste of labor power is not found at the bottom of the social scale in the form of an unemployed class; it is found at or near the top of the social scale, in the form of a voluntarily idle or leisure class. Generally speaking, the leisure class is made up of the most capable members of the community, though this is not necessarily true in every individual case. As a rule, the most successful farmer will lay up a fortune more rapidly and be able to retire from active farming earlier in life than the less capable farmer, whose rate of accumulation is less rapid. So with the capable business man. The more capable business man will acquire a competence earlier in life than the less capable man, and if he is inclined to retire at all the more capable he is the more likely he will be to retire, and the earlier in life he will retire.

Now economic capacity is largely a matter of need and scarcity. A kind of labor power, mental or physical, for which the need is far in excess of the supply, counts as high ability. But no matter how great the need for it, if there is as much of it as is needed, it does not count as high ability. The scarce forms of ability, relatively to the need for them, are the kinds which command the highest salaries, or secure the largest profits in any healthy and well-governed community. But if, as a result of the scarcity of their talent, a certain class of men grow prosperous, and as a result of their prosperity, they retire from business early in life, the active talent is thereby made still scarcer, and a bad situation is made worse. If, in addition, he not only retires from active business himself, but brings up his sons in idleness, they, in turn, expecting to be able to live on their inherited wealth, the scarcity of active business talent is made still scarcer. This, however, will be considered under the discussion of inherited wealth.

Probably the scarcest form of productive power is genuine investing ability; the ability to see just where new industrial enterprises are needed, coupled with the courage to act, and the skill to get the new enterprise started in the right way. A few more men possessing this kind of ability in any community would remake that community by causing an expansion of industries, creating new employment for labor, and increasing the products for the satisfaction of wants. But there are productive and unproductive investments. If I invest in a real productive enterprise, I help to start a new enterprise, and the community is benefited by my action. But if I invest in land, intending merely to hold it for a rise in value, I have done nothing for the benefit of the community. No new land is created by my investment, and the community is in the same condition as though I had never invested. The most that could be said of my investment would be that I had released the capital of the seller and that he might, if he chose to do so, invest the capital thus released in productive work. But this could not be said of land investors as a class. There would, therefore, be this important difference. The more men there are buying tools, machinery, buildings, etc. — for that is virtually what investment means — the greater will be the demand for such things, and the more their production will be stimulated. The normal result of this kind of investment is to increase the world's stock of tools, machinery, buildings, etc. But the more men there are buying land, but not themselves improving it, the higher the price of land goes, and that is the end of the process. No more land is produced, because land cannot be produced, and the world is no better supplied with land than it would be if men did not invest in it. Much of the investing talent of the country is perverted to this unproductive purpose. If this opportunity for unproductive investment were closed, some of this talent would be forced into other and productive channels. Instead of buying land, men would buy other sources of income, that is, other means of production. The increased purchases of these things would stimulate their production and thus the world would be better equipped. By taxing away the selling value of land and thus making it an unprofitable field for the investors, the scarcest and most precious form of industrial talent would be made somewhat less scarce than it now is. If we could prevent its being diverted into the useless channels of land investment, and turn it into useful channels, it will count for something. Because this kind of talent is so scarce and so precious, it is of vastly greater concern to us to save it and utilize it than it is to save and utilize a kind of labor power which is abundant relatively to needs.

If that is virtually what investment means, the more men there are investing in tools, machinery, buildings, etc., the more of such things there will be produced. The result, therefore, of increasing the number of this class of investors, especially the number of wise investors, will be an increase not only in the number of tools, machines, and buildings, but in the quality and value of these instruments of production. But, as pointed out above, if the higher forms of investing ability are absorbed in useless speculation in land, speculation which neither increases nor decreases the supply of anything, there is that much less left for the kind of speculation which really draws the productive forces of the community into the manufacture of other productive agents.

Because a considerable extension of the land tax would tend to force into productive use a certain amount of land which is now held out of use for speculative purposes; because it would tend to relieve active production from the repressive burdens of taxation, and because it would tend to cut off the incomes which now support capable men in idleness thus forcing a certain amount of talent into action, we must conclude that an extension of the land tax would work well for the nation. However, one cannot be called a single taxer who believes also in the inheritance tax.

CHAPTER XII

THE QUESTION OF INHERITANCE

THE inheritance tax has made more headway than the land tax. The arguments for one seem to be about as strong as for the other. The inheritance tax, however, has stood on its merit and has not been championed as an engine of social reform. It has had no body of ardent apostles to set up a fiery cross and preach a crusade against a fortunate class. The land tax has been thus handicapped, which may account for its slow progress. In the ardency of reform, arguments are used which ignite certain inflammable spirits but repel all thinking men. This makes constructive reform impossible and nothing can be done until the inflammable spirits gain control in a sweeping and destructive revolution. This, however, seldom happens. For one such movement which grows to a general conflagration at least ninety-nine flicker out.

There are two points of view from which to approach the question of inherited wealth. Each method of approach leads to such contradictory conclusions that it seems necessary to follow each in turn to its logical result and then see what can be done toward harmonizing them.

From the point of view of the present generation, or the generation which has accumulated the wealth in question, the following considerations will appeal to most men as reasonable. Assuming, to begin with, that a man has earned his income, there is no good reason why he should be compelled to consume it all and save none of it. In fact it can easily be shown that it is very much better for society that he should save a part of it, — all of it, in fact, beyond what it is necessary that he should consume in order to maintain his working efficiency at its maximum.   If he saves a part of his income it is better that he should invest it in productive or useful tools rather than that he should hide it away.   If he saves a part of his income and invests it wisely in useful or productive tools, there is no harm in allowing him some control over them, in other words, there is no harm in regarding them as his property.   If they are his property there is no harm in allowing him some freedom in disposing of them.   If he chooses to give them away, it would seem inexpedient and unjust to forbid him to do so. And if he is to be permitted thus to dispose of them, there could be no harm in permitting him to give them to his children or near relatives rather than to strangers.

All this is, of course, based on the assumption with which we started, viz., that he has actually earned his income.   If he has not earned it, the obvious thing to do is to correct the evil at the source by cutting off his unearned income.   It would be exceedingly unintelligent to permit him to receive an unearned income and thus build up a swollen fortune, and then try to correct the evil after he is dead by depriving his heirs of their inheritance.   This unintelligence would amount to a crime if fortunes actually earned and honestly accumulated by saving, were swept away by the abolition of inheritances merely because some other fortunes were unearned.   This would be worse than punishing the just with the unjust for sins which the unjust had committed; it would be punishing the *heirs* of the just and of the unjust for sins which the unjust had committed.

Looking at the question of inheritance apart from the question of the source of income, and looking at it also from the point of view of the generation which accumulates the wealth, there seems to be no good reason why the individual who saves a part of his income and accumulates a fund of wealth should not be permitted to transmit it to his widow and orphans.   How wide the circle of relatives should be who should be allowed a legal claim on the inheritance is another question.   Undoubtedly it should be much narrower than is at present permitted.   Since one of the strongest motives to accumulation is the desire to provide for the members of one's own family, and since accumulation is socially desirable, there is a positive reason why the right of transmission by inheritance should be sustained.   One effect of the destruction of this right would be to encourage lavish consumption, and discourage accumulation.   Each man who loves to gratify himself would be tempted, somewhat more strongly than he is at present, to say, as soon as he had accumulated a competence, "Soul take thine ease. Thou hast much goods laid up for many years, eat, drink and be merry."   If he could not leave anything to his family, they would be just as well off if he were to consume his fortune as if he were to save it.   Under such conditions, unless the law were evaded by gifts during the lifetime of the accumulator, capital, which is tools, would tend to grow scarce or increase less rapidly, industries to contract, or to expand less rapidly, the effective demand for labor to decline and wages to fall, while interest would rise in response to the scarcity of capital.[1]

Thus far we have considered the problem exclusively from the standpoint of the generation which accumulates wealth, forgetting succeeding generations.   If, now, we consider the matter exclusively from the standpoint of succeeding generations, forgetting the generation which accumulated the

[1] Cf. Chapter VII.

wealth in question, the whole situation has a different look. From this new point of view we shall notice, first, that certain individuals, — the inheritors of wealth, — start in the race of life with a sum of capital in addition to their natural powers, while others start with nothing but their natural powers.   It is obvious that the inheritors have an advantage in the race, and therefore it is also obvious that it is not a fair race.

It is perhaps desirable at this point to consider the meaning of the word " fair " as applied to any form of competition.   In a foot race, for example, the competition is sometimes said to be fair when all the runners are given an even start and given an equally good track on which to run.   Of course there will be great differences in the speed of the different runners, and it is certain that there will be great unevenness among the runners at the end of the race, even though they were all even at the start and all had equally good outward conditions.   Inequality of results, when it can be attributed exclusively to inequality of power, and not to an uneven start or any *outward* advantages or disadvantages, may, from this point of view, be considered fair.

In other cases, there is a deliberate attempt to predict the relative speed of the various runners, and to arrange a series of handicaps, in order that the race may be as nearly even *at the end* as possible.   In this case they are deliberately given an uneven start, in order that there may be an even finish, or a finish as nearly even as the handicap committee can arrange.   If the handicaps are intelligently and fairly calculated, this kind of a race is also said to be fair.

The same principles would apply to economic competition.   If all the competitors were given an even start, and if all were given a fair field with no favors, it would be called, from one point of view, fair competition. On the other hand, if it were possible to arrange a series of handicaps, giving each of the weaker competitors an advantage commensurate with his weakness, such a competition might also be said to be fair. The competitors would be given an uneven start and uneven advantage in order that they might be as nearly even as possible at the end of the race.

But it must be remembered that a system of handicaps must be intelligently arranged, otherwise it becomes outrageously unfair. If, instead of giving some outward advantage to the slower runner, it were given to the swifter runner, and the prizes awarded on the basis of the results of such a race, every sentiment of fairness would be outraged. And in the field of economic competition, if the handicaps were arranged in inverse order to the power of the competitors, every one would say that it was unfair. Again, if the handicaps were arranged in a haphazard fashion, without any regard to the power of the competitors, so that the stronger were as likely as the weaker to be given an outward advantage, the case would be only a little better. No one would even pretend that it was a fair competition. This is exactly what happens to economic competition under the system of inherited wealth. From this point of view, forgetting the other, there can scarcely be two opinions on the subject. Inheritances ought not to be allowed, because they make competition unfair. The strong competitor is quite as likely as the weak to be given the advantage of a fund of capital with which to start the race of life.

These two points of view, from which such opposite conclusions are reached, may be harmonized, or compromised, by considering the family rather than the individual as the unit of society, and considering the family as a permanent unit, unaffected by the brevity of individual lives. We should then assume that economic competition takes place between families rather than between individuals. And the family being a permanent rather than a transitory unit, the race or the competition cannot be considered as having a beginning or an end. What is called the inheritance of wealth is therefore not to be considered as giving an individual an unearned advantage in competition so much as keeping in the possession of the family the advantage which it has already earned.

In proportion as one is in the habit of thinking in terms of the family rather than of the individual, and of emphasizing the solidarity and perpetuity of the family and the unity of its interests, in that proportion will one emphasize the first point of view and minimize the arguments which are used against the inheritance of wealth. But in proportion as one is in the habit of thinking in terms of the individual rather than the family, or of thinking of the family as a temporary biological unit, beginning with marriage and ending with death, existing for the purpose of producing children and bringing them to maturity, in that proportion will one naturally emphasize the second point of view and minimize the arguments in support of the inheritance of wealth. Before considering the merits of the two conceptions of the family, it is safe to record the fact that the undoubted tendency of popular opinion is away from the conception of the family as a solid and perpetual social unit, and toward that of the family as a temporary, biological unit. There are even evidences of a tendency toward the purely individualistic conception which eliminates the family as an institution, though recognizing the necessity of a mating of males and females for the propagation of the species.

While there is an undoubted popular trend at least toward the theory that the family is a temporary biological unit, it does not follow that this is the direction of progress rather than degeneracy. The issue is, at bottom, one between family building, on the one hand, and spawning on the other, as rival methods of perpetuating the social group. The conception of the family as a temporary biological unit, beginning with marriage and terminating either with the maturity of the children, who then establish new families, or with the death of the parents, which is the final dissolution of the group which began with marriage, is only a compromise between the two conceptions of family building and spawning. It does not have the elements of permanency even as a theory. If the family is only a biological unit, existing for the purpose of propagating children and of bringing them safely to maturity, it may be found easier to turn the latter function over to the state, leaving propagation as the sole function of marriage. This obviously does not necessitate permanency. Spawning is the next step, where children are begotten without any sense of responsibility on the part of parents, the spawn being left to the tender mercies of an impersonal state.

Both methods, — both family building and spawning, — are always with us, together with every graduation between the two extremes. The difference between communities is largely one of emphasis. The question is, toward which extreme the variations tend to concentrate. Aristocratic families tend to emphasize family building, and to plan for the future of the family, and the family name, even for remote generations as well as for the present generation. But the mass of the people in most modern nations, appear to care little for family name, tradition, pedigree, or remote posterity. Their domestic instincts may be strongly developed, and family affection intense, but it is limited in its

scope to the present generation and those immediately preceding and following.

In almost every age the family builders have ruled the
spawners. This is no accident. They in whom the instinct
for family building is strong, who habitually look beyond
their individual lives; who are willing to sacrifice present
gratification in the interest of the remote future, not simply
the future of their own individual lives, but the future
of their families, grow in prosperity, power and influence
generation after generation. They who live in the present
generation alone have no such cumulative advantage, and
are gradually outdistanced. The amazing prosperity of the
last century and a half, however, has tended to obscure this
law. Under the rapidly developing conditions of this period,
stupendous fortunes are built up in a single generation,
and as quickly dissipated by the next. In the midst of
these rapid changes it is not always easy to perceive any
advantage on the side of the family-building part of the
population. So many are carried on to fortune by favorable turns in the tide of human affairs, and so many others
are carried down to misfortune by unfavorable turns, that
we are encouraged to think and speak slightingly of those
who still take pride in family name and tradition, or sacrifice
present gain for family name and honor. Nevertheless, it is
more than probable that out of even these cataclysmic
changes there will emerge a few families who have held
themselves true to the family ideal. If business and finance
continue to furnish satisfactory fields for the exercise of
their ability and training, they will dominate business and
finance. If these fields are closed by socialistic legislation,
so that politics and government employment become the
only large fields for the exercise of ability and training, then
these families will dominate politics and government. Even

in the strategy of politics for the control of the popular will, and in the communities which have thought themselves most democratic, the aristocratic families, with their accumulated knowledge, skill, and influence, have pretty generally outmaneuvered the products of the spawning process.

The abolition of inheritance, or any step in that direction would tend to destroy or undermine the prosperity, power and influence of the family-building part of the population and to put them more nearly on an equality with the spawning part. The latter will, as rapidly as they are brought to an appreciation of this fact, work toward the abolition or curtailment of inheritance. Popular education, particularly the popularization of the study of economics, may be expected to acquaint the masses more and more with the principles involved, and show them where their advantage lies. Consequently we may confidently expect that the right of inheritance will be more and more curtailed even if it be not eventually abolished altogether in new and prosperous countries.

But this would not settle the matter. The question would still remain whether the nations which moved most rapidly in this direction would not degenerate most rapidly and eventually become a prey to those countries which remained truer to the family ideal, and gave more encouragement to the family builder. If such should be the case, the world would still remain in the possession of the family builders, even though the spawners did, in certain countries, outnumber them and carry popular elections against them. There are other elections by certain " ancient elemental powers " whose results overrule those of even the most powerful human governments. In other words, the nation which decides, by however large a majority, upon a wrong course will weaken itself, and may eventually destroy itself if it ever comes into competition with another nation which has decided upon a wiser course.   In the end it is the wisdom or unwisdom of the policy which counts, not its popularity or unpopularity.   No one but the cheapest kind of a politician tries to find out what is popular.   The constructive leader of men tries to find out what is right and then tries to make it popular.

In a state of civilization where competition is intense, where only the efficient can flourish, the advantage on the side of the family builders is more easily seen.   They will not only succeed better than the spawners, on the average and in the long run, but, as the result of this success, they will remain numerous enough to dominate the whole political and economic situation.   The spawners are kept from becoming numerous by their sheer inability to survive under the stress of severe competition.   Under such conditions there is little likelihood that they will ever make much headway in their attacks upon the right of inheritance or any other institution which works to the advantage of the family building class.   But the marvelous prosperity of the western world since the age of machinery was ushered in, has enabled the spawning class to flourish and increase in numbers.   They have, therefore, risen to a position of power and influence, many of them to positions of enormous wealth and authority.   Even the most incompetent and thriftless have been able to spawn and to survive in vast numbers. The result is that a severe struggle is now going on, not only over the subject of the inheritance of wealth, but over the moral and social precepts of the family builders.

This struggle is more profound and far reaching than most of us appreciate.   So long as civilization was dominated by the family-building type, the qualities of that type were elevated to the position of virtues.   Industry, frugality, thrift and foresight, together with the domestic qualities, were prized and commended.   In proportion as the spawning type approaches to a position of dominance, in that proportion do the qualities of that type tend to be elevated to the position of virtues.   Leisure, unthrift, the type of good fellowship which manifests itself mainly in eating and drinking, and the general qualities which make one an agreeable member of a crowd in a carousal, come to be prized.   The old-fashioned domestic qualities are poorly esteemed, while thrift and the instinct for accumulation are hated.   Arguments on the fallacy of saving, the vice of thrift, and in praise of luxury make an appeal even to the quasi-intellectual classes.   The family becomes unstable, marriage being regarded merely as an arrangement for the pleasure and convenience of the contracting parties. Women become emancipated from the duties which belong to them, and men cease to regard family building as their chief ambition and begin to allow their own pleasure, or their business or profession to take precedence over the duty of founding or perpetuating a worthy family.

The more the spawning process gains ground, and the more unstable marriages there are, the stronger becomes the popular argument in favor of doing in public institutions what was formerly done in the home.   It becomes more and more easy to show that many children come into the world with few home advantages.   They who were responsible for their existence have no sense of responsibility for their education or training, therefore the state must educate and train them.   The arguments grow stronger every year for more and more state help.   We must expect that eventually this tendency will grow until the state not only educates, but feeds and clothes the children of the spawning process, and perhaps pensions mothers as well.

So far has opinion already drifted in this direction that it is difficult to find any who even understand the counter-arguments when they are presented. As to pensioning mothers, for example, how many even understand the real meaning of the ancient formula " With all my worldly goods I thee endow " ? To men and women of the family building type this means the endowment of motherhood. To the spawning type it is a mere form or ceremony. To the former it means that he who pronounces those words is thenceforth consecrated to the endowment of motherhood *and to nothing else.* That is thenceforth his chief business; that is why he labors at his business, trade or profession. It also means that she to whom those words are pronounced is thenceforward consecrated to motherhood and *to nothing else.* That is her chief business, and her only reason for accepting a share of his earnings.

It follows from this that he who does not mean to give himself exclusively to the endowment of motherhood is a blasphemer if he pronounces those words. It also follows that he who is not in a position to endow motherhood, that is, has no income with which to endow it, cannot honestly pronounce them, nor can any church honestly permit it. But, as already suggested, the growth of the spawning class, and the consequent increase in the volume of the spawning process, is making this formula meaningless. Men are allowed to pronounce the words who have no worldly goods and no income. While many of those who have both have not the slightest intention of doing anything resembling what they say they will do. They are, to all intents and purposes, spawners, though conforming to an ancient rite which was intended for family builders alone.

But after all, the question is not whether we are or are not departing from ancient standards, but whether the new standards are better or worse than the ancient.   The question is whether the state which is dominated by the spawning element, and all of whose policies and institutions are shaped in their interest, can be as strong as the state which is dominated by family builders, and all of whose policies and institutions are shaped in their interests ?   If so, it will succeed, and eventually dominate the world; if not it will fail and eventually be eliminated from the world.   Specifically, can as good and useful a type of citizenship be developed by taking the spawn of biological matings and caring for them in public institutions as can be developed by the social group which we call the family, where motherhood is endowed by the man who begets the children, and where the responsibility for the care of children is laid definitely upon those who are responsible for their existence ?   The reasons in favor of the negative seem more weighty than those in favor of the affirmative.

In the first place, the removal from parents of all responsibility for the welfare of those for whose existence they are responsible, removes the only automatic check on numbers. No matter how beneficent the state might be toward its individuals, it would never be able to keep some of them very far above the starvation line.   This is a law of the very widest applicability.   Whenever any kind of competition is open to all comers, without limit as to number, some of the competitors will always be on the margin of existence.   No matter how rich in opportunity a certain spot may be, if it is open to all comers, and there is no limit to the number, so many will flock to that spot as to bring some of them down to as low an economic position as those in less favored spots. The only difference will be that the more favored spots will have more people than the less favored.

It is this principle which makes protection so futile when applied to favored industries. No matter how high the protection, or how prosperous the industry may become temporarily, so many will rush into it as to reduce some of their profits to a minimum. Then it becomes impossible to reduce the protection without bankrupting some of the weaker establishments. This is always used as an effective argument against reduction. In fact it is cunningly used in favor of further and higher protection. It never can be high enough but that some establishments will still be on the verge of bankruptcy, and therefore, it is claimed, in need of further protection. The same rule applies to the rate of wages in protected industries. So long as any number of laborers can come into the industry, protection does not raise wages; at most it merely enables a larger number to be employed within the protected territory, and a smaller number in the territory discriminated against.

In proportion as the family-building type dominates the social system, and shapes the policy and institutions of that system, in that proportion will there be automatic checks upon the population. If the family-building policy should become universal, there would never be any more people in any class or occupation than could live comfortably and worthily in that occupation. This would happen automatically because family builders do not have any more children than they can support worthily and train properly for the work of life.

But seeing that not all are family builders, there being many spawners, in whose interest shall our social policies and institutions be shaped? It would seem wiser to shape them in favor of those whose habits and purposes accord most closely with the permanent interests of the state, even though, in so doing, we sacrifice many of those whose purposes and habits are less in accord with these permanent interests.

This requires that one shall view the state in a larger aspect than is commonly done. One must view it as something more than an aggregation of individuals, and feel that the interests of the state are something more than an arithmetical average of the interests of all its individuals. It is more to the interest of the state to cherish the individual who in turn contributes largely to the growth of the state than it is to cherish him who in turn contributes little. The state is also a permanent entity, and must regard the interests of future generations as of equal importance with those of the present. Since future generations do not vote, the most democratic state conceivable is necessarily controlled by a very small minority of those whose interests it must conserve. The interests of this great non-voting majority are safe in the hands of the present generation only when this generation is dominated by family builders with a vital interest in posterity.

Just what is meant by the state in its larger and more permanent aspects may be made clear, perhaps, by personifying it. Let us imagine the Great State to have a mind and a will of its own. Though its body is made up of people, as the individual body is made up of members, organs, and tissues, yet let us imagine that the Great State is something more than an aggregation of members, organs, and tissues, it is a personality. As such a personality, it could scarcely regard one organ or bit of tissue as of equal importance with every other. In fact, it might find itself with a surplus of adipose tissue and therefore compelled, in the interest of its own health, to reduce that surplus. But if the body were democratically ruled with a view to the interests of individual tissues, or if the interests of the whole were regarded merely as an arithmetical average of those of all the parts, this might be difficult to do.   In fact, in an extreme case of corpulency, the adipose elements might outvote all the rest and refuse to be reduced in number.   It would be useless to argue with them that unless they voted their own destruction the life of the whole body would be destroyed.   They might well ask, what good is the life of the body to us after we are destroyed ?

But without going to the extreme of considering abnormal tissues, the wise person will exercise some preference for the normal and useful portions of the body.   Those organs, like the brain and the heart, or even the eye and the ear, upon which the life or welfare of the whole body depends, will be given more care and consideration than some of the others which, though perfectly good and normal, are not so indispensable to the whole organism.   Yet if it came to a question of " rights," the thumb or the big toe could argue as stridently and perhaps as plausibly, as the eye or the ear.   The exaggerated notion of individual rights is, of course, inconsistent with this conception of the Great State.

Again, a careful farmer will exercise some preference for certain plants in his field, or certain animals in his flock, as compared with others.   If we may conceive of the State as a husbandman, cultivating its people as a farmer cultivates plants and animals, we shall come very near a correct conception.   Those people are to be cherished who are in turn capable of contributing most largely to the growth and welfare of the state, and consequently, of other people.   A state made up of persons each of whom was exceedingly capable of contributing to the welfare of others, would, of course, be very much stronger and better in every way, than a state made up of persons each of whom had little capacity in this direction.   By favoring those of the former type, even to the disadvantage of those of the latter type, the state may strengthen itself and eventually possess an exceedingly capable and prosperous people.   A group of people, each of whom is contributing largely to the prosperity of the whole, must necessarily become a very prosperous group.   The group, that is, the state, should therefore aim to cultivate people of this type.

This, however, would look unfair from the standpoint of our present conception of democracy.   It means giving advantages to the capable rather than to the incapable.   It means the arranging of handicaps so as to give the stronger rather than the weaker runners an outward advantage, a start, in the race.   This violates all our present sentiments of justice and fair play.   But that is exactly what the farmer does.   The strongest plants and animals are the ones which he tends with most care and nourishes most abundantly. The reason we do not think it fair or just for the state to do likewise is because we have never learned to think in terms of the state as an entity, or of society as an entity, having an interest of its own which transcends the interests of individuals.   We have learned to think rather in terms of individual rights.   If we thought in terms of the individual rights of the members of the farmer's herd we should demand that he do the precise opposite of what he does.   The weak bull has, from this point of view, apparently as much " right " to procreate as the strong and vigorous; but not from the point of view of one who is interested in maintaining and improving the quality of the herd, that is, not from the point of view of the herd itself.   Thinking in terms of the individual animal leads to one conclusion: thinking in terms of the herd, or group, leads to another.

The reason we are more inclined to think in terms of the individual than of the herd is probably because individuals are present and able to push their claims.   The weak bull is on hand to demand his rights or appeal for sympathy.   The thousands of generations that are yet unborn have no spokesman.   Here as elsewhere, our sympathy is short-sighted.   Just as the shameless beggar who presents him-self personally before us, exhibiting apparent misery, and exercising his arts of persuasion, gets our sympathy and our help, and causes us to forget much greater misery which is borne in silence all around us, so the individuals of the pres-ent generation who can in person present their claims and exercise their arts of persuasion, cause us to forget the vastly greater claims of future generations who are yet silent and unfranchised.   Justice is only sympathy with a long look. It aims to do the greatest kindness to all concerned, but realizes that an individual a thousand generations in the future is as much concerned, and entitled to as much con-sideration as an individual who is present and voting.

At this point, it is interesting to note one of the great economic paradoxes.   They who call themselves socialists, and who might therefore be supposed to look at things from the standpoint of the group or the state, are the very people who are least inclined to do anything of the kind.   To them the group or the state is only an agency through which in-dividual rights and advantages are to be obtained.   The kind of reasoning which necessarily follows from the con-ception of the group as an entity, having interests more per-manent and greater than those of individuals, is peculiarly abhorrent to them.   Such an idea as that the advantage should be given to the strong rather than the weak, in order that the herd, group, or state, may become eventually a herd, group, or state of strong members, is diametrically op-posed to all their ideals and ways of thinking.

In what may, from a certain point of view, be called normal conditions, that is, in conditions of severe competition, requiring hard and efficient work for survival, the most effective way of giving an advantage to the stronger families, in order that they may expand and flourish, is the legal right of inheritance.   By virtue of this legal right, each family is permitted to hold, generation after generation, any advantage gained.   Since normally the strongest and most economically useful individuals, that is, they who supply the greatest wants, will accumulate most rapidly, their families are permitted to hold this advantage and add to it if they are equally capable, and lose it if they are incapable. The net result is that, in the long run, where conditions are hard, the most capable are enabled to flourish, and to expand more rapidly than would be possible without inheritance.

Under such hard conditions as we have assumed, this furnishes an excellent reason in favor of the legal right of inheritance.   But under such prosperous conditions as we know at the present time, the argument is weakened.   Fortunes have become so large as to hinder in many cases rather than help, in the process of family building.   Such enormous fortunes as encourage idleness, vice and luxury tend to destroy rather than to expand the families which are so unfortunate as to possess them.   This situation argues undoubtedly in favor of a limitation upon the right of inheritance.   Leaving to the heirs as much as is amply necessary to conserve the family idea, and to enable the family, by careful management and efficient work, to expand without limit and without danger of want, the surplus should be taken by the state.   This is as much in the interest of the heirs as of anyone else.   The best method of accomplishing this is by a heavily graduated inheritance tax, leaving untaxed a moderate fortune going to an individual heir, but taxing the excess more and more heavily as it increases in amount, making the tax much heavier in the case of the larger fortunes than anything yet devised.

This plan will also satisfy the argument that the right of inheritance is necessary in order to encourage the accumulation of capital.   The desire to safeguard one's offspring, and provide for the prosperity and happiness of one's family after one is gone, is unquestionably one of the strongest motives to accumulation, and the accumulation of capital is unquestionably desirable in the interest of the expansion of industry and the increased demand for labor.   As much in the way of inheritance as is necessary to safeguard one's offspring and provide for the genuine prosperity of one's family ought therefore to be untaxed.   But after one's accumulation has increased beyond that which is necessary for these purposes, the motive to further accumulation changes.   One then engages in business enterprises because of a love of action and a love of power.   Accumulated capital becomes then one of the instruments of the game.   So long as the player is left in possession of this instrument while he is one of the players, he is not likely to be discouraged from accumulation merely by the fact that the state rather than his heirs get it after he is through with it. This surplus accumulation serves his purpose exactly as well if it passes to the state in an inheritance tax as it does if it passes to some of his heirs, especially if he is wise enough to see that such an inordinate fortune would injure rather than benefit his heirs.

CHAPTER XIII

THE QUESTION OF MONOPOLY

The Devil is never very far away from those who are responsible to none but God for their actions. — GUSTAVUS ADOLPHUS.

MONOPOLY is very old, but the form of monopoly which now agitates the public mind is an outgrowth of the joint stock corporation which has become the dominant form of business organization. We must therefore begin with a brief examination of the corporation problem. A business corporation is a special form of organization by means of which a number of individuals combine their capital for the purpose of carrying on a business enterprise jointly. The ordinary corporation differs from the ordinary partnership in five main particulars. (1) The partners in a firm have control over the business, but the stockholders in a corporation delegate their authority to a board of directors who have full control. (2) The partners in a firm are individually responsible for all the debts of the firm, but the stockholders of a corporation are, unless otherwise provided by statute, liable only to the amount of their stock. (3) A partner in a firm cannot sell his interest to another and thus introduce a new member into the firm without the consent of the other partners, but the stockholder of a corporation may transfer all or a part of his stock to any one without asking the consent of the other shareholders, in which case the new stockholders have all the rights of the old. (4) The corporation is treated, under a fiction of the law, as a person separate and apart from its stockholders, and may sue or be sued by any of them. (5) The corporation dies no natural death and is not affected by the death of any or all of its stockholders, whoever receives a share of the stock by gift, devise or inheritance being a member of the corporation as a matter of course.

The advantages of this form of organization are so great, from the standpoint of the participants, as to have made it the dominant factor in our business and industrial life. In the first place, it makes possible the organization of larger aggregations of capital than would be possible under any other form. A partnership, where each member is responsible for the acts of the whole, is possible only among mutual acquaintances, each of whom is confident of the honesty and solvency of every other. Except in a few cases this would make it impossible to gather together under one management such vast aggregations of capital as are necessary to carry on some of our modern business enterprises such as railways, steamship lines, mines, and factories. But since there is no need for such mutual acquaintance among the shareholders of a corporation, capital can be drawn from a larger field and a larger number of sources, and a larger quantity can be brought together than is possible under the partnership. In the second place, the perpetual character of the corporation enables it to carry out enterprises which require a long period of time for their maturity, undisturbed and unaffected by such circumstances as the death of its members. In the third place, it enables men of small means to share the benefits of large scale business which would otherwise go exclusively to men of large means.

The last named advantage, however, is realized only where there is a high sense of business honesty on the part of the membership generally, and where there is an honest and efficient government to interpret and administer the laws. For, with all its possible advantages, this form of business organization is peculiarly subject to abuses. In the first place, the officers of a large corporation are in a position similar, in one respect, to that of the officers of government, viz., they are handling other people's money. Whether in business or politics, this is a standing temptation to extravagance and corruption, and it is, today, a question whether it leads to more extravagance and corruption in politics than it does in business. It is fundamentally just as dishonorable for the officers of a corporation to vote themselves immense salaries, to be paid out of the dividends due to shareholders, as it would be for the officers of government to vote themselves similar salaries to be paid out of the taxes of the people. It would be universally condemned if the officers of a city or state should vote themselves salaries of fifty thousand or seventy-five thousand dollars. It is a sign of a distinctly low standard of business honesty that such things are tolerated in the field of corporation management. Again, the system of corporation management under which the voting is done by shares makes it possible for a small clique to get control of a majority of the shares and vote themselves into office, and vote themselves also such salaries and other privileges as they choose. These other privileges are numerous and varied. One of the commonest and most vulgar forms of corruption has been for the inside clique to form another corporation to furnish supplies to the original corporation at prices determined by themselves, thus enriching themselves at the expense of the other shareholders. In politics this would probably land the perpetrators in prison, but the officers of a corporation do not commonly go to prison for defrauding in this way the people whose money they handle.

As a remedy for this evil it is sometimes suggested that the plan of giving every shareholder one vote, whether he owns many shares or only one, be substituted for the plan of giving each share a vote. This would, of course, prevent a small number of men from controlling the corporation by the simple device of getting control of a majority of the shares. It opens up, however, other possibilities which are quite as dangerous as those which it prevents. It makes it possible for a majority of small shareholders to exploit in their own interest the larger wealth of the larger shareholders. This is a standing temptation which human nature has never been able to resist, and the result is that men with large means will not go into such a corporation. Its operations are, therefore, limited to small affairs where large quantities of capital are not needed.

This form of corruption is not changed in principle, when, instead of forming a new corporation to do business with the old, a similar basis of reciprocity is established between several large corporations whereby one serves the other — to the advantage of the few who happen to have stock in all of them. The machinery by which this kind of fraud is perpetrated is the " interlocking directorate," that is, an arrangement where several different corporations, supposed to be independent of, and competing with, one another, have the same men on their several boards of directors. While each of this group of corporations is, in the eyes of the law, a separate *fictitious* person, they all constitute, in the light of human intelligence, only one real person. Since they are all ruled by the same group of flesh and blood persons, they have only one set of real interests and purposes. One of the common varieties of this species of legal creation is the union of a business enterprise with a bank. A group of gentlemen interested in promoting certain business enterprises, and desiring to gain some advantage over their competitors in the same field, also form a banking corporation. Through the bank they invite deposits, thus getting other people's money to invest. The industrial corporations which they are promoting furnish them an opportunity for investing the money thus received. Having thus secured money to start the industrial corporation and having bought their own stock with it, the public is then invited to buy the stock of these corporations which are now going concerns. The stock is then sold to the public at a profit to the gentlemen who are operating the brilliant scheme.

In the second place, the impersonal character of the corporation tends to destroy any feeling of responsibility, on the part of shareholders and officers alike, for the acts of the corporation. This is always and everywhere a dangerous moral situation. The difference between a moral being and a monster is precisely this: the moral being feels a sense of responsibility, but the monster feels none. The combination of great power with a lack of responsibility has produced the worst crimes of history. The enormous power which goes with the mere size of the corporation, combined with the lack of responsibility which members feel for its acts, makes the corporation a monster which needs the most careful and rigid control. This control may come in three ways. (1) It may come through an aroused moral sense on the part of the shareholders of the corporation itself, which will lead them to take to themselves the responsibility for the deeds performed by the corporation of which they are a voting part. (2) It may come through an enlightened and discriminating public conscience which will not stop with a general condemnation of corporations as such, but will look beyond the corporation and blight with social disgrace and obloquy the individual members of a corporation which does dishonorable deeds, and reward with honor and esteem the individual members of a corporation whose deeds are honorable. (3) It may come through an efficient and discriminating interpretation and administration of law, which will visit individual punishment upon the particular persons who are responsible for corporate misdeeds, instead of fining the corporation as such.

That the irresponsibility of the corporate form of organization is an important factor in the problem of control is generally admitted.   Every boy with the instincts of a gentleman must have realized on more than one occasion the disadvantage of dealing with boys lacking those instincts. The boy who has no such instincts, who does not feel any responsibility for his conduct, or who does not care what he does or says, has certain well-known advantages in certain forms of contest, though not in all, over the boy who will not stoop to certain things.   That being the case, there are certain forms of contest which self-respecting boys will avoid, and leave in complete possession of the rowdy element. Similarly in certain forms of business competition, though not in all, the competitor who has scruples as to what he does is at a disadvantage as compared with those who have no scruples or sense of responsibility.   That being the case, the self-respecting and responsible competitors tend to avoid those forms of business competition and leave them in complete possession of the unscrupulous and the irresponsible. This is one of the reasons, in addition to certain real economic advantages of the corporate form of business enumerated above, why corporations are displacing private business men and partnerships, even in those lines of enterprise where immense aggregations of capital are not required.

It is sometimes asserted that the mere size of a corporation should not affect its standing before the law, or its rights and obligations.   In the sense in which this assertion is probably intended, it is correct; but if it is intended to imply that a corporation requires no more legal control when it is large than when it is small, it is untrue.   The larger the corporation, the greater is its power, either for good or evil, and that makes it especially important that its power be under control.

A decade or so ago the social psychologists were engaged with the problem of the mob mind.   Before the analysis was carried very far, it was discovered that the mob mind did not present any special mystery as distinct from the individual mind.   The mob thinks and acts precisely as any of its individuals would think or act were his power greatly increased and his sense of responsibility greatly diminished. That is precisely what the presence of numbers does for the individual when they are all moved by a common impulse; it gives him a sense of power proportionate to the numbers and, at the same time, the very fact of numbers diminishes his own sense of responsibility.   That is why the mob is so like a monster, for the difference between a man and a monster is precisely that the monster feels a sense of power and does not feel a sense of responsibility.

Something of the same kind exists in the case of an industrial corporation.   There also you have the circumstance of increased power combined with diminished responsibility. The sense of power comes, not so much from the presence of numbers as it does in the case of the mob, as from the larger fund of competitive capital which is brought together.   The diminished sense of responsibility comes partly from the mere fact of numbers, no individual of which feels the full responsibility for the acts of the whole, partly from the impersonal character of the conduct of the corporation, and partly from the limited liability feature of most of the char-

ters. Most of the evils of corporation practice grow out of
this simple situation and the remedy must be applied at this
point. The sense of responsibility must be made commensurate with the sense of power.

This is to be accomplished, not by reducing the power of
corporations so much as by increasing the sense of responsibility of the individual members. If they can be made to
feel the same responsibility for the acts of the corporation
which they feel for their individual acts, the corporation
problem as such, will be solved, and it will be solved in no
other way. This means the frank adoption of Governor
Harmon's maxim that crime is always personal, and that
corporate law-breaking is to be dealt with in precisely the
same way as individual law-breaking.

In fact, it may be necessary to go even further and enforce stricter responsibility upon members of corporations,
particularly the larger corporations, than we do even upon
individuals. If the principle we have laid down be sound,
it furnishes no support to the view that the mere bigness of
a corporation is not a matter for the law to take into account. From our point of view, bigness is an important
factor in the problem, for the bigger the corporation the
greater its power and the less the sense of responsibility on
the part of each member. That situation alone calls for
more and more strict regulation and enforcement of responsibility the bigger the corporation becomes. Its increased
power is a good thing provided that power be used productively and not acquisitively, but there is no certainty that it
will be used productively unless subjected to the strictest
control. This does not mean that large corporations have
worse dispositions than small, nor that their members are
meaner men than the members of small corporations. It

only means that the disproportion between power and responsibility increases with the size of the corporation.

If I may use a homely illustration, I will take the common house cat, whose diminutive size makes her a safe inmate of our household in spite of her playful disposition and her liking for animal food. If, without the slightest change of character or disposition, she were suddenly enlarged to the dimensions of a tiger, we should at least want her to be muzzled and to have her claws trimmed, whereas if she were to assume the dimensions of a mastodon, I doubt if any of us would want to live in the same house with her. And it would be useless to argue that her nature had not changed, that she was just as amiable as ever, and no more carnivorous than she always had been. Nor would it convince us to be told that her productivity had greatly increased and that she could now catch more mice in a minute than she formerly could in a week. We should be afraid lest, in a playful mood, she might set a paw upon us, to the detriment of our epidermis, or that in her large-scale mouse-catching she might not always discriminate between us and mice.

There is another problem, not strictly a corporation problem, but a social problem growing out of the prevalence of the corporate form of industrial organization. That is the problem of the widening gap between employers and employed, or, more strictly, between capitalists and laborers. It may be laid down as a general social law that anything which separates people into sharply distinguishable groups, whether it be a geographical boundary, a racial difference, religious creeds, or a class distinction, will produce between the groups thus separated, first, ignorance of one another, then suspicion growing out of that ignorance, then misunderstanding growing out of that ignorance and suspicion, and finally open warfare whenever a pretext is found; whereas anything which bridges over these gaps, or brings people together regularly and normally, creates, first, knowledge of one another, then confidence instead of suspicion, then understanding instead of misunderstanding, and finally, lasting peace because no difficulty seems large enough to serve as a pretext for war.

Now the joint stock form of organization, though a most effective industrial device, has produced at least one serious social result. It has widened somewhat the gap which would otherwise have existed between the employing group and the employed group. When employers are known by their personality, and can come in some kind of personal or direct contact with employees, and when, therefore, employer and employee know something about one another, there can be no such degree of ignorance of one another as now exists. And where ignorance disappears, suspicion tends to disappear also; but when employers stand as the shareholders of a corporation in a purely impersonal relation to employees, when the average employer or shareholder knows nothing personal about the employees of the corporation, and also the employees know absolutely nothing personal about the shareholding employers, there is about as great a degree of ignorance on either side of the line of those on the other as can be found anywhere in modern social life.

The gap which separates the two groups is made so wide as to produce very much the same result as is produced by a difference of color between races, or a difference of religion between too widely contrasted religious groups. Such a state of things never failed in the history of the world to produce suspicion, jealousy, misunderstanding, and on the slightest pretext, open hostility; and so far as we are able to see into the future, there is not the slightest ground for hoping that such a condition will ever fail to produce these same undesirable results. In other words, we need not hope for social peace, or for any cessation of the conflict of classes until that chasm is in some way bridged over or made to disappear.

This result can hardly be achieved by doing away with joint stock corporations. They are too effective as industrial devices to make such a program tolerable, but if we are ever to have anything resembling social peace, some way must be found to bring employing classes and the employed into personal relationships one with another. The ideal is undoubtedly that of having the workers in our industrial establishments become also the owners of the stock of the corporation. If that result could possibly be achieved, there would be an end of the present phase of warfare.

How this is to be achieved is another question. It will never be achieved until our corporation laws and our judicial procedure relating to corporations are made efficient enough to make it a safe venture for a man of small means to buy a share in an industrial corporation. So long as these things are so inefficient as to enable large shareholders and rings to freeze out the small shareholders, or in any way to make it hazardous for a man of small means, such as the average working man, to invest in a share, it will never be accomplished. This looks like a legal problem rather than a legislative problem, and it is for the legal fraternity and the courts to solve. If they will not solve it, or if they ultimately prove incapable of solving it, it may be necessary to reform our courts. Many discriminating persons are beginning to believe that the judicial branch of our government, instead of being the most efficient branch, is less efficient even than the legislative or the executive branches. Its inefficiency is measured by its inability to grasp the underlying economic facts of the social system with which it is dealing.

As to those extreme developments of the corporation principle commonly called trusts, it is becoming more and more apparent that their power for evil lies wholly in their power of controlling and manipulating prices. If that power could be taken out of their hands we should then have nothing to fear from them.

If they could not succeed and survive in competition through their power over prices they could then succeed only through their power of production. If they should then survive, the mere fact of their survival would prove their fitness to survive. This has been pointed out many times by scholars; but the self-styled practical men, and politicians with their unerring instinct for the wrong way, have ignored it and have been trying various hard and useless methods of dealing with the problem. Eventually, after having tried every possible way of going wrong, we shall apply the simple and direct remedy of governmental control of prices wherever a monopoly exists.

I do not wish to indulge in any sentimental nonsense about the people and their control over affairs of this kind. The people never did, do not now, and never will control these things or anything else connected with the government. These and all other governmental affairs are controlled by politicians, and politicians are no more interested in the people than the trust magnates themselves. But the choice is a hard one. Where competition fails to regulate prices, these prices are going to be fixed arbitrarily by some one. In the absence of governmental control they are fixed by the trust operators alone. Where there is governmental control, they are fixed by the joint action of politicians and the trust operators. Their interests are not the same, and as the result of their pulling and hauling, prices will not be fixed quite so exclusively in the interest of the trusts, but more in the interest of both the trusts and the politicians. Since the people can control trusts after a fashion by refusing to buy of them, and politicians after a fashion by refusing to vote for them, it will happen that through this double control the interests of the people will be somewhat better safeguarded than now.

Incidentally, this would destroy most of the trusts. No trust exists by virtue of its superior productive power. Every one depends for its existence upon its superiority in buying or selling, that is upon its power over prices. Take away this power and enable the outside concerns to match their productivity against that of the trust, and outside competition will increase, and force the trust to break up into its most efficient *productive* units, as distinguished from the most efficient *bargaining* units.

A great deal is written and said, nowadays, about the monopolistic character of corporations, but they are not necessarily monopolistic. Fundamentally there are only two kinds of monopoly — monopoly of privilege and monopoly of knowledge. Monopolies of privilege are the creatures of government, and when they abuse their privileges it is an invariable sign of a corrupt or an inefficient government. Trusts, for example, never have existed, and do not now exist where government is honest and efficient. Monopolies of knowledge are the result of the general ignorance of the mass of the people. Where only a few men know how to do a thing which needs to be done, they have as complete a monopoly as though they had been granted a special privilege by the government. The cure for this kind of monopoly is widespread knowledge. Such monopolies as corporations possess, which are not due to the weakness or corruption of government, are due to the fact that our people do not generally understand how corporations are organized and managed, or how their business is done. So long as corporation law, and corporation finance, corporation management, and corporation accounts are all impenetrable mysteries to the mass of the people, the few who are initiated have as complete a monopoly as the priests of a heathen cult ever had. A widespread and thorough knowledge of these subjects is the obvious cure for the evils of this kind of monopoly. In this case knowledge is not only power, but it is a power which makes for righteousness. More important even than a knowledge of accounts is a knowledge of the processes of buying and selling, of devices and machinations by means of which the few who are initiated can control the market. Of this, more later.

The perpetual character of corporations creates another problem, which has not yet become acute, but which may sometime give us trouble. Such a corporation is like the grave in that it never gives up anything. While individuals must die and pass from the scene, corporations may remain in possession of the situation. This creates the possibility that every form of business enterprise may eventually pass into the hands of a corporation, and the individual have no opportunity whatever in business except by becoming a shareholder in a corporation. To be sure, such opportunities will always be open, even to men who have not inherited shares, and therefore such a situation would not be intolerable. It would leave vastly more room for individual enterprise and for the reward of the economic virtues and the penalizing of the economic vices than any form of collectivism. Moreover, our greatest industries and those which are most fundamental to our well-being, the various agricultural industries, have shown as yet no tendency to pass into the hands of corporations. So far, therefore, as we can now see into the future, the world will remain predominantly and fundamentally individualistic, even though all the large urban industries should pass permanently into the corporation stage.

One danger from the perpetual nature of corporations lies where we least expect it. Our various endowed educational and charitable institutions are, like the daughters of the horse leech, crying, " Give, give." These institutions are perpetual and what they receive they never give up. A few centuries of such rapid accumulation of endowments as the last half-century has witnessed may leave these various institutions in possession of a large share of the invested capital of the country. When the country is fully developed, and the opportunities for new investment are nearing exhaustion, this situation will cause agitation and a possible revolution similar to that which dispossessed the mediaeval monasteries of their lands. In many ways the present situation resembles that. Together with the fact that the monasteries had been accumulating endowments for centuries there was the feeling on the part of the public that they were no longer serving a useful purpose, or justifying their possession of so much valuable land. It remains for these modern institutions which are accumulating endowments even more rapidly than did the monasteries, to see to it that the public secures a genuine service commensurate with the vastness of the accumulations they are allowed to enjoy.

A score of years ago it was confidently predicted, in certain circles, that the day of the small business unit was at an end. We were declared to be at the threshold of an era of vast concentration in industry. These predictions have not been realized and people should now be willing to listen to reason. There never was, and there is not now, any reason to expect great concentration except where bargaining is a more important factor than productivity in the success of a business enterprise. Wherever productivity is the more important factor there tends to be diffusion, except in a few cases of natural monopoly.

The reason for the movement a generation ago, toward the extreme concentration of business organization, was the fact that, in the business strategy of that day, bargaining was, in many fields, more important than productive efficiency. When an association of steel manufacturers could form a great selling organization and, through that organization, outsell or underbuy its competitors, the latter could be driven out of business in spite of their superior productivity.

The question of monopoly is largely a question of trading or bargaining where it is not based on a government grant or a limited natural resource, such as mineral deposits. Here all modern governments in all their branches are weak and inefficient, and our own government is probably more weak and inefficient, in this respect, than that of any other civilized people. One reason for this is that economics is not considered an essential part of the education of our lawyers or even our judges, who must be relied upon to apply in detail the laws of the land. Back of this, perhaps, is the fact that economics is an occult science to most of our legislators and executives. If consistent and intelligent efforts are made to equalize bargaining power, the question of monopoly will take care of itself. In fact, monopoly would disappear except where it is based upon some physical factor, like a limited natural resource or a right of way. If, however, it expects to succeed through unfair bargaining, this would prove an effective check. As a matter of fact, no new trust would be formed under these conditions, and those now in existence would soon disappear.

The question as to what constitutes a monopoly may not, in every case, be easily decided. But because a thing is hard to do is no reason for not doing it. In general terms, a monopoly may be said to exist whenever and wherever there is an organization which can, in any degree, set its own prices. This can be done, of course, only through the control of supply or of demand. It would probably be necessary, in legislation, to adopt a fixed and arbitrary rule to the effect that a monopoly exists whenever one organization controls say fifty per cent of the total supply sold within a prescribed area, or when it buys fifty per cent of the supply produced within a prescribed area. Such a rule would still leave room for minor abuses, but would correct the larger ones and re-establish the reign of small or moderate sized industrial units, that is, units of such a size as to give the maximum economy in production. We should then have real competition in production, which always works well, even though competitive bargaining sometimes has its disadvantages, while competitive consumption always works badly.

In that class of cases which are commonly known as common carriers, the state has usually reserved the right to fix rates. There is not the slightest reason for this rule which does not apply equally well to any other monopoly of a necessity of life. A very little examination will convince one that it is not because they are common carriers that the state has a moral right to regulate prices, but because, without such regulation, common carriers have an extraordinary bargaining power, that is, a power to exact unfair prices. Wherever the same power exists the state has the same right and obligation to regulate prices, whether the subject of regulation be known as a common carrier or by some other name.

Instead of trying to force the dissolution of those business organizations commonly known as trusts, the more intelligent method would be to permit any and every sort of combination; but to require them to submit to public price regulation. This will give them every possible opportunity to introduce their assumed economies of production. If they really believe in these economies, price regulation need not deter them.

Earlier in this chapter reference was made to the distinction between productive power and bargaining power. This distinction, though clear as daylight, is not perceived by many of those who discuss the trust problem. Most of the supposed economies of the trust, as compared with the smaller competitive unit, are found, upon analysis, to resolve themselves into advantages in bargaining. A huge organization which can dominate the market, or control the sources of raw material, may be able to secure its raw materials on more favorable terms than a smaller organization. This is bargaining power and not productive power. It may be able to secure better transportation rates from the railroads. This likewise is bargaining and not productive power. It may be able to control its labor supply. Again, this is bargaining and not productive power. It may be able to maintain a bigger selling organization, and to sell its products where others cannot sell at all, or sell to a better advantage than others can. This likewise is bargaining and not productive power. Finally, it may be able to organize its own banking system and thus secure other people's capital for its own operations on more favorable terms than its smaller rivals can do. This, as in all the other cases, is bargaining and not productive power.

If we could put the trusts on the same basis with respect to bargaining as their smaller rivals, then we should have a real contest on the basis of productivity. If the trusts could hold out or gain ground under these conditions, it would be a demonstration of their productivity. If they should lose ground it would be a demonstration of their inferior productivity. A willingness on the part of trust magnates to submit to this kind of a test would indicate that they really believed in the superior productivity of their organizations and were not lying when they talked about the superior economies of the trust form of organization. If they were unwilling to submit to such a test it would indicate that they did not themselves believe what they were saying when they prate about their productivity. As a matter of fact, if we leave out of account the whole bargaining process, and confine our attention strictly to the question of productivity, there are no peculiar economies in the trust form of organization which are not more than compensated by superior economies peculiar to the smaller organization.

It is important to remember that, from the national point of view, productive power and not bargaining power is of value. What one gains by superior bargaining in domestic trade is always at the expense of some one else, and the nation as a whole gains nothing. In international trade, where the superior bargainer is a citizen and the inferior bargainer a foreigner, there may sometimes accrue some gain to the nation as a whole, but not, of course, to the world as a whole. But what one gains by superior productive power is not at the expense of the other members of the group. It results in a definite addition to the national wealth. The nation as a whole, therefore, promotes its own strength and prosperity by developing superior productive units rather than superior bargaining units in its industries.

Many large classes of citizens, however, lose sight of this important fact, seeing only the advantage that comes to themselves. A certain large department store, for example, is an excellent place at which to buy certain classes of goods. That is as far as the purchasers see. They do not see that, in order to offer these bargains, the store, by reason of its size, is able to bulldoze producers and wholesalers into giving it lower prices on its own purchases, or that it makes use of a large quantity of very cheap help, — young girls, for example, who are supported at home and are willing to work for pin money. Not seeing these and other similar facts, the mass of purchasers are easily persuaded into believing that the department store is a superior economic unit, whereas in reality, from a national point of view, it is an inferior unit.

The wisest and soundest economic movement now afoot is that known as the rural organization movement, or the coöperative movement among farmers. This movement is not toward coöperative farming, it will be observed, but toward coöperation among farmers. By coöperative farming is meant a system where the work of farm production, the growing of crops and livestock, is carried on coöperatively on a large scale. By coöperation among farmers is meant a system under which the work of production is carried on, as now, on individual farms, but under which certain other activities are carried on by coöperative effort among individual farmers. The field wherein this coöperative effort proves to be economical is mainly where bargaining is the dominant factor in success. In production, the small or moderate sized individual farm has proved itself superior to all others. In bargaining it is weak. Coöperative action for the purchase of farm supplies, for the marketing of farm products, for securing farm credit, for insuring farm property, is therefore needed by the farming class. This furnishes the large field for voluntary coöperation.

Certain other problems such as the combating of pests, the eradication of disease, etc., also call for coöperation, but, in the end, these things will be taken over by the police power of the state, and thus taken out of the field of voluntary coöperation.

The peculiar merit of this movement for coöperation among farmers is that it preserves the most efficient unit of production, the small farm, and establishes a superior bargaining unit, which to be efficient, must be large. So long as this coöperative movement confines itself to this kind of work it deserves to succeed because it is following sound economic lines. When it departs from these lines and undertakes to establish, through coöperation, large productive units, it will deserve to fail because these large productive units are less efficient.

Sometimes, however, in the case of an agricultural specialty, which is always difficult to market, the large unit may succeed for a time. If so, it will be for the reason that the question of efficiency in buying and selling is more important than that of efficiency in production. Its superiority as a selling unit may for a time more than compensate for the inferiority as a producing unit. A small farm, though it could produce more economically, might not be able to sell its product to advantage. (We are still talking about agricultural specialities which are hard to sell.) But if a large number of small farmers, with their superior productive power, should coöperate in buying and selling, thus establishing a bargaining unit equal to that of the big farm, they could eventually drive the big farm from the field of competition.

It may be asked, of what advantage is it to the nation that the farmers should thus increase their bargaining power ? Does not some one else lose in proportion as they gain ?

That is undeniably true. If it were a question of the farmers' taking an unfair advantage of other people, particularly the consumers, this coöperative movement would have nothing to commend it. But if, on the other hand, the farmers as well as the consumers have suffered a positive disadvantage because, while they bargain in small units, they have had to deal with others who are so organized as to bargain in large units, it puts a different aspect on the case. An organization which will put them on an equal footing in the bargaining process with those with whom they must deal, only equalizes things and prevents exploitation.

Again the successful marketing of farm products is not primarily a matter of shrewd bargaining or higgling of the market, by which one bargainer gains an advantage at the expense of the other. It is primarily a matter of an intelligent distribution of products among the various consuming centers. To have one consuming center flooded with a product while another is suffering from a dearth, is bad economy from the national as from the individual point of view. So long as a vast multitude of small producers are shipping their products indiscriminately, without any system or plan, it will frequently happen that one market will be glutted while in another there is a dearth of the product in question. This is bad national economy and also unprofitable to the shippers. It is bad national economy because it is always a waste for one group of people to have more than they need while others have less than they need. It is a loss to the producers because they are forced to take a low price in the glutted market when they might be getting a higher price if a part of the product could have been diverted to the undersupplied market. Marketing under a well-considered plan or with full information as to the conditions in the various markets will permit the producers to secure the maximum profit without any attempt to control prices or restrict production. Even a group of small farmers, however meritorious they might be in other respects, would be guilty of a social wrong, and, therefore, deserve punishment if they undertook to restrict production or control prices in any artificial way.

The proposal that the state should have a hand in the fixing of prices whenever and wherever a monopoly exists must apply, of course, not only to the price of what the monopoly has to sell, but what it has to buy as well; that is to say, it is just as clearly within the power of a monopoly to beat down the price of its raw material and thus rob the producer as it is to put up the price of its finished product and thus rob the consumer. Among its raw materials must be included the labor which it has to buy as well as material goods.

On the other hand, a caution must be thrown out at this point against any attempt on the part of the public to overreach itself in its efforts to punish a monopoly. Even a monopoly may be a producer, though the purpose for which a monopoly is organized is always a bartering rather than a producing purpose; that is to say, if production pure and simple were its aim, there would be no motive or inducement to the formation of a monopoly; but with production there is always the desire to buy and sell to a better advantage than can be done by the ordinary competitive concern. This desire to barter to advantage is the effective reason for changing from the competitive to a monopolistic basis. If state regulation of prices should go so far as to destroy the profits of production, it would stop production. Therefore, the principle according to which prices should be regulated is as follows: The price should be such as to induce the producer to continue his production. Anything more than that is unnecessary, it merely enriches the producer without increasing production. Anything less than that is injurious in that it will discourage production and cause it to diminish, thus depriving the public of the products.

Be it observed that this is really the principle of competitive price. Under competition, wherever it exists, there is or tends to be such a level of price as will just be sufficient to induce producers to continue producing as much as consumers are willing to buy at that price. This is what is called the equilibrium of demand and supply. If, under competitive conditions, the price should for some accidental reason be too low, purchasers would be demanding more than producers were willing to produce. If, on the other hand, the price should happen to be too high, producers would be stimulated to supply more than purchasers were willing to buy. Under free competition (which, by the way, does not often exist, though there are various approximations to it) this equilibrium of demand and supply produces the maximum economy in the expenditure of productive energy. Wherever this equilibrium is disturbed there is, or tends to be, a waste of human energy. This principle of competitive price, therefore, should be the guide to the state in attempting to fix monopoly prices. Prices, in other words, should be fixed authoritatively at that point which will produce an equilibrium of demand and supply, that is to say, a price at which consumers will be willing to purchase just as much as producers are willing to produce. If the price of a monopoly product is made too low, then consumers will be demanding more than anybody is willing to produce. If it is fixed at too high a point, producers will be willing to supply more than consumers are willing to purchase. In either case there is a waste of human energy.

The machinery by which this fixing of monopoly price shall be carried out is an administrative problem and not a problem in economic justice. Therefore it does not enter into the present discussion.

The essence of monopoly, however, is the suppression of production on the part of others, in order that the monopolistic producer may sell his products to better advantage. The monopolist is, therefore, both a producer and a preventer of production. Our efforts at correction of the monopolistic abuses should be directed against the repressive measures of the monopolist rather than against his own production.

All monopolistic enterprises are essentially like the following: A gentleman of the Far West was running a ferry boat across a certain river. This was a productive enterprise for the service of travellers. He also adopted the playful custom of using his Winchester on any one else who attempted to run a ferry boat across the same stream. That was repressive and intended to prevent the serving of the traveller. His purpose was to enable himself to collect a somewhat higher fee for his own service. Be it remembered that this service was a genuine one. Obviously, the proper method of dealing with this gentleman was the one which the citizens finally adopted. They paid him for the service of transporting travellers across the river: they hanged him for preventing others from performing the same service. This was rough and ready justice, but it was in strict conformity with our highest ideals of abstract Justice.

The same principles are involved in the more refined and complex cases of modern monopoly. The monopolist usually renders a genuine service for which he should be paid, but he also prevents others from rendering the same service. For this he should be punished.

CHAPTER XIV

THE CURE FOR POVERTY

POVERTY is as unnecessary as malaria or yellow fever. Let that be stated once and for all. But there is a right way and there are multitudes of wrong ways of trying to cure any of these maladies. Each method has its own violent partizans. He who opposes any of these methods is, from the standpoint of its advocates, a standpatter, an advocate of a *laissez faire* policy. We are all *laissez faire* economists on some points; there never was a *laissez faire* economist on all points. Even the socialist turns out to be a standpatter and a stickler for a *laissez faire* policy when it comes to a remedy for poverty which operates in accordance with what economists are accustomed to call economic law. The so-called orthodox economist believes that if the state would do a few right things it would then be unnecessary to do the thousand and one wrong or ineffective things now being advocated in behalf of " labor." With respect to the few right and necessary things, he is an advocate of state interference. With respect to the many wrong and ineffective things, he is an opponent of state interference.

Not only is poverty unnecessary, but we can have any degree of equality we want, if we are willing to pay the price and if we are willing to work in harmony with economic law rather than against it. Moreover, we can have this equality without attacking the competitive system, the institution of private capital, of freedom of contract, of freedom of initiative and enterprise, or any of the social institutions which have helped us thus far in our progress. We can have equality as between different occupations, and still leave every man to conduct his own business, every one to find his own employment, every farm, shop, store and factory to be run as private enterprises. This would be as much better than socialism as a living organism is better than a machine.

Many ardent reformers become exceedingly impatient when the economist begins to speak of economic law. Some of them even go so far as to declare that such economic laws as that of diminishing returns and the principle of population are mere inventions of the economist to postpone social reform. As well might the bacteriologist be accused of having invented the germ theory of disease in order to prevent the cure of human ailments. One result of the studies of the bacteriologist is to throw discredit upon certain favorite remedies, but at the same time they point the way to genuine remedies. So it is with the studies of the economist. Though there are many doctors who still antagonize the teachings of the bacteriologist and bio-chemist, there are even more who antagonize those of the economist.

After all is said that can be said about poverty, we come back in our saner moments to the question, why does the poor man's labor sell for so little ? Why does his service bring so low a price ? This is a question of value and price. Until we are willing to face this question, and reason it out as we would the question of the price of anything else, we shall never get very far. The question of the low price of the poor man's labor resolves itself into the two questions, why is the demand for his labor so small, and why is the supply so large ? When we are in a position to answer these two questions, we shall then, but not before, be able to suggest constructive remedies. That is, we can then begin to study how to make the demand greater and how to make the supply smaller. Working along this line, we can go as far in the direction of equality as we really care to, provided we are willing to work consistently, and accept the consequences of equality when they come. We shall also find that equality is quite consistent with the private ownership of capital, with the competitive system, with freedom of initiative, freedom of enterprise, etc.

The best way of increasing the demand for labor is to increase the supply of other things which have to be combined with it in production. If there were no bread on which to spread butter, there would be a much smaller demand for butter. With an abundant supply of cheap bread, we are willing to buy a good deal of butter to eat with it. Thus the increase in the *supply* of bread tends to increase the *demand* for butter. Vice versa, if there were no butter to spread on our bread we should doubtless find bread less appetizing and buy less of it, unless we could find some good substitute for butter. But with a good supply of cheap butter or its substitutes, we find bread satisfying, and buy a good deal of it.

This case of bread and butter is only one illustration of a general economic law with innumerable applications. Where two articles are substitutes for one another, and they compete with one another on the same market, an increase in the supply of one will decrease the demand for the other. They satisfy the same demand, and if one increases, the total demand is more nearly satisfied, and there is accordingly less demand for the other. But where one is not a substitute for the other, but where, on the other hand, one article does not satisfy a demand unless the other is joined with it, then they do not compete with each other. The increase in the supply of one increases the demand for the other.

Where two kinds of labor, say native and foreign, or white and black, do the same kind of work, they satisfy the same demand. One is a substitute for the other. Consequently the increase of one kind diminishes the demand for the other. But if they do not do the same kind of work, but different kinds which have to be combined in production, as hand labor and managerial labor, or as the labor of farmers and millers, or millers and bakers, then they are not substitutes for one another, they do not compete with one another, and an increase in the supply of one increases the demand for the other. It is obvious that the more farmers there are growing wheat the greater will be the demand for millers, somewhere, to grind that wheat, and the more farmers and millers there are, the greater will be the demand for bakers. That is to say, this case comes under the same law as bread and butter.

Not only is it necessary to unite different kinds of labor to produce a given article, it is also necessary to have land and tools to combine with labor in order to get the best results. With an abundant supply of good land, there is a large demand for labor to work the land. Reduce the available supply of land, and, other things equal, you reduce the demand for labor. The abundant supply of fertile land which we have had in this country has had more to do with our high wages than any other single factor.

One way of increasing the available supply of land is that pointed out in Chapter XI, namely, the forcing into use of the land which is now held out of use for speculative purposes. When land is held out of use for any purpose it is, temporarily at least, subtracted from the supply. For the time being it might as well be non-existent, so far as it affects production and the opportunities for labor. A tax on such land which would absorb all possible speculative profits would tend to force it into use. If it is put into use, men would have to be employed upon it. This in itself would increase the demand for labor.

This increase in the available supply of land, or in the quantity of land in actual use would, unless the labor supply increased correspondingly, increase the acreage for each laborer, tend somewhat toward extensive cultivation, and thus toward a larger product per man. It is this larger product per man upon which the average well-being of the whole population depends. There is a popular opinion to the contrary, that is, in favor of intensive rather than extensive cultivation. This opinion seems to be held as largely by the laboring people as by the employing classes, though it works to the disadvantage of the former and to the advantage of the latter. So persistent is this error that it seems necessary to examine it in some detail.

Mr. Henry A. Wallace,[1] writing in *Wallace's Farmer* for December 27, 1912, makes the following exceedingly pertinent observations regarding the comparative merits of Bavarian and Iowa farming. After calling attention to the larger yield of farms in Bavaria he says:

But when we consider that the Bavarian farmer puts at least five times as much human labor on each acre of farm land, is it surprising that he gets from one-fourth more to double the Iowa yields ? Really, he should get far larger yields if the man who works on the land is to get anywhere near as large returns as in Iowa. . . . To make a long story short, I figured the total number of therms of sun's energy imprisoned in Iowa by farmers with the corn, oats, wheat, barley, rye, potato, and hay crop, and also Bavaria. As a result, I found that for every man, woman, and child connected with farming in Iowa, 14,200 therms of sun's energy were imprisoned, while for every man, woman and child connected with farming in Bavaria, only 2,600 therms were stored up. In other words, the average Iowa farmer is

[1] From a paper read by the author before the American Economic Association, at the twenty-fifth Annual Meeting.

six times as successful in his efforts to capture the power of the sun's rays as the average Bavarian farmer.　On the other hand, the average acre of Iowa land is only about one-seventh as successful as the average acre of Bavarian land in supporting those who live upon it.　If we look on land as the unit, then the Bavarians get better results than we in Iowa; but if we look on human labor as the unit, then the Iowa farmers are far ahead of those in Bavaria.

Here is a clearly drawn issue.　Before we can determine which is the better system of agriculture, we must first decide whether we are to look on land or labor as the unit. Before we can decide this question we must distinguish between the interests of the individual farmer and those of the general public.

From the point of view of the individual farmer, the question as to what constitutes good farming depends entirely upon circumstances.　If he is farming where land is scarce and dear, while labor is abundant and cheap, wise management will require him to economize land rather than labor. If his land costs him a great deal, he will fail unless he can make every acre produce a great deal, whereas, if his labor costs him very little, he may succeed if each unit of labor produces only enough to cover its cost.　But if the conditions are diametrically opposite, — that is, if land is relatively cheap, but labor scarce and dear, — then he must be particularly careful to economize labor.　Since each unit of labor costs him a great deal he must see to it that each unit produces at least as much as it costs, otherwise he will fail; and, since each acre of land costs him very little, he may succeed even if each acre produces very little, always remembering, of course, that whether the acre produces much or little, each unit of labor *must* produce a great deal. Wise management will always require such an adjustment to circumstances as will economize most carefully the most expensive factors of production.

It happens that in Bavaria land is scarce and dear and labor cheap, at least according to American standards. During the greater part of the history of the United States, land has been abundant and cheap and labor scarce and dear, at least according to European standards. In these fundamental conditions we find a perfectly clear and satisfactory explanation of the facts recorded by Mr. Wallace. Now that both land and labor are becoming dear in the United States, the wise farm managers will try to increase their products per acre, but, if they are wise, they will not try to achieve this result in any way which will reduce the product per man. Labor is still so dear as to cause the speedy bankruptcy of any farmer who would try to increase his crop by the European or Asiatic method, or by putting five times as much labor into its cultivation as he now does. He must still hold rigidly to the use of all the labor-saving devices, but add to them such land-saving devices as he can find, such as underdrainage, commercial fertilizers, etc.

Some larger and deeper problems arise when we turn from the point of view of the individual farmer and assume that of the general public. Is it good that land should be scarce and dear and labor abundant and cheap, or is it better that land should be abundant and cheap and labor scarce and dear ? The latter is, without any question, better for the laborer. It is also better for the farmer who does his own work, for he is, to that extent, a laborer. If labor becomes abundant and cheap, the farmer who does his own work will get very little for his work, though the value of his land and its rent will be increased. When labor is abundant and cheap, either the price of farm crops will fall to the level of the lower cost of production, or else land will rise in value because of its sheer and absolute scarcity. In the former case the whole farming class will lose. In the latter, they who do the work will lose while they who own the land will gain. The farmer who is both a landowner and a laborer will lose in one way and gain in another. It may be a matter of indifference to him if his wages fall while his rent rises. But there are great social difficulties certain to arise under these conditions.

So long as labor is dear and land relatively cheap, the road is easy from the condition of farm laborer to that of farm owner. Wages being high, it is easy for the frugal and far-sighted farm hand to accumulate a fund of capital. Land being cheap, it does not take a very large fund with which to buy a farm. Under these conditions we shall never have an agricultural proletariat, nor a permanent class of farm laborers who can never be anything but farm laborers. But when labor is cheap and land dear, the road is steep and difficult from the condition of farm hand to that of farm owner. Wages being low, it is difficult for the laborer to accumulate capital. Land being high, it takes a great deal of capital to buy a farm. Few farm hands, under these conditions, will succeed in traveling this road successfully. We should then have an agricultural proletariat, — a permanent class of agricultural laborers most of whom can never hope to be anything else. This has never failed to happen in any country where labor is abundant and cheap while land is scarce and dear. We must make up our minds, and that right soon, whether we want this condition in the United States or not.

Under the law of diminishing returns, which may be regarded as one of the fundamental laws of economics, an adequate supply of land is necessary to a large product per man. Just what is an adequate supply of land will differ with the kinds of crops grown and the market for them. Where the market calls for small fruits and vegetables, and is willing to pay a high price for them, a small acreage per man may be enough. But where the market demands the coarser products of the farm, — hay, grain, livestock, and the coarser vegetables, — a larger acreage will be found necessary to the largest product per man.

But land is not the only thing which has to be combined with labor. Russia has an abundance of fertile land but lacks other things which are as important as land, and which also have to be combined with her enormous supply of unskilled labor in order to get the best results. She needs wise rulers to govern her laborers well. What is more important, she needs more business talent to direct that labor intelligently. If she could train up two business men where she now trains one, if her nobility could be made to feel that a business career is the most respectable because the most useful career, it would benefit the laboring classes enormously. It would have the same effect on the labor market that an increase in the supply of saltpetre would have on the charcoal market in a previous illustration. Or again, what she needs most of all is a supply of wise teachers to make over a large proportion of her unskilled labor into skilled labor, and a large portion of her skilled labor into business ability or employing talent, capable of conceiving new productive enterprises and carrying them out successfully. Again, an adequate supply of capital, that is, tools, provided there were enough skill to use them, and, which is quite as important, provided there were enough business talent to organize and direct them and the laborers in a productive manner, would add greatly to the well-being of the laborers.

But so long as labor is not the limiting factor, that is to say, so long as there are more laborers than can be satisfactorily combined with the limited quantity of something else which has to be combined with them, so long will laborers be at a disadvantage. When a few laborers could be spared with no loss to the total production, and when a little capital cannot be spared without considerable loss, so long will capital have the advantage in distribution. Create the opposite condition under which not a single laborer could be spared without a considerable loss, and a considerable fund of capital could be spared with little loss, and labor will have the advantage in distribution besides being in a position to dictate terms to capital. This is mainly a question of making capital so abundant that it ceases to be the limiting factor in production. The way to do this is to encourage saving and the accumulation of capital.

The first problem of reform in any system of distribution is to search for the limiting factor or factors. Find the factor which is so scarce, relatively to the opportunities for using it, that a little more or a little less will make a marked difference in the total production, and you will find the factor which is in a strong economic position, and commands a large share of the product. Find the factor which is so abundant, relatively to the opportunities for using it, that a little more or a little less will make very little difference in the total production and you will find the factor which is in a weak economic position and commands a small share of the total product. Whether the limiting factor be land, as in densely populated countries, capital as in countries where thrift has not developed, mechanical skill, as in countries where technical education has received little attention, or managing ability, as in countries where business education is difficult to acquire, and also where the business man is held in low esteem, the problem is essentially the same. The remedy is, of course, to increase the supply of the limiting factors. The remedy for a scarcity of the higher forms of skill and managing ability is, of course, vocational education.

The well-being and general economic situation of the laborer and the small farmer are so much alike, and depend upon such similar conditions, that a further consideration of this problem is desirable. The large industrial unit, where hundreds or thousands of men are organized and directed under one head, has so impressed itself upon the imagination of the world as to lead men generally to accept it as an economic necessity. Farming alone seems to be, as yet, unassailed by the big capitalistic unit. Perhaps we are too hasty in concluding that it has come to stay in manufacturing and merchandising. Some examination of the economic position of the small farmer may throw light on that question.

It is a common error to suppose that justice would eliminate poverty.[1] If by justice is meant merely that each individual should get exactly what he produces, or what he is worth, it is certain that poverty would not be eliminated, and might not even be materially diminished. If each one gets only what he produces, or what he is worth, and if he does not produce enough to live upon, or if he is not worth enough as a worker to earn a wage which will support him, he will still be poor. Before we can eliminate poverty, therefore, we must not only secure justice for each individual, but we must also see to it that each one is made worth enough, or productive enough to enable him to live comfortably upon his earnings.

Nor would this result come about automatically under a regime of strict justice. The bad distribution of human

[1] From a paper on *The Redistribution of Human Talent*, read by the author before a meeting of the Vocational Guidance Association, held in Cambridge, Mass., 1911.

talent would still exist unless measures were taken to redistribute it according to needs. By the bad distribution of human talent is meant something quite similar to what would exist if material commodities were badly distributed in proportion to the need for them. If there is more of one commodity in a certain place than is needed, and less of another, the one will have no price and no purchaser, while the other will have a high price and many purchasers for each unit. Or, if there is almost as much of the one as is needed, and much less of the other, the one will have a low price, and it will be difficult to find buyers enough, whereas the other will have a high price and buyers will have difficulty in getting enough of it.

This law is particularly effective when we consider factors which have to be combined in the production of a given article. In a dry country where there is an abundance of nitrogen, phosphorus and potash in the soil, but no water, there may be a great demand for agricultural products, but these elements of fertility will be of little value. The man who tried to sell commercial fertilizer in such a community would starve. But water, being the scarce factor, or the limiting factor, and everything depending upon it, will command a good price. The man who can supply such a community with water will have no difficulty in selling it. Moreover, this would be just. Fertilizer, in that situation, is unproductive in the only sense in which the word productive has any real place in economics. Ask the question, how much more grain could be grown on that land if there were more fertilizer, and you will get some idea of the value to such a community of the services of the fertilizer man. He might be getting all he was worth, and yet be poor, in spite of the fact that he might be a thoroughly good man and his fertilizer first class. But ask yourself the same question respecting water and you get an idea of the productivity of the water company. More water more crop. The men who bring water to this land may be no better than the men who bring fertilizer, and the water may be no better as water than the fertilizer is as fertilizer, yet if the water men get what their service is actually worth, they will get a large share of the product of the land, whereas the fertilizer men would, on the same terms, get a small share. This inequality in the distribution of the products of agriculture would not be due to social injustice, but to the bad distribution of the factors of production. This is the fundamental difficulty, of which the bad distribution of products is but the symptom. One who thought he could cure this bad distribution of products by merely changing the social system of distribution would only be covering up symptoms. In a rain-soaked country where fertilizers are scarce, the conditions and the results of the illustration would be exactly reversed.

Take any illustration you choose where several ingredients have to be mixed to get a given commodity, or several factors combined to get a given product, and you will invariably find that if the factors do not exist in the proportions called for, some being scarce and others abundant relatively to the need, those which are abundant will have little real productivity per unit according to any rational economic test, and those which are scarce will have a high productivity per unit. One unit more or less of the abundant factor will make little difference with the product: Very little product depends, therefore, upon any given unit. A new unit of this abundant factor will not be much needed, will not be worth much. But the factor which is scarce, which does not exist in sufficient abundance to combine with all the other factors, is really the limiting factor. One

unit more or less makes a large difference in the product.
Much product, therefore, depends, under these circumstances, upon each and every unit of the scarce factor.
This is what is meant by saying that, economically speaking,
the productivity *per unit* of the scarce factor is greater than
that of the abundant factor.   It would be a greater gain to
production to have a new unit of the scarce factor than to
have a new unit of the abundant factor.   It would be a
greater loss to production to lose a unit of the scarce than
to lose a unit of the abundant factor.

Returning to the gunpowder illustration of a previous
chapter, the following observations will apply to this argument.   Assume that charcoal is abundant and saltpetre
scarce, and then ask the question, " More charcoal, more
gunpowder ? " and the answer is, " no."   But to the question, " More saltpetre, more gunpowder ? " the answer is,
" yes."   The production of gunpowder varies directly with
the supply of saltpetre and only slightly, if at all, with the
supply of charcoal.   Every new unit of saltpetre increases
the production of gunpowder, but a new unit of charcoal
would be of practically no use.

This relation between conditions and results may be
termed an economic law.   It is a law which lies deeper than
forms of social organization.   It is grounded in the laws of
physics.   No scheme of social reform which would try to
get at this inequality of prices by merely changing the social
machinery would be worth a moment's consideration.   It
would not have advanced beyond the policy of treating
symptoms rather than causes.

It happens, under the modern system of production, with
its elaborate division of labor, that many different, non-
interchangeable kinds of labor have to be combined in the
production of a given article.   These different kinds of

labor are to be treated as different factors, and bear precisely the same relation to one another as fertility and moisture in the soil. All that was said of moisture and fertilizer in the growing of crops, or of charcoal and saltpetre in the making of gunpowder, may be repeated of two different kinds of labor power, or talent, in the manufacture of any commodity. Where two or more non-interchangeable kinds of labor power, or human talent, have to be combined in production, and one is found in greater abundance than will combine satisfactorily with the limited supply of another, you have precisely the same condition in the labor market that you have in the fertilizer market where there is more fertilizer than will combine with the limited supply of soil moisture, or in the charcoal market if there is more than will combine with the limited supply of saltpetre. In other words, wherever you have a bad distribution of human talent, more of one kind than will combine satisfactorily with the existing supply of another kind which has to be combined with it in production, there you will have a bad distribution of the products of industry. Moreover, this bad distribution of products cannot be attributed to social injustice if by social justice is meant merely that each one shall get exactly what he produces. For, if one kind of labor power exists in greater abundance than will combine satisfactorily with the existing supply of some other factor, you have a situation in which any unit of that kind of labor can be eliminated with very little loss to production, and the addition of a new unit would bring very little gain to production; all of which means that, unit by unit, this kind of labor would have a very low productivity. Yet it might be very good labor, and under other conditions it might have a very high degree of productivity. That is to say, bring to this labor a larger supply of those factors which have to be combined with it, but which we have assumed to be scarce, and every unit of this kind of labor will then be needed to combine with those new factors. Then the loss of a unit of this kind of labor would mean a larger loss to production, and the addition of a new unit would mean a larger gain to production, all of which means that, unit by unit, this kind of labor has literally become more productive, not through any change in itself, but through the increase of the other factors which have to be combined with it. This proposition is likely to be an occasion of stumbling to some, but it need not be to any one who can see that, in one of the foregoing illustrations, the chemical elements of fertility in the soil in a dry country may be made literally more productive by increasing the supply of another factor, viz., moisture.

It is a sad commentary upon the intelligence of our social reformers that so many of them fail to see the significance of this elementary economic principle, and continue to apply their remedies to symptoms rather than to attack the causes of the bad distribution of wealth. Because vocational guidance and vocational education go at the underlying cause, instead of attacking symptoms, they must appeal to every real progressive. By training the rising generation out of those occupations where labor power is over-abundant and into those where it is under-abundant, you not only increase the productivity of every individual so trained, and therefore of society at large, which is very important; but you accomplish the still more important result of tending to equalize incomes in different occupations. If the talent commonly understood to be possessed by the employing classes, so-called, can be made as abundant relatively to the demand for it as that of the so-called laboring classes, there will be no great difference in the incomes of the two classes.

There is danger, however, that this program may fail if it is carried out in a half-hearted and incomplete manner. If it aims merely at redistributing the supply of human talent among the laboring classes, that is, at making a more efficient body of employees, increasing the supply of skilled labor, it will result only in reducing the wages of skilled labor and enabling the employing classes to get skilled help at a lower cost than now, and thus increase their profits. What is particularly needed is a more numerous and more skilled class of employers. Of all classes of human talent, the scarcest, relatively to the need for it, is genuine entrepreneur ability. So scarce is this ability that it is like water in a thirsty land, where fertility and every other factor of production are abundant, only needing moisture to make them productive. We have enormous quantities of unskilled labor, but few men who know how to use them. This knowledge — the " knowing how " — is the scarce factor. If we can increase the supply of this rare kind of knowledge, then these vast stores of unskilled labor, now with a low degree of productivity, will be made more productive. More men who know how, — know what to do, — will fructify this mass. Ability to discern genuine opportunities for new enterprise, which is investing ability, and probably the rarest of all; ability to coördinate and organize the factors of production, which is managing ability in the higher sense, and which is, next to investing ability, the scarcest of them all; and ability to direct men in the actual work of production, which is administrative ability, and is also somewhat scarce, need especially to be increased. The scarcity of these kinds of talent reduces the effective demand for the lower grades of labor, just as the scarcity of water reduces the demand for fertilizer in the foregoing illustration. Conversely, the enormous supplies of labor, needing to be directed, create an enormous demand for these scarce forms of talent, just as the supply of fertility in the soil needing to be irrigated, creates a demand for water, in the foregoing illustration. An abundance of entrepreneur talent and a scarcity of labor will bring down the price of the one and bring up the price of the other as surely as an abundant supply of water on a western plain, and a scarcity of fertilizer would bring down the price of the one and bring up the price of the other. In this direction, and in this direction alone, must we look for a solution of the problem of the bad distribution of wealth.

From the standpoint of a country which receives considerable numbers of laborers by immigration, the problem of the distribution of wealth is materially affected thereby. Migrations of laborers are brought about by a bad territorial distribution of the labor supply. When there is an excess in one region and a dearth, or a milder excess, in another region, the obvious remedy is a territorial redistribution. This tends toward equality as between different regions. But there may also be a bad occupational distribution, with an excess in one occupation, and a dearth, or a milder excess, in another. The remedy is equally obvious. Instead of a migration from one region to another, there needs to be a " migration " from one occupation to another. This, however, can usually take place only as a result of vocational training, which should have one and only one purpose, to train men for those occupations where men are scarcest and most highly paid. This will, at the same time, relieve those where men are abundant and poorly paid.

One of those half truths which are more dangerous than falsehoods is the statement, which so frequently emanates from the sapient minds of editors and magazine scientists, that since laborers are themselves consumers as well as producers, there must of necessity always be work enough. It is scarcely conceivable that one of those who repeat this statement would go so far as to say that there must necessarily be work enough for each laborer at the exact spot where he happens to stand. If one once admits that it may be necessary for the laborer to move from the spot where he happens to be standing, the way is then open for a rational solution of the problem. Why should it be necessary for him to move ? If he is an agricultural laborer, and he is standing on a crowded street corner, he must at least go where there is land to cultivate. This is an admission that something else besides labor is necessary. There must be land. But if he is in the country where there is land, but every farm is equipped with as many laborers as can be satisfactorily employed, he may have to go farther, until he finds a place where land is more abundant, or labor scarcer, which means the same thing. That is why agricultural laborers migrate.

But he might be at a spot where there is an abundance of land, but no tools with which to work. Unless he is prepared to make his own tools he may have to migrate again, until he finds a place where there is such a combination of land and tools as will furnish him the opportunity he is seeking. Or again, there may be no farmer with sufficient business ability to see how to use any more men to advantage; again he will have to migrate until he finds one who can, unless he can become his own manager. It is also conceivable that there might be so many farm laborers in his community, and so few factory laborers, miners, etc., to produce things to exchange for farm products, or so few carriers to transport them, as to destroy the opportunity for enlarged farm production. In that case our farm laborer, or others like himself, may find it necessary to change their occupation. In short, to say that there must be work for everybody means nothing unless you qualify it by saying that there is opportunity for any conceivable number of men provided they can be properly distributed, both territorially and occupationally. If they are not so distributed, it is quite possible that there might be more on a certain spot than can possibly be employed on that spot, and more in a given occupation than can possibly be employed in that occupation.

This part of our discussion may be summarized as follows:

I

A.[1] One large factor in the bad distribution of wealth is the bad distribution of men among the different occupations, too many crowding into the unskilled and too few going into the skilled and the learned occupations.

B. Children born of parents who have not been able to rise out of the poorly paid occupations are themselves more likely, *on the average*, to remain in these occupations than are the children of parents who have risen into the more highly skilled and better paid occupations to sink back into the poorly paid occupations.

C. Therefore, it would help matters if the birth rate could be reduced among those who remain in the overcrowded, underpaid, and unskilled occupations, and increased among those who succeed in rising into the more highly paid occupations.

[1] From a paper on *The Occupational Distribution of the Labor Supply*, read by the author, before The American Economic Association, in Washington, D. C., 1910.

II

So long as immigrants enter a country in considerable numbers, and enter the ranks, particularly the lower ranks, of labor[1] in larger proportions, and the ranks of the business and professional classes in smaller proportions than the native born, continuous immigration will produce the following results:

A. As to Distribution. It will keep competition more intense among laborers, particularly in the lower ranks, and less intense among business and professional men, than it would otherwise be. This will tend to increase the income of the employing classes, and to depress wages, particularly the wages of the lower grades of labor.

B. As to Production. It will give a relatively low marginal productivity to a typical immigrant, particularly in the lower grades of labor, and make him a relatively unimportant factor in the production of wealth, — a few more or less will make relatively little difference in the total production of national wealth.[2]

C. As to Organization of Industry. Because of their low individual productivity, they can only be economically employed at low wages *and in large gangs.*[3]

[1] Cf. Commons, *Races and Immigrants in America*.   Table between pages 108 and 109.

[2] A disproportionately large supply of one grade of labor as compared with the supply of other grades of labor with which it has to be combined in production, tends to make each laborer in that grade an unimportant factor in production, so that one laborer more in that grade adds very little to, and one laborer less subtracts very little from the total quantity which can be produced.   By way of illustration, the reader is again referred to the gunpowder illustration.

[3] Just as scarce labor and abundant land lead inevitably to extensive farming where a small quantity of the scarce factor, labor, is combined with a large quantity of the abundant factor, land, so a relatively small supply of managing ability and a relatively large supply of the kind of labor which

D. As to Agriculture.   If immigrants go in large numbers into agriculture, it will lead to one or the other of the following results, *in all probability the latter.*

1. The continuous *morcellement* or subdivision of farms, resulting in an inefficient and wasteful application of labor, and smaller crops per man, though probably larger crops per acre; or

2. The development of a class of landed proprietors on the one hand, and a landless agricultural proletariat on the other.

III

If there are large numbers of immigrants belonging to races or nationalities which do not fuse with the rest of the population by free intermarriage, or with which the rest of the population will not intermarry freely, there will result one of the three following conditions:

1. Geographical separation of races; or

2. Social separation of races, i. e., in the formation of classes or castes, one race or the other becoming subordinate; or

3. Continual race antagonism, frequently breaking out into race war.

Of equal importance with the increase in the demand for the labor which is now poorly paid is the decrease in the supply.   For a country such as the United States of America, which receives such large supplies of unskilled labor by immigration, the first and most obvious remedy is a restriction of immigration.   This is in no way to be asso-

---

must be superintended, leads inevitably to a combination of a small quantity of the scarce form with a large quantity of the abundant form, i. e., one superintendent, foreman, or boss, over a large gang.   Again, just as in the former case there will be high wages and low rent, so in the latter case there will be high salaries and low wages.

ciated with race prejudice. It is wholly a question of the occupational redistribution of our labor supply.

Wherever any particular class of labor is, for a considerable period, scarce and hard to find, there the conditions of labor are good for that class and it needs no social legislation for its protection; but wherever any particular class of labor is abundant and easy to find, there the conditions of that class of labor are bad except where mitigated by the kindliness of individual employers, or by various kinds of social legislation, most of which are ineffective.

When any employer can hang out a shingle saying " men wanted " and have ten men apply for every job, so that he can merely take his pick and send the rest away, conditions are very easy for employers, but correspondingly hard for laborers. When any laborer can hang out a sign reading " job wanted " and have ten employers apply for his help, so that he can take his pick and send the rest away conditions will be as easy for laborers as they were under the first named conditions for employers, and as hard for employers as they were for unskilled laborers. So long as the former conditions prevail, the term " wage slavery," while inaccurate, will continue to convey a real meaning to the laboring man. Where the latter conditions prevail no one can use that term with a straight face. So long as the former conditions prevail, there will be a widespread feeling, and this feeling will be justified, that the laborer is in a helpless situation, so far as economic laws are concerned, and that his only hope is in numbers and brute strength. When this feeling is widespread, laboring men will be excused, if not justified, in the use of violence. There will be no effective public opinion to support the state in its efforts to preserve law and order. When there is some approach to the latter conditions there will be an easy recognition of the fact that the laborers are not in a helpless condition, that they do not need to rely on numbers and brute strength, and public opinion will then support the state effectively and promptly in its maintenance of law and order.

While it may not be possible or desirable to reach such extreme scarcity of laborers and abundance of employers as described under the last named conditions, it is both possible and desirable to make some progress toward that condition and away from the first named condition. We can train a few more men to become employers, creators of new business enterprises, and thus increase somewhat the number of jobs for laboring men. This will do our present laboring population little good if the new jobs are promptly filled by immigrants. There must also be a restriction of immigration.

If immigrants entered the class of employers in the same proportion as do the native born, they would not materially disturb the balance. But they enter the laboring class almost exclusively, and the class of unskilled laborers predominantly. If they were excluded (which is not here proposed) our free education and liberal institutions would encourage them to rise rapidly out of the class of unskilled laborers, into the scarcer and better paid occupations. This would soon make unskilled labor, and ultimately all poorly paid labor, so scarce and hard to find as to put laborers in a strong position economically and make it unnecessary for them to resort to numbers and brute strength. Moreover, employers would have to offer satisfactory inducements to persuade laborers to work for them, and very little social legislation for the alleged protection of the laborers would then be necessary.

Better than exclusion would be a plan of restriction which would select those who were capable of entering the well paid occupations and exclude those who would crowd into occupations where wages are already too low. The best way to do this would be to reverse our present contract labor law, and admit only such immigrants as could present contracts, signed by responsible employers, guaranteeing employment at two dollars a day for at least a year. (It is not necessary that the wage should be exactly two dollars. That is about the minimum on which a family can be supported in comfort and decency in any large city in this country.) This would admit all the laborers who were really needed. No employer can say, with a straight face, that he needs a man so very badly unless he is willing to pay him as much as two dollars a day. At the same time it would prevent the coming of hordes of cheap laborers whose influence is to depress the wages of unskilled labor. It would make the lower grades of labor so scarce as to eventually make two dollars a day the actual minimum wage without the difficulty of enforcing a minimum wage law.

If this reversal of the contract labor law is considered politically impossible, the literacy test comes as near an ideal as anything that has been proposed. This is said with a full recognition of the fact that literacy is not an invariable test of character. Neither is it an invariable test of fitness for the civil service, or for entrance to college. It is believed, however, that if all literate immigrants are arranged in one group, and all illiterates in another, the *average* of the literates would be better than that of the illiterates. Excluding illiterates would therefore improve the average quality of our immigrants.

Again, the illiterates go predominantly into the unskilled trade where wages are low. The exclusion of illiterates would therefore tend to make unskilled labor scarce, while the admission of literates would permit us to get all the skilled labor we need, that is, to increase our supply of any kind of labor which can in any sense be said to be scarce.

It will be observed that nothing has been said in the above statement, about race, religion, eugenics, or anything of the kind. The reasons for favoring the restriction of immigration are purely economic. They relate wholly to the problem of improving the conditions of labor. The time is probably coming when any one's protestations of interest in the cause of labor in America, or of social welfare, will be laughed out of court unless he is willing to do the one thing which will really help labor, that is, make it scarce and hard to find, or jobs abundant and easy to find, which means the same thing.

The increase in the prosperity of the small farmer, who does most of his own work on his own farm, is quite as important as that of the laborer. His salvation depends upon his ability to compete with the large farmer or the farming corporation. Two things threaten to place him under a handicap and to give the large farmer an advantage over him in competition. If these two things are allowed to operate, the big farmer will beat him in competition and force him down to a lower standard of living and possibly to extinction.

One thing which would tend in that direction is a large supply of cheap labor. The small farmer now has an advantage in America because of the difficulty which the big farmer has in getting help. So great is this difficulty that many of the bonanza farmers are giving up the fight and selling out to small farmers. That is, the big farms, the farms that can only be cultivated by gangs of hired laborers, are being divided up. Give the owners of these farms an abundant supply of cheap labor, — make it easy for them to solve the problem of efficient help — and they will begin again to compete successfully with the small farmer who, because he does his own work, has no labor problem. If we can keep conditions such that the capitalistic farmer has great difficulty in getting help, the small farmer will continue to beat him in competition, and the bonanza farm will continue to give way to the one-family farm.

By pursuing a consistent policy of reducing the supply of unskilled labor, of increasing the supply of the scarcer kinds of employing talent, as well as the supplies of land and capital, we can, by progressive stages, approach as near to equality of incomes as between occupations as we care to. If we do not do this, the only honest reason we can give will be that we do not care for equality in the concrete, however unctiously we may preach equality in the abstract.

CHAPTER XV

THE RESPONSIBILITY OF THE RICH FOR THE
CONDITION OF THE POOR

THE rich *are* largely responsible for the condition of the poor. The author wishes to be very clearly understood on that point. Nevertheless, he is convinced that this responsibility is very different from that which is commonly proclaimed. The poor may sometimes be poor because the rich are rich, but it is usually just the other way about. The rich are more frequently rich because the poor are poor. This does not mean that the rich rob the poor. Where that is the case, the rich are the cause of the poverty of the poor. More frequently the rich are a help to the poor as individuals and yet, in spite of that, are responsible for the persistence of large masses of poverty. These cases are more numerous than those of downright robbery, even admitting, as we ought, that robbery includes adulteration, shoddy manufacturing, monopolization, and mendacious advertising. In the class of cases which we are about to consider, the riches of the rich are the result, rather than the cause, of the poverty of the poor. Moreover, it can be shown that the rich are still, many of them, trying to keep the poor poor in order that they, the rich, may remain rich.

No truer or braver words were ever spoken than were recently spoken by a southern gentleman in discussing the negro question. He told his fellow-southerners that it was impossible to have a mass of ignorant laborers without breeding up a race of scoundrels to prey upon and exploit

them. He could wisely have extended this remark to cover
a great many other cases besides the negro problem. And
on the negro problem itself he might have made some very
pointed remarks to that type of southern mind which fears
that if negroes are educated it may be difficult to get good
servants. If it is difficult to get good servants, the servant-
keeping class will suffer some disadvantage. In proportion
as it is easy to get good servants at low cost, in that proportion will the servant-keeping class gain. They become
richer in the sense that, with the same income, they can live
more luxuriously. The poverty of the servant class contributes to the riches of the servant-keeping class.

A northern lady lamented the scarcity of good servants,
and the high wages demanded by them in her city. She had
formerly lived in London, and spoke approvingly of the fact
that, in that city, one could get very capable women to do
any kind of housework for very low wages. Yet this lady
was possessed of the most generous impulses, and imagined
herself to be a social reformer. Her ideas of social reform,
however, did not include the improvement of the wages of
household servants. She was herself an employer of household servants. She was an ardent advocate of higher wages
for the employees of other people. In short, she was an
adorable and unconscious humbug.

A gentleman of conspicuous literary power and eminent
public service has recently written, apropos of the simple
life, that one increasing difficulty in the way of real simplicity (!) was that of entertaining in a genteel manner
without good servants who were becoming very expensive.

But we need not confine ourselves to the question of
household servants in order to find illustrations of the concern which certain well-to-do persons have lest the poor
should cease to be poor, that is, cease having to sell their

services cheap, and begin selling them at a high price. How, it is frequently asked, can we develop our resources unless we can import cheap laborers ? How can we run our factories and our mines, how can we build our railroads and trolley lines if we have to pay the wages demanded by American laborers ? In short, how can we accumulate great wealth unless we have a mass of poverty, otherwise *called* a large supply of cheap labor ? Is it not obvious that our wealth would be less if this mass of poverty were reduced, that is, if there were fewer laborers ? Under such circumstances, we should each have fewer of them, and we should have to pay them higher wages. That would reduce *our* prosperity.

There is a certain European city which has long been noted as a center of enlightenment. Popular education and a virile religion combined to lift the masses of the people into a condition of prosperity, in strong contrast with the surrounding territory where the people remained ignorant, and, because of their ignorance, poor. Because of the intelligence and prosperity of the masses in this city it became increasingly difficult to hire them to do rough and unskilled work. They could all do something better. In fact, it was necessary to pay them almost as high wages for unskilled as for skilled work, and the skilled worker got almost as much as the business man. The reason was that every man had a wide range of choices in selecting an occupation. No one would enter a poorly paid occupation if there was a well paid occupation open to him. The result of this was that there were no poorly paid occupations. In other words, poverty was about to disappear.

But in the outlying regions there were masses of poor people, kept so by a repressive religion and a lack of popular education. Certain inhabitants of this enlightened city found that they could make more money by hiring these poor and ignorant people from the outside than by hiring the prosperous and intelligent people of their own town. Accordingly they began importing laborers in large numbers. They grew rich thereby, but they filled their city with poor people. Now it would be idle to say that these poor people were poor because the rich were so rich. They were probably a little less poor on that account. The real truth is that these rich people got richer because of the presence and availability of these poor people.

Wherein, then, does the responsibility of the rich lie ? In the case of the city just mentioned, it was the greed of the rich which led them to import those masses of poor and ignorant laborers. In other cases it is the greed of the rich which opposes measures which will make labor scarce and hard to find. They know too well that where labor is scarce and hard to find, there labor is well paid and well treated. But they know also that the opportunity for profitable exploitation is there reduced. The rich cannot get so very rich because there are none so very poor.

There is another and more important sense in which the rich are responsible for the condition of the poor. It is the rich who set the pace in the worst form of competition known to the economic world, that is, competitive consumption. This works to the disadvantage of the poor in several ways. In the first place, the poor, like all the rest of us, have their social ambitions. They dislike to fall behind their neighbors in matters of dress, furniture, food and general appearance. They are led like all the rest of us to imitate the rich in this vicious habit of competitive consumption, to spend so much on appearances that they have hard work buying the necessaries of life. We all spend more trying to live like our neighbors than in trying to live comfortably.   If competition in consumption could be made less intense, if our neighbors would spend less on appearances, and *their* neighbors likewise, all of us would feel just as respectable as we now do, and we would have more to spend on the necessaries and comforts of life.   The rich have it within their power to reduce the intensity of this kind of competition.   They can do better than they are now doing.   Therefore they are under obligation to do so.   *He who does less well than he can does ill.*

Again, by setting so high a pace in competitive consumption, the rate of accumulation of capital is retarded.   If we would all consume a little less and save and invest a little more, capital (that is, tools), would accumulate very much more rapidly than it now does.   The accumulation of capital creates new opportunities for labor.   A new stock of tools is a new and standing invitation to labor.   Over-consumption retards the accumulation of capital and reduces the number of invitations to labor.   By setting a high pace in competitive consumption the rich therefore retard the accumulation of capital and reduce the demand for labor.   That makes interest higher and wages lower than they would otherwise be.

But, it is asked, what would happen if everybody began accumulating capital ?   Would it not become over-abundant ?   How could we use it all ?   That is just the point.   It would become so abundant that the owners of capital would have difficulty in finding employment for it.   That is to say, they would have difficulty in finding laborers enough to use their tools and machinery.   In that case it would be capital and not labor which would have to hunt for employment and have difficulty in finding it.   If one could not find labor to use his capital, that would mean that no labor was out of employment.   If there was anything unemployed it would be capital.   Labor would then be independent, capital dependent.

If I had inherited or married a fund of capital and wanted to get the most out of it, and were narrowly selfish, I should advise everyone to consume lavishly and not to save; to spend his money " like a gentleman " and not invest it " like a shopkeeper "; to buy consumers' goods with it and not tools.   Every time my neighbor buys tools, they begin to compete with mine, but every time he buys consumers' goods, he creates a demand for my tools.

Moreover, if I cared more for money than for the truth I should studiously promulgate a lie.   I should tell all my neighbors that by lavish consumption they would be giving employment to labor and benefiting the poor.   I should refrain from telling them that by buying tools they would be giving employment to the laborers who make tools, and that, besides, the tools would then continue increasing the laborer's product and his wages.   By thus encouraging lavish consumption and discouraging the accumulation of capital I should be increasing my own income from my own capital, and reducing the wages of labor.   At the same time, I should be responsible for the condition of the poor because I had helped create that condition.

Immigration from Europe is not the only method of keeping up a large supply of cheap labor.   Immigration from Heaven into the ranks of unskilled laborers has much the same result.   That is to say, if the ranks of unskilled laborers are kept abnormally full by large families among the very poor, it has the same result as immigration.   It makes unskilled labor abundant and easy to find, which means necessarily that jobs are scarce, relatively to the number looking for them, and hard to find.   That is to the advantage of the employing class.

The result is greatly accentuated by a lack of immigration, either from Europe or from Heaven, into the ranks of the employing class. If most of our immigrants entered directly into business, bringing their own capital, competing with our present employers not only for markets, but for employees as well, the profits of business would fall and the wages of employees would rise. The shoe would then be on the other foot. The same result would happen if it were the rich rather than the poor who had large families. By encouraging large families among the poor, but seeing to it that they themselves do not follow their own advice, the rich can increase their own riches and the poverty of the poor at the same time. Are they responsible ? They might do better. *He who does less well than he can does ill.*

For the benefit of sonorous moralists, they are again reminded that foxes approve large families among rabbits. They add to the riches of the foxes. The people who profit by the poverty of the poor must be held under suspicion of being responsible for it, until they can clear themselves by showing proof that they have done something to reduce the number of men looking for jobs, or to increase the number of jobs looking for men. It is time for a searching of hearts. Moreover, it is time that every unctious expression of interest in, or sympathy for the poor were laughed out of court, unless the speaker or writer can show proof that he or she has done something which would really help the poor. The only thing which will really and permanently help the mass of the poor is the raising of their wages, — that is the price of their labor. That is precisely what most of the unctious social reformers are unwilling to do. It would add to their expenses. The price of labor, like the price of everything else, is finally determined by the ratio of supply to demand. He who has consciously and intelligently done something to increase the demand for labor, or to reduce the supply of it, has a right to speak on the labor problem. All others who exercise their verbosity in this field are mere charlatans.

CHAPTER XVI

SOCIAL SERVICE

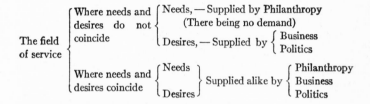

PEOPLE either desire what they need, or they do not. If they do not, and I happen to know what they really ought to have, I have two opportunities before me. In the first place I may undertake to give them what they need, or do for them what they ought to have done, even though they do not care for my product or my service. That is one kind of social service, but it is not the only kind and it is not business. It is a noble work, provided I am correct in my judgment as to what they need, and am not mistakenly trying to force upon them a favorite panacea of my own; but it calls for self-sacrifice. There is no profit in it for me, because if the people do not want my service they will not pay for it, however valuable it may really be. I am in some sense a missionary. In the second place, I may say, " Who am I that I should presume to know what is good for these people ? They desire this product or this service and are willing to pay for it though it is not good for them and they do not need it. But I will give them what they want." That is one kind of business, but it is not the only kind, and it is not social service. It will be profitable for me because the people will pay well for it. It is not profitable for them because they desire what is not good for them.

But if people know what they need and desire it, — and they sometimes do, — then their desires and their needs will coincide. If I satisfy their desires I am at the same time supplying their needs. That is both business and social service. It is business because the people will pay for my product or my service. It is social service because it supplies the real needs of the people.

We may lay down the general principle, therefore, that when people do not know what they need, or when desires and needs do not coincide, social service is one thing and business quite another. But when the people really do know what they need, or when desires and needs really do coincide, then social service and business are the same thing. In the former case, social service must be performed on a more or less philanthropic basis. There is no other way to support it. But in the latter case, social service is carried on on a purely business basis and calls for no philanthropy at all, at least not in the ordinary acceptation of the term.

Let us put aside, for the present, all consideration of the former class of cases and give our attention exclusively to those where desires and needs coincide. This is the field of worthy business enterprise, or the proper field for the exercise of business talent. And let us consider, for a moment, what the requirements of and opportunities for social service are in this field. In order to help us in this analysis, let us assume that I am a pure altruist, with no selfish interests whatever, and no desire except to render as large a service as possible. How should I proceed to find the largest opportunity for service in this field, and how should I proceed to meet the opportunities presented ?

In the first place, I should seek an industry or an occupation where more men are needed, or where more products are needed. Since desires and needs coincide, the evidence of the need will be the market demand. If I find that the supply of farmers is scarcer relatively to the demand than the supply of any other class which I am capable of entering, obviously I should become a farmer, if my talents fit me for that work, or if I can fit myself for it by hard study. If among farm crops, I find that potatoes are somewhat over-supplied, it would obviously be no great service if I should begin growing potatoes. But if I find that the community is less well supplied with apples than with anything else which I can grow, then my greatest opportunity for service would be in the growing of apples. There is where I could do the most good to my fellow-men.

In the second place, if I should decide upon an industry whose products seem to be in great demand, I may find it so highly organized as to call for a great many different kinds of skill or talent, ranging all the way from unskilled muscular labor up to the higher forms of business management. Here a new problem presents itself. I must choose among the various kinds of work within the organization and try to find the one where I can be of greatest service in increasing the output. If I go into a kind of work where I affect the total product or output to a very slight degree, when I possess talent which would enable me to go into another kind of work where I can increase the product more, I am obviously not performing as large a service as possible. I am a poor kind of a servant if I do not go into a line of work where my service will have the highest productivity.

Now the different kinds of labor power which have to be combined in a given industry, or in the production of a given product, come under a very important law. This law, which may be called the law of variable proportions, is one of the most important laws of economics, and it is the most fundamental of all. Under this law, the scarcest factor in a combination becomes the limiting factor, and, unit for unit, the most productive of all, while the most abundant is, unit for unit, the least productive.

The different kinds of labor power which have to be combined in the production of a given product come under the same law. If there is more of one kind, say unskilled muscular labor, than will combine satisfactorily with the existing supply of another, say managing ability, then one more unskilled laborer would add very little to, and one less would subtract very little from, the total output. But one good man added to the managerial staff would add a great deal to, and one subtracted would subtract a great deal from, the total output. These also would be physical facts, lying deeper than the form of social organization. Reverse the conditions, making managerial ability the abundant and muscular labor the scarce factor, and the results would be reversed.

Under the conditions assumed, I should not be a good social servant if I should go into muscular work, provided I had the ability to join the managerial staff. If there are already more muscular workers than can combine satisfactorily with the limited supply of managerial ability, I should add very little to the producing power of the whole organization if I should merely add one more to the existing oversupply. But by adding one more man to the managerial staff where men are scarce, I can enable the whole business to expand. Here, under the terms of the present illustration, would be my largest opportunity for social service,—where I could contribute the maximum to the supply of human needs, — could do the most good to my fellow-men.

In the third place, I should be a poor kind of a social servant if I only tried to give as large a service as I could today and did not try to increase my power to serve from day to day and from year to year. One way of increasing my power for service would be to improve my knowledge and skill. If hard study will do this, it is obviously my duty to study hard. Another way of increasing my power for service would be to improve my tools, to increase their size, their number and their quality. I can increase my tools either by making them myself, or by buying them of some one else. The latter is usually the better way. I can buy them only by setting aside a part of my income for that purpose. If my income is more than sufficient to buy those consumers' goods which are necessary to maintain my working strength and efficiency at their maximum, the surplus should be expended on more and better tools so long as more and better tools will increase my production or improve my service in any way.

One of the most persistent fallacies is the notion that lavish consumption is good for industry and a benefit to labor. If I have a dollar to spend, over and above what I need to maintain my working power, I can spend it for an article of consumption, or I can spend it for a tool. If I spend it for an article of consumption I do, it is true, stimulate the industry which produced it. But if I spend it for a tool, I equally stimulate the tool-making industry. I set labor to work quite as much in one direction as in the other. Thus far the accounts balance, or the benefit is equal, whichever way I spend my dollar. But this is not all. After I have got my article of consumption, I consume it and that is the end. The world gets no further benefit. But if I have a tool, my productive power is thereafter increased, and the world will thereafter be better supplied with goods by reason of my having it. If, however, I do not happen to need more tools in my particular line of work, I shall find, if I look about, that there are other industries or occupations where more tools are needed. If my income is more than sufficient to maintain my working power at its maximum, it then becomes my duty to do what I can to supply tools to other industries and to other workers. I can do this by buying such tools, which is virtually hiring others to make them. The reasons in favor of doing this are quite as strong as those in favor of buying more tools for myself, the only difference being that when I buy more tools for myself I increase my own productive power but when I buy tools for others I increase their productive power. In either case the world's productive power is increased and its wants thereafter more fully satisfied.

The question may be asked, at this point, why not give my surplus income away, if I have more than I need for my maximum working power. The answer is that there is probably no way in which I can give it away to such good advantage as by increasing my productive power — which is power to serve — or by increasing the productive power of others. If I give to them outright, I benefit neither them nor the rest of the world; but if I increase their power to produce I increase their earning power and their power to serve at the same time. That is the very best kind of benevolence if it be not something very much better than any kind of benevolence.

Another way of putting the same question is to ask why not give my service free, or require in payment at most only enough to maintain my working power. If I really thought that I could render a larger total service in this way than by asking the full value of my service and then giving the surplus back in the form of more tools or instruments of service, that is what I ought to do.   But it is more than doubtful if that would be the best way.   I could not greatly enlarge my own productive power in that way, and it would be uncertain whether those who receive the service free would pass it on in the form of increased production, or whether they would absorb it themselves.   But if I put this surplus income into tools, I am at least certain on this point.   Moreover, they who are to profit immediately by the tools must themselves work to secure the benefit.   They, at least, must pass the service on.   What eventually becomes of it is still a matter of uncertainty, but I am at least certain that my service has been passed on one stage further when I choose this alternative than when I give my service free.   If I am not only benevolent but wise, I shall therefore probably ask all that my service is worth and then, if this gives me more than is necessary to maintain my maximum working power, give the surplus back in the form of more tools and instruments of service.

But should I give the service of my tools free, or should I ask what their service is worth ?   The same reasoning will apply here as to my personal productive power or service. I shall probably do better if I ask for the service of my tools what it is worth and give back the surplus in the form of still more tools, so long as more tools are needed.   I shall probably be serving the world more wisely and effectively by that method than by any other.

Now it so happens that all these things which I should do as a pure altruist in the field where the desires and needs of my fellow-men coincide are precisely the things which I should find it to my interest to do if I were wisely self-interested.   For, to go back to the former illustrations, if the world needs and desires the service of farmers more than any other which I am capable of performing, this is not only the occupation where I can be of greatest service, it is also the one where I can earn the largest income. And if apples are scarcer relatively to the demand than any other crop which I can grow, that is not only the crop in the growing of which I can supply the largest needs and render the largest service, it is also the most profitable crop I can grow. Again, in a highly organized industry where many kinds of labor power are employed, the kind which is scarcest relatively to the demand is not only the kind which will give me greatest power to serve, if I possess it, it is the kind which pays best. Or, again, if I can increase my productive capacity by supplying myself with more and better tools, I not only increase my power to serve, I increase my income as well. Finally, if I can increase the productive power of other industries and occupations by providing them with tools, by hiring men to make tools for them, that is, by investing in such tools, I not only render a social service by so doing, I also increase my capital, my control over the productive forces of the world, and my income. In every particular, therefore, good business and good social service coincide so long as we are in the field where human desires and needs coincide. Bad business is quite another thing.

Where needs and desires coincide, it is literally true, without the least bit of mysticism, poetic license, or oriental imagery, but with the most occidental and matter of fact regard for scientific accuracy, that whosoever would be chief among you, *must* become your servant. He who performs the greatest service becomes richest, acquires greatest popularity or secures the largest number of votes, according to the method which people choose for rewarding their servants.

CHAPTER XVII

HOW OUGHT THE BURDENS OF TAXATION TO BE DISTRIBUTED?

IF taxes [1] were voluntary contributions for the support of the state, it would be important that we should recognize some principle by which to determine how much each individual ought to give. Since the payment of such a tax and its amount would be matters for the individual conscience, it would be pertinent to ask what principle of obligation the individual ought to adopt as his rule of action. But since taxes are not voluntary contributions but forced payments, we need not so much to know what the duty of the individual is as what the duty of the state is: not how much the individual ought in conscience to give, but how much the state ought in justice to take from him, and under what conditions the state ought to take it. In the matter of taxation the state alone is the voluntary agent, and consequently the duty of the state alone is to be determined. It is one thing to say that the individual ought to contribute to the support of the state in proportion to the benefit which he receives, or to his ability to pay, or to his faculty, but it is quite another thing to say that the state ought to make him do any of these things.

These two questions, though distinct, may be resolved into one by assuming that it is the duty of the state to make its citizens do whatever they ought in conscience to do. It

[1] From an article on the "Minimum Sacrifice Theory of Taxation," in the *Political Science Quarterly*, vol. xix, no. 1.

would still be the duty of the state which would have to be determined, but under such an assumption that duty would be clear whenever we had found out how the individual ought to act. Such was the assumption upon which states acted in an earlier and darker age, but it has generally been abandoned except in discussions of the basis of taxation, and it is time that it was abandoned even here.

It is doubtless true *in some cases* that the state ought to make the individual do whatever his duty requires, as in the payment of a debt or the keeping of a contract, but there are many other cases where the duty of the state has to be determined on other grounds. It may be that each citizen ought to contribute to the support of the church " according as the Lord hath prospered him," but none of the more advanced nations would think of trying to compel him to do so. It may be the duty of each laborer to join a union, but no state ought to force him into one, much less ought the union to be allowed to appropriate that prerogative of sovereignty to itself. It may be, and very likely is, the duty of each individual " to produce according to his ability and consume according to his needs," but no one but a communist would claim that the state ought to make him do so. The illustrations might be multiplied, but enough has been said to show that there are no *a priori* reasons for assuming that because the individual ought to pay for the support of the state according to his ability, for example, that it is therefore the state's duty to make him do so.

It is not to be inferred that the question of taxation is entirely divorced from ethics. Neither is it to be inferred that there are two kinds of moral obligation, one for the individual and the other for the state, nor that the ultimate test of right action is not the same for the one as for the other. A very distinct ethical problem is involved in the question of the apportionment of taxes: viz., what is the duty of the state in the matter ?   Moreover, there is only one kind of moral obligation, and the same test of right action, whatever that test may be, must be applied in determining the duties of both the individual and the state.   But even when a general principle of obligation has been agreed upon, no one is in a position to decide upon the specific duty of either the individual or the state until he knows what would be the general consequences of their various possible acts.   Recognizing that each act is, for his purposes, the first link in a chain of causation, he must be able to trace that chain from its initial act to its general results before he can tell whether or not the act in question conforms to his general principle.   As applied to taxation, for example, he must know how the effort to collect a certain tax will affect industries and morals and other social interests before he can say whether the state, in levying the tax, would be acting in harmony with the general principle of obligation agreed upon.   If, to be more specific, he should find that the attempt to collect a certain tax would discourage certain desirable industries and commendable enterprises, that would be at least a partial reason for condemning it.   That is to say, if the industry which is suppressed meets the test of the ethical principle, the tax which suppresses that industry cannot possibly meet the same test.

The question of the general principle of obligation lies so far outside the field of economics that one may be justified in borrowing such a principle ready-made from the moral philosophers.   Let us therefore accept, for purposes of this discussion, the principle of utility, and assume that the state, as well as the individual, ought to promote the general welfare — or the greatest good to the greatest number. How can the state promote the general welfare in the matter of taxation ?   In discussing the duty of the state the present writer cherishes no illusions as to the nature of the state. Realizing that the state is merely an abstraction, a convenient name for certain forms of joint action on the part of a multitude of individuals, and that the state can have no duties separate and apart from those of the individuals who compose it, yet the duty of the individual in imposing his will upon other individuals through legislation is so distinct from his duty in other matters that it is much more convenient, and fully as accurate, to speak of the former class of duties as if they belonged to the state itself.

The question of the duty of the state in matters of taxation is, of course, to be kept distinct from the question of its duty in the expenditure of revenue after it is raised.   By the expenditure of a given revenue the state may, in various ways, add positively to the general welfare.   But it may not be so obvious how the state can, in merely collecting revenue, promote the general welfare.   There are certain ways of collecting revenue which are generally believed, and no doubt correctly, to positively promote well-being.   When, for example, a tax or a license suppresses or holds in check an industry which is regarded as more or less deleterious, such a tax or license meets the utilitarian test, and is justified only because it meets that test.   Writers on taxation generally, even those who uphold the benefit theory or the faculty theory, accept this as a justification, even though it does not conform to their special canon of justice.   But if the general utilitarian principle, or the general welfare argument, can, in this special case, override their special canon, why may it not in other cases as well ?   It is at least an admission that the general utilitarian test is a more fundamental test than that of their special canon.   If so, the more fundamental test ought to be applied in all cases.

While, as already suggested, there are certain taxes whose collection adds to the public welfare by suppressing undesirable industries, yet, generally speaking, the collection of a tax is in itself an evil. It is the cost which we have to undergo for the advantages which may be secured by means of the revenue after it is collected. Since a tax is, speaking thus generally, an evil, a burden, a sacrifice imposed, it is obvious that the utilitarian principle requires that that evil, that burden, that sacrifice, shall be as small as possible in proportion to the revenue secured. When the taxes are so levied and collected as to impose the minimum of sacrifice, and the revenue so expended as to confer the maximum of advantage, or when the surplus of advantage over sacrifice, of good over evil, is at its maximum, the state has fulfilled its obligation completely: it has met the utilitarian test.

If it is once admitted that the state's obligation in the matter of taxation is to be determined on the basis of a broad principle of public utility, then it is apparent that the argument in favor of either the benefit theory or the faculty theory must be reconstructed. Instead of basing the argument upon the duty of the individual, as is usually done,[1] the upholder of either of these theories must show that if the state should apportion taxes according to benefits received, in the one case, or according to ability to contribute, in the other, such apportionment would impose the least burden, all things considered. This is possibly the sub-conscious basis of the arguments of those writers who have championed either of these theories, but it does not seem to have been explicitly recognized by any of them. The champion of the faculty theory, for example, may conceivably have reasoned somewhat as follows:

---

[1] If such is not the argument, then the leading expounders of these theories are at least guilty of inaccurately expressing their views.

Major Premise. The burdens of taxation ought to be so distributed as to involve the least possible sacrifice on the part of the community as a whole.

Minor Premise. When each individual contributes in proportion to his ability, the whole burden of taxation is most easily borne — i. e., with the minimum of sacrifice.

Conclusion. It is the individual's duty so to contribute.

Granting the premises, the conclusion follows as a matter of course, so far as the individual's duty is concerned; but, as we shall see later, the minor premise is not sound, and, as we have already seen, the conclusion is not conclusive so far as the duty of the state is concerned. For, whatever might be true if all men were willing to contribute according to their ability, the fact is that they are not willing so to do. Being unwilling, they will resort to various methods of avoiding such contribution. The attempt of the state to compel them to contribute according to their ability will not be without injurious results: it will cause various changes in the direction of business enterprise. One of the ways of avoiding the necessity of paying a tax is to avoid the occasion which the assessor, acting under the law, seizes upon as a pretext for collecting a sum of money. If, for example, the possession of a certain kind of property is such an occasion, men will tend, within certain limits, to avoid the possession of that kind of property. In so far as men generally try to avoid the possession of such property, or to avoid the other occasions for which the assessor is on the look-out, in so far is industry and enterprise disturbed and readjusted. These disturbances and readjustments may be more or less injurious, or more or less beneficial. If some taxes are to be approved because they repress certain undesirable industries, others must on the same reasoning, be condemned because they repress desirable industries. Since almost every tax has some effect in determining the direction of business enterprise, it is obvious that such considerations must enter into the determination of the duty of the state. The matter is therefore not settled when we have found out what the individual ought to do.

By an argument precisely similar to, though somewhat sounder than, that in favor of the faculty theory of taxation, the socialist could support his claim that the state ought to assume the direction of all industry and apportion to each individual his work and his income.

Major Premise. The individual ought to work for the economic welfare of the whole people.

Minor Premise. If each individual would voluntarily work according to his ability and consume according to his needs, the economic welfare would be promoted in the highest degree.

Conclusion. It is the duty of every individual to produce according to his ability and consume according to his needs.

Both the premises are probably sound, and, if so, the conclusion follows as a matter of course; but like the former argument it is inconclusive when applied to the question in hand, which is: What ought the *state* to do ? This question is complicated in both cases by the fact that individuals are not willing to do what the conclusion points out as their logical duty, and will therefore adopt methods of avoiding such necessity if the state should attempt to impose it upon them. Such an attempt would therefore produce unlooked for, and, it is generally conceded, highly undesirable consequences. All this amounts to saying that it is not the duty of the state to try to do anything which it cannot accomplish, or in trying to accomplish which it would work mischief. What is here affirmed regarding the state is equally true of individuals. It is, for example, in the

opinion of the present writer, highly desirable that all who
read this chapter should agree with its conclusions, but
even he does not consider it any one's duty to try to force
them to do so — for the simple and only reason that such
an attempt could never succeed, or if it did, it would produce other results more undesirable even than disagree-
ment.

McCulloch alone among the leading writers on taxation
seems to have grasped this fundamental truth when he
wrote:

> It would, no doubt, be in various respects desirable that the inhabi-
> tants of a country should contribute to the support of its government
> in proportion to their means.   This is obviously, however, a matter of
> secondary importance.   It is the business of the legislator to look at
> the practical influence of different taxes, and to resort in preference to
> those by which the revenue may be raised with the least inconvenience.
> Should the taxes least adverse to the public interests fall on the con-
> tributors according to their respective abilities, it will be an additional
> recommendation in their favor.   But the *salus populi* is in this, as it
> should be in every similar matter, the prime consideration; and the tax
> which is best fitted to promote, or least opposed to, this great end,
> though it may not press quite equally on different orders of society,
> is to be preferred to a more equal but otherwise less advantageous tax.
> . . .   The distinguishing characteristic of the best tax is, not that it is
> most nearly proportioned to the means of individuals, but that it is
> easily assessed and collected, and is, at the same time, most conducive,
> all things considered, to the public interests.[1]

Far from ignoring all ethical considerations, as Bastable
suggests,[2] this is a distinct recognition of an ethical principle
more definite and more fundamental than any which Bastable himself recognizes in his discussion, or shows any signs
of being aware of.

Leaving out of consideration for the present all benefits
which the levying and collecting of a tax may confer, such

---

[1] *Taxation and the Funding System*, London, 1845, p. 19.
[2] *Public Finance*, London and New York, 1895, p. 314.

as the suppression of an undesirable industry or the deepening of the taxpayer's interest in the affairs of the state, let us turn our attention to the sacrifices involved. There is, of course, to be considered the direct sacrifice on the part of him who pays a tax. Having his income curtailed by the amount of the tax, his power to consume, or to enjoy the use of wealth, is correspondingly reduced. This form of sacrifice is the most prominent, and has, naturally enough, generally appealed most strongly to writers on taxation. But there is also another form of sacrifice quite as important and fully as worthy of attention. Any tax which represses a desirable industry or form of activity not only imposes a sacrifice on him who pays it, but also upon those who are deprived of the services or the products of the repressed industry. Taxes should therefore be apportioned in such a way as to impose the smallest sum total of sacrifice of these two kinds.

While it is essential that both forms of sacrifice should be considered before reaching any final conclusion as to the best system of taxation, nevertheless the preliminary discussion may be facilitated by first considering them separately. If one were to consider only the first and more direct form of sacrifice, with a view to determining how the total sacrifice of this kind could be reduced to a minimum, he would be driven to conclude in favor of a highly progressive rate of taxation on incomes, with a somewhat higher rate on incomes derived from more permanent sources, such as secure investments, than upon income from insecure sources, such as salaries. From the gross income which comes to him in the form of a salary, the receiver must make certain deductions in the way of insurance premiums, e. g., to provide for the future, before he is on a level, in point of well-being, with one whose net income comes to him from a permanent investment.   The man with a salary of five thousand dollars would be no better off than another with an income of four thousand from a permanent investment, if the former would have to spend one thousand dollars of his salary in life insurance premiums in order to provide as well for his family as the latter's family would be provided for by the investment itself.   Under these conditions, the sacrifice involved in the payment of an equal amount to the state would be equal, though the nominal incomes are unequal.

Leaving such matters out of consideration, a highly progressive rate of taxation would be necessary in order to secure the minimum of sacrifice, and for the following reasons.   In the first place, a dollar is worth less, generally speaking, to a man with a large income than to a man with a small income, and a dollar taken from the former imposes a smaller sacrifice than a dollar taken from the latter.   Moreover, if after the first dollar is taken from the first man, his income is still greater than that of the second man, the taking of a second dollar will occasion him less sacrifice than would the taking of a first dollar from the second man; so that if only two dollars were to be raised, they should both be taken from the first man.   Applying this principle rigorously, we should continue taxing the largest income until it was reduced to such a level that the last dollar of the remaining income was worth as much to its owner as the last dollar of the next largest income is worth to its owner, and then only should we begin to tax the latter at all.   Then the two should be taxed until they were reduced to a similar level with respect to the third largest, before the third largest is taxed at all, and so on until a sufficient revenue is raised.[1]

---

[1] For a fuller discussion of this point, see an article by the present writer on " The Ethical Basis of Distribution and its Application to Taxation," in the *Annals of the American Academy of Political and Social Science*, July, 1895.

Such an application of the principle involves the assumption that wants are equal, which, though obviously not true, approximates more nearly to the truth than any other working assumption that could possibly be invented. Since the state must collect a revenue, it must have some definite assumption upon which it can proceed. The question is not, therefore, whether men's wants are equal, but whether there is any rule of inequality of wants upon which the apportionment of taxes could be made with a nearer approximation to the truth. If there be such a rule, it has not yet been discovered. To assume, for example, that the man whose income is greater than five thousand has correspondingly greater wants than the man whose income is less than five thousand, would be obviously unsafe, because there are even chances that the opposite would be true. Where the chances are even on both sides, it is safer to assume equality. Of a given number of men of the same age and the same general standard of health (by way of illustration) it is obviously untrue to assume that they will all live the same number of years, yet it is nearer the truth to assume that than any other definite workable principle. Consequently the life-insurance company acts justly when it assumes that they will live the same number of years, and apportions their premiums accordingly.

This in no way ignores the fact that wants expand with the opportunity of gratifying them. This objection, however, could only apply at the time when the tax was first imposed. At such a time it would doubtless be true that the five thousandth dollar taken from a man with an income of ten thousand would occasion him a greater sacrifice than the taking of the first dollar from an income of five thousand dollars would occasion its owner. But the reasons for this are twofold. In the first place, by taxing the first man so heavily the state would be depriving him of so many things which he was accustomed to enjoying that by the time the five thousandth dollar was reached, the taking of each particular dollar would be keenly felt.   The last dollar of his remaining income would represent a greater utility to him than would the last dollar of the five thousand dollar income to its owner.   In the second place, by taxing the second man so lightly as compared with his present taxes, the state would be allowing him to consume some things to which he had not become accustomed.   The taking of the particular dollar in question would not involve a very high sacrifice, for the reason that it would deprive him only of some enjoyment which had not yet entered into his standard of living.   But both these reasons would disappear after the new tax had been in operation for a generation, or long enough to bring the standards of living of the two men to the same level.

Drastic as this method of taxation would be, yet the writer contends, this is the method which would be logically forced upon us if we should adopt the utilitarian test, and should, in applying it, have regard only to the direct sacrifice on the part of those who pay the taxes, ignoring the indirect forms of sacrifice which a system of taxation inevitably imposes.   J. S. Mill, who advocated equality of sacrifice as the rule of justice in taxation, was guilty of faulty reasoning on this point, doubtless because he had not made the analysis which subsequent writers have made into the nature of wants and their satisfaction.   He was too good a utilitarian to advocate equality of sacrifice if he did not believe that it would involve the least sacrifice on the whole.   This is shown by the following quotation, the italics of which are mine.

For what reason ought equality to be the rule in matters of taxation ?

For the reason that it ought to be so in all affairs of government. As a government ought to make no distinction of persons or classes in the strength of their claims on it, whatever sacrifice it requires from them should be made to bear as nearly as possible with the same pressure upon all, *which, it must be observed, is the mode by which the least sacrifice is occasioned on the whole.* If any one bears less than his fair share of the burden, some other person must suffer more than his share, and the alleviation to the one is not, *caeteris paribus*, so great a good to him, as the increased pressure upon another is an evil.[1]

The last proposition in the above quotation would be true only of persons whose incomes were approximately equal. If A's income is twice as great as B's, or, to state it more accurately, if A's income were enough greater than B's so that a dollar is worth half as much to A as it is to B, then equality of sacrifice would be secured by making A pay twice as many dollars as B: by collecting $100, for example, from A and $50 from B. But the last dollar of A's remaining income would still be worth less to A than the last dollar of B's remaining income is worth to B: and the last dollar taken from A would occasion him less sacrifice than the last dollar taken from B has occasioned him. Then by taking more than $100, say $110, from A, and less than $50, say $40, from B the same revenue would be raised with a smaller sum total of sacrifice, for the gain to B by this change would be greater than the loss to A. This will appear at once to any one who at all understands the principle of marginal utility. The only conclusion one can draw is that the least sum total of direct sacrifice is secured, not by equality of sacrifice, but by equality of *marginal* sacrifice. Equality of marginal sacrifice would be secured by so apportioning taxes that, as a general rule, the last dollar collected from one man should impose the same sacrifice as the last dollar

[1] *Principles of Political Economy*, bk. v, ch. ii, sec. 2.

collected from any other man, though the total amount collected from each man might impose very unequal total sacrifices.

We are now in a position to test the validity of the minor premise in the argument on page 397: viz., if each individual would voluntarily contribute in proportion to his ability, the whole burden of taxation could be most easily borne — i. e., with the minimum of sacrifice. If one's ability is assumed to be measured by one's income, real and potential, and to vary with that income, then the minimum of sacrifice would not be secured by each one's paying according to his ability. If the rich would volunteer to pay more than in proportion to their ability, allowing the poor to pay less than in proportion to their ability, the burden would be more easily borne — i. e., with less sacrifice — than if all should pay proportionally. As a statement of individual obligation, even, the faculty theory is untenable, unless modified and defined more rigidly than has yet been done. From the strictly utilitarian standpoint, the individual who measures his obligation to society by his total income is less to be commended than the individual who determines whether he has fulfilled his social obligations by considering, not how much he has given, but how much he has left. The latter type of individual is well illustrated by the example of that religious and philanthropic leader who found, early in life, that he could live in comfort and maintain his maximum efficiency by the expenditure of a certain small income. Later in life, as his income increased, he continued living on his earlier income, devoting all his surplus to the service of society. This is mentioned merely by way of further elucidation of the proposition that if there were no indirect consequences of the attempt to collect taxes, the utilitarian test would require an enormously high rate of progression in the apportionment of taxes, and that, if the state were able to apportion and collect taxes on this basis, it would only be making individuals do what they ought to do voluntarily.

But there are indirect results, the most important of which is, as already pointed out, the repression of certain desirable industries and enterprises. The importance of this consideration becomes apparent when we reflect on the probable consequence of a system of taxation so drastically progressive as that suggested above. If a large share of one's income above a certain sum should be seized by the tax collector, it would tend to discourage the effort to increase one's income beyond that sum. In so far as this reduced the energy of the individual in business or professional life, the community would be deprived of his services. This deprivation would be a burden on the people, all the more regrettable because it would not enrich the public treasury in the least.[1]

Such considerations become still more important when we come to the discussion of various forms of taxation, especially the taxation of various kinds of property. Since different kinds of property come into existence in different ways, taxes must affect them differently. A kind of property which is produced by labor, or comes into being as the result of enterprise, may be very seriously affected by a tax. Tax the makers of it and they will be less willing to make it. Tax the owners or users of it and they will be less willing to own or to use it. They will therefore pay less for it, and thus discourage the makers of it as effectively as if the latter had to pay the tax themselves. In either case, there will be less of that kind of property made and used, and some mem-

---

[1] See also Ross, " A New Canon of Taxation," *Political Science Quarterly*, vii, p. 585.

bers of the community who would otherwise have enjoyed the use of it will now be deprived of that use. This is a burden to them, and, moreover, a burden which in no way adds revenue to the state. Such a tax is repressive. On the other hand, a kind of property whose existence does not depend upon individual labor or enterprise, will be less affected by a tax. Tax the owner of a piece of land, and, while you make him less anxious to own it, you will not cause him to abandon it. While you lower its price, you do not reduce the amount of land nor deprive the community of the use and enjoyment of anything which it would otherwise have had. Such a tax is not repressive.

As a general proposition, it is safe to say that, other things equal, a tax which represses desirable enterprises or activities, and thus deprives the community of the use and enjoyment of certain desirable goods, is more burdensome in proportion to the revenue raised than a tax which does not entail such results. In other words, a repressive tax is more burdensome than a non-repressive tax. A proposition much more to the point is that a tax on any form of property or income which comes into being as the result of the productive industry or enterprise of its owner is more repressive than a tax on any form of property or income which does not thus come into being. By productive industry and enterprise is meant such industry and enterprise as add something in the way of utility to the community, and not such as merely cost something to their possessor. Skill in buying land may cost as much study and care as skill in making shoes; but, whereas those who exercise the latter kind of skill increase the number of shoes, it has never been shown that those who exercise the former kind add anything whatever to the community's stock of useful goods. Tax shoe factories and, in so far as it represses the industry, the community will have fewer shoes. Tax the land and the community will not have less of anything than it would have without the tax. What is said of a tax on land could also be said, within limits, of a tax on inheritances. From the standpoint of non-repressive taxation, therefore, both the land tax and the inheritance tax have much to be said in their favor.

Any one who is familiar with the subject of the shifting and incidence of taxation will see at once that there is a close connection between the repressive effects of a tax and the shifting of it. A tax can be shifted, generally speaking, only when it affects the demand for, or the supply of, and consequently the value of, the thing taxed. The more easily a tax affects the supply or demand, the more easily it is shifted. A tax which does either of these things is repressive: it affects supply by repressing production; it affects demand by repressing consumption. A careful analysis of the conditions under which taxes may be shifted is, therefore, very much to be desired. Such an analysis would enable us to form conclusions as to the repressive or non-repressive effects of various taxes.

As applied to incomes in general, without regard to their source, a progressive, even a highly progressive, tax will occasion, on the whole, less direct sacrifice to the taxpayers than a proportional tax. A progressive tax is therefore to be commended, unless the rate of progression is made so high as to discourage the receivers of large incomes from trying to increase them. If the rate of progression is so high as this, the indirect form of sacrifice, growing out of the repressive effects of the tax, will counteract, wholly or in part, the reduction in the direct form of sacrifice. A moderately progressive income tax would, therefore, seem to be more desirable than a proportional one. But as between different kinds of income and different kinds of property, the preference should be given to those taxes which fall upon natural products, such as land, rather than upon produced goods, and upon increments of wealth which come to an individual through natural causes over which he has no control — inheritances, for instance — rather than upon incomes earned by the individuals themselves. Such taxes are less repressive than most other special forms of taxation, and therefore occasion less sacrifice of the indirect kind.

It is well known that the payer of the tax does not necessarily bear the burden. He may, under certain circumstances, shift the burden onto some one else. The problem of justice in taxation has to do with the distribution of the burdens of taxation. Therefore it is important that we understand the laws which determine the shifting of these burdens, before we are in a position to determine whether a given tax is a just tax or not. In other words, we must know where the burden of a tax rests before we can possibly know whether those burdens are justly distributed or not.

More specifically, it may be laid down as a sound principle of taxation that a tax which is easily shifted from one person to another, and which therefore tends to diffuse itself widely throughout the community, is suitable for temporary or emergency purposes, while a tax which cannot be shifted, and is therefore not diffused at all, is suitable for the raising of permanent revenues. A tax which diffuses itself throughout the community is suitable for the raising of temporary or emergency revenues, because no matter who pays it in the first place, others will be compelled to help bear the burden. Therefore the government can begin quickly, and with no very elaborate machinery, collecting such a tax and securing immediate revenue, without feeling that it is committing an act of flagrant injustice or expropriation. That is why stamp taxes have long been recognized as effective means of raising emergency revenues. A few people, or a few forms of property, may be selected for the first payment of the revenue into the public treasury. They who pay the tax, in turn, collect from other people in the form of higher prices or higher fees.

While such a tax as this is widely diffused, there is no certainty that they who ultimately bear the burden are the ones who ought to bear it. The government merely seizes the nearest source of revenue and trusts to luck that the tax will diffuse itself in such a way as not to work a very great or positive injustice. For a permanent income it is obvious that a more intelligent method of distributing the burdens of taxation is desirable. If a tax is easily shifted from one person to another, it is, humanly speaking, impossible to trace it to its final incidence and determine who really bears the burden. If it is impossible to tell who really bears the burden of a tax, it is equally impossible to distribute that burden intelligently. The less a tax is shifted the easier it is to tell who bears it, and it is proportionally easier to devise a series of taxes whose burdens are intelligently distributed.

More important still, a tax which cannot be shifted, such as a tax on land values, tends to be capitalized and, if it lasts over a long enough period of time, becomes a burdenless tax. It is paid once and for all when the tax is taken out of the capitalized value of the thing taxed.

For example, if a piece of land is normally yielding $1000 a year in rent, over and above taxes and other necessary expenses, and if the current rate of interest is five per cent, the selling price of that piece of land will normally be $20,000 unless a future rise or fall in the rent is anticipated. That is to say, $20,000 at five per cent interest would yield $1000 a

year.   This piece of land would be approximately as desirable as $20,000 in money, since each would yield the same
income.   But suppose that an extra tax of $500 were put on
that piece of land, leaving the owner a net income of only
$500.   The land would then be only as desirable as $10,000
in money, since each would yield the same income, viz. $500;
$10,000 would then normally be the price at which the
land would sell.

It is popularly supposed that such a tax as this would
raise the rent of the land and thus enable the owner to shift
the burden upon the tenant, or upon the purchaser of the
products of the land.   Such is clearly not the case.   Such a
tax would neither increase nor decrease the supply of land
or of its products.   It would not cause a single new acre to
go out of cultivation, because no one would throw away a
piece of property which was still, in spite of the tax, yielding
him a clear income of $500 a year.   The supply of land
would be the same as before, likewise the supply of its
products, and their prices.   The owner, therefore, would not
be able, by reason of the tax, to get any more out of the
land than he would have been able to get out of it if the tax
had not been levied.   In other words, he could not shift it
either upon the consumers or upon the tenant if there were a
tenant.   The tenant would not be more desirous of getting
the use of the land with the extra tax on it than he would
have been if there had been no extra tax.   On the other
hand, the owner would be no less anxious to rent his land
than he otherwise would have been.   There being no
change in the supply of land, and no change in the attitude
of the owner or renter, it is difficult to see how the renter
could be made to pay a higher rent.   Unless he can be made
to pay a higher rent, the burden of the tax is not shifted
upon him.   The owner must bear it.   That is, in the fore-

going illustration, he must be content with a net rent of $500 and a price of $10,000.

Moreover, the owner, if one there be, at the time the tax is first instituted, is likely to bear the whole future burden and to relieve all future generations of it. In the foregoing illustration, the value of his land has fallen from $20,000 to $10,000. The future purchaser, therefore, will be able to buy it for $10,000, by reason of the tax, whereas if the tax had not been put on the land, he would have had to pay $20,000. He still gets, after paying the tax, five per cent on his purchase price. That is all he would have gotten if he did not have to pay the tax, because, in that case, the purchase price would have been $20,000. Or, if he has $20,000 to invest, he could spend $10,000 on the land, and put the other $10,000 at five per cent interest. The income from the $10,000 thus put at interest would pay his tax, and leave him a net income of $1000, the same as he would have had if there had been no tax and he had had to pay the whole $20,000 for the land.

While such a tax is a great advantage to future generations, enabling them to provide a public revenue without burden to themselves, it is a severe blow to the owners of land at the time the tax is first levied. This absolutely destroys the value of such a tax for temporary purposes. The concussion is so severe that it ought not be repeated. Once is enough. The whole merit of such a tax lies in its permanency. The longer it endures without change the better it becomes, that is, the more completely are the wounds of the first concussion healed.

All that has been said about a land tax can be repeated of any other tax which is not shifted. An inheritance tax is an example. In this case, not only can one say everything that was said in favor of the permanency of a land tax, but something else besides. Since inheritances come to men very infrequently, an inheritance tax might be collected for one year, or several years in succession, without striking everybody. If the tax were then removed for a few years, the people who paid it when it was in force might receive no benefit from its suspension, and they who paid no tax, because receiving no inheritances while it was in force, might be the very ones to benefit by its suspension, that is they might be the ones who would receive their inheritances during the period of suspension. Obviously, therefore, the inheritance tax should be a permanent rather than a temporary or emergency tax.

Let us now examine a little more in detail the conditions which determine whether a tax can be shifted or not.[1]

In the present state of economic knowledge it is scarcely worth while to attempt the task of locating the final incidence of all kinds of taxes. When the process of shifting a tax is started, it is difficult to tell when or where it will stop. That such knowledge is greatly to be desired goes without saying. It is truism that equity in taxation consists in distributing the burdens of taxation equitably; but how can this be done, even in theory, unless we know where the burden will rest? As a step in this direction it may be worth while to examine the conditions which will permit a tax to be shifted, leaving the question of incidence for future investigations.

A tax is shifted only when it affects value and prices so as to enable the taxpayer [2] to reimburse himself for the tax at the

---

[1] From an article on the " Shifting of Taxes", in the *Yale Review*, November, 1896.

[2] For convenience, the following terminology is adopted: The taxpayer is the one who pays the tax in the first place, or the one from whom the tax collector receives it. The bearer of the tax is the one upon whom the burden finally rests. The thing taxed is that upon which the taxpayer's tax is

expense of some one else. The shifting of taxes forms a special class under the general phenomena of value,[1] and must, therefore, be brought under the general law of value and price. The first question to arise is: Under what conditions will a tax affect the value of the thing taxed; or, in other words, under what conditions will it bring about such a change in the market and such a modification of values as to furnish the taxpayer an opportunity to shift the burden upon some one else.

A tax is no exception to the general law that nothing can change the value of an article without first changing the relation between demand and supply. In order to raise the price of anything a tax must either increase the demand or reduce the supply; and to reduce the price it must either decrease the demand or increase the supply. A failure to appreciate fully the universality and persistency of the law of demand and supply lies at the basis of much incorrect thinking on the subject of the shifting of taxes. There is a more or less general opinion that the value of anything is determined directly by what it costs; and as a tax adds to the cost it must therefore be added to the price. This overlooks the true relation of cost to value. The cost of anything affects its value only when it puts a check upon production and limits the supply. Whenever an addition to the cost will cause a decrease in the supply or an increase in the demand, it will raise the value of the article in question. But this will not occur in every case. It is scarcely conceivable that a tax can increase the demand for the thing taxed.[2] If it ever does so, the instances must be so rare that

rated, or according to which it is estimated. This seems to be in accord with Professor Seligmann's idea as set forth in the *Political Science Quarterly*, vol. 7, p. 715, and also in his *Essays in Taxation*, p. 395.

[1] See *Marshall's Principles of Economics*, 3d ed., p. 519.

[2] Though it may increase the demand for some other commodity by induc-

we can safely ignore them. This leaves us to the conclusion that a tax can only raise the price of the thing taxed when it occasions a diminution in the supply.

Under what conditions will a tax cause a diminution in the supply of the thing taxed ? Whenever it will make the production of any part of the existing supply a source of loss to the producer at the existing price. The supply of different commodities is determined by wholly different factors. In order to arrive at definite conclusions as to the effect of taxation upon the supply of different taxable things, it will be necessary to adopt the following classification:

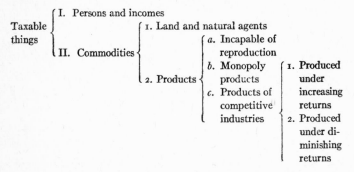

Persons and incomes belong to a class by themselves, since they are not commodities. Consequently, if a capitation or an income tax is shifted at all, it must be by affecting the price of some commodity which is inseparably connected with personality. In other words, such taxes cannot be shifted unless they either increase the price of labor or decrease the price of the necessaries of life. Capitation and income taxes respectively correspond in a rough way to

ing people to substitute it for the thing taxed. But there are many general and indefinite social effects of taxation which need not be discussed under the shifting of taxes, since they do not give the taxpayer any special opportunity, nor any special advantage over the other members of the community.

specific and *ad valorem* taxes on commodities. It is difficult
to see how a general income tax could be shifted at all. It
could not make the possession of an income undesirable, and,
if it applies proportionally to all incomes, it could not drive
men from one industry to another. If, however, it applies
only to a special class of incomes, or to incomes derived from
certain special sources, it might drive some men out of certain occupations; and wherever this results, the diminished
competition will enable those who remain in these occupations to earn more and thus reimburse themselves, in part at
least, for the tax. A capitation tax necessarily bears most
heavily upon the poorer classes, but may, under certain conditions, enable these classes to earn more and thus escape a
part of the burden of the tax. For example, if a certain local
community should levy a heavy capitation tax it might drive
a certain number of the laborers elsewhere. If the industries
of the place were localized, the scarcity of labor would
enable the remaining laborers to earn better wages. But
the wider the area over which the tax is levied, the more
difficult it will be to shift it. What the effect of capitation
or income taxes will be upon the price of the necessaries of
life will depend on the use that is made of the money that
is collected. The probability of such taxes being shifted by
causing a reduction in the cost of living, seems too remote
to call for a detailed discussion here.

Since land and natural agencies are not the products of
industry, the only way of reducing the supply of these things
is by causing the abandonment of some portion which is already in use, or by preventing the appropriation of some portion that would otherwise be used. A tax of less than one
hundred per cent of the rental value could do neither of these
things. Since rent is a pure surplus, no individual owner
could have any reason for abandoning his property so long

as the tax collector leaves him any part of this surplus. Since such a tax would make no difference in the amount of land cultivated, and would not change the factors which determine the intensity of cultivation, it could not affect the price of the products of the land nor raise its rent. From the standpoint of the tenant, a given piece of land would be neither more nor less desirable on account of the tax; the landlord could collect neither more nor less rent and would have to bear the burden of the tax.

But, on the other hand, the fact that the landlord must bear the tax makes land a less desirable kind of property after the tax is levied than before. This will so diminish the demand for land as property as to reduce its selling value and enable the future purchaser to shift the future taxes upon the present owner. In other words, the present owner must bear the whole of the future taxes, so far as they can be foreseen.[1] If a certain tax is levied and it is expected that it will continue to be levied indefinitely in the future, it will reduce the selling value of the land to the amount of the capitalized value of the tax. The future owner will, therefore, be able to buy it so much cheaper that he will realize as large a percentage on his investment as though the tax had never been levied. Our conclusions are that a tax on the rental value of land cannot reduce the supply of land and, therefore, cannot raise its rent. Consequently the owner of the land at the time the tax is first levied cannot shift the tax at all; but such a tax will reduce the demand for land as property and consequently will lower its selling price. Therefore the subsequent purchaser will be able to shift the tax upon the one who owned it at the time the tax was first levied.

[1] See Seligmann on the *Shifting and Incidence of Taxation*, pp. 52–62, for a historical and critical examination of this theory.

If, however, the tax is specific, and the land is taxed at so much an acre without regard to its value, it is almost certain that some of the poorer land will not be worth the taxes. Where this is the case it will be abandoned and thrown out' of cultivation. The resulting diminution in the supply of the products of land will increase their price and enable the owners of the better qualities of land to collect a larger rent. They will thus be able to shift a portion of the tax upon the consumers of the products of the land.

Those products of human industry which cannot now be reproduced form a small and unimportant class which includes rare old coins, curios, and works of art. A universal or world-wide tax would affect them in precisely the same way that it would land; but since they are movable and land is not, a local tax would affect them differently. A local tax on such articles would have so little effect on their general market price that the future purchaser could not have the opportunity of escaping the burden by shifting it upon the present owner.

The supply of monopoly products is limited more or less arbitrarily by the will of the monopoly. The general tendency is for a monopoly to fix the price of its product at the point that will yield the largest net return, and to limit the supply to such an amount as can be sold at that price. A tax on the product would necessitate a new calculation of expenses and profits and a new adjustment of prices and production to suit the new conditions. The price that would yield the largest net profit before a tax was put upon the product would seldom or never yield the largest net profit afterwards. A higher price and smaller product would ordinarily give better results. Let us suppose that a certain article can be produced by a monopoly at a uniform cost of four cents a pound. At four cents a pound, two million pounds could be sold; at four and a half cents, one and a half million pounds; at five cents, one million pounds; at five and a half cents, six hundred thousand pounds; at six cents, four hundred thousand pounds; and at six and a half cents, two hundred thousand pounds. Clearly the monopoly would prefer to put the price at five cents and limit the production to one million pounds. But if a tax of one-half cent a pound were added to the expense, a larger net profit would remain if the price were put at five and a half or six cents and the production limited to six hundred thousand or four hundred thousand pounds. Therefore, if a monopoly is taxed in proportion to its gross product it will shift the tax, in part at least, by charging higher prices for its product.

If the monopoly is taxed in proportion to its net profits, or if it is taxed a lump sum regardless of either profits or production, it will have to bear the burden of the tax. In neither case could the monopoly gain anything by reducing the amount of its production. Such a tax would not change the conditions which determine the net profits of the business.

The supply of commodities that are produced under competitive conditions is not fixed by nature nor by the arbitrary will of a monopoly. The tendency is for the supply to increase until the price falls to a level with the cost of producing the most expensive increment. If the cost were greater, the production would be checked sooner, and there would be a smaller supply which would command a higher price. If the cost were lower, the production would be checked later, and there would be a larger supply which would have to sell at a lower price. The effect of a tax on the production of an article of this class would be the same as an addition to the cost of production. If the same amount continued to be produced after, as before the tax was added, it would have to sell at the same price and some of the more expensive increments would then be produced at a loss. But this fact alone would make it certain that some of the former producers would be driven out of the business, and, if it were an industry of diminishing returns,[1] this would result in a smaller supply and a higher price. Those who remain in the business and continue to pay the tax would thus be able to shift a part of the tax upon the consumers of the article. But if, on the other hand, the tax were collected directly from the consumer rather than from the producer of the article, it would make no material difference in the distribution of the burden of the tax. Such a tax would make the article a less desirable possession, and would, therefore, diminish the demand for it. This diminution in the demand would lower the price and shift a part of the burden back upon the producer. This may be illustrated by the diagram on the following page.

Let us suppose that the supply of a certain article is measured along the line OA, and its value and cost of production along the line OB. Let GC represent the demand curve and EC the cost curve; in other words, let us suppose that the price that could be had for any definite supply of the article is represented by the perpendicular distance from the point on OA which marks the limit of the supply to the curve GC, and that the perpendicular distance from the same point on

---

[1] It is quite conceivable that a tax on an industry of increasing returns might simply drive some of the weaker competitors out of the business and enable the survivors to produce on a larger scale, and consequently, more cheaply. They might even be able to sell the product at the original price, being reimbursed for the tax by the reduction in the cost of production. In the absence, however, of satisfactory data, this is only a tentative conclusion. But where the tax falls only on a part of the competitors, as in the case of an import duty on an article that is also produced at home under the law of increasing returns, the case is clearer. This will be discussed later.

OA to the curve *EC* represents the cost of producing the most expensive increment of the supply. Obviously, the tendency will be for the supply to increase to an amount represented by *OD*, where it would be checked, because a further production would involve a loss. When the supply is represented by *OD* the price would be represented by *OF*. But if a tax equal to *EE'* were laid upon the production of

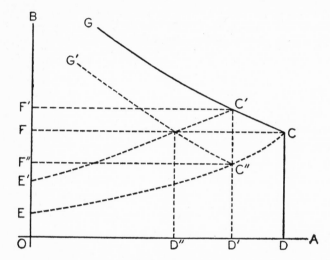

the article it would have the effect of raising the cost curve from *EC* to *E'C'*. This would have the effect of checking production and limiting the supply to an amount represented by *OD'*, and this supply would sell at a price represented by *OF'*. This would shift a part of the tax upon the consumer.

But if the taxes were collected from the consumer, instead of the producer, it would lower the demand curve from *GC* to *G'C'*, check the supply at *OD'*, and reduce the price to *OF''*. This would shift a part of the tax back upon the producer. If, however, the tax were collected equally from the producer and consumer the supply would be reduced to OD''; but the price would not be materially changed.   We have still to consider the case of a tax which is collected upon an article in some advanced stage of its production, or while it is in the hands of the merchant or importer.   This will be taken up later.

According to the foregoing illustration, only a part of the tax is shifted in either case, i. e. whether it is originally collected from the consumer or from the producer, what the effect of the tax will be upon the price of the thing taxed depends upon two conditions: 1. The elasticity of the demand for the article; 2. The amount of rent which its production affords in proportion to the cost.   If, as is the case with commodities for which there are many substitutes, the demand is highly elastic, it means that a comparatively slight change in the price will occasion a considerable change in the amount consumed.   This gives the consumer a decided advantage in the struggle to shift taxes.   Other things being equal, the consumer will bear a smaller share of the burden of the tax when the demand for the thing taxed is elastic than when it is inelastic.   When the demand is elastic, the only condition upon which he will use the thing at all, or in anything like the usual quantities, is that it shall cost him no extra expense.   An attempt to make the consumer bear the burden of the tax would result in a greatly diminished consumption.   Consequently, the producer must either bear the tax or go out of business.   But if the demand is inelastic, as is the case with commodities for which there are few substitutes, the producer has the advantage. Other things being equal, the consumer will have to bear a larger share of the tax than he would if the demand were elastic.   The additional expense of the tax would not occasion any considerable falling-off in the amount consumed.

On the other hand, the elasticity of the production or the supply depends upon the extent to which rent enters into the production of the article in question. If very little rent is afforded, it is because there is very little difference in the cost of producing different increments of the supply. If all increments of the supply are produced at a nearly uniform cost, which cost approximates very closely to the market price, any addition to the current cost, or any subtraction from the current price, would occasion a considerable falling off in the amount produced. Unless the producers could shift a tax, they would stop producing rather than pay it. So the consumer would have to bear a large share of the tax or do without the product. But if the production of the article in question affords a large share of rent, it is because there is a considerable difference in the cost of producing different increments of the supply. Where this is the case, an addition to the cost, or a subtraction from the price, will occasion a comparatively small diminution in the supply. The effects of a tax would be only to cause a small diminution in the supply, and the consumer would have the advantage.[1] Other things being equal, the consumer will bear a larger share of the tax when the production of the thing taxed affords a small amount of rent than when it affords a large amount. For convenience in the following discussion let us agree to use the term, " elasticity of production or supply," to mean the extent to which a fluctuation in the value or in the cost of production will affect the amount produced. Thus, the production of a given article is highly elastic when a comparatively slight addition to the price or subtraction from the cost will occasion a considerable increase in the amount produced, and a comparatively slight addition to the cost or subtraction from the price will

---

[1] The probabilities are that the tax will come out of the landlord's rent.

occasion a considerable decrease in the amount produced. When the opposite conditions obtain, the production is inelastic. Then we can lay it down as a general principle that the distribution of the burden of any particular tax on the products of competitive industries, depends upon the comparative elasticity of the demand and the supply of the thing taxed.[1] If the demand is more elastic than the supply, the consumer will bear a small share of the tax; but if the supply is more elastic than the demand, the consumer will bear a large proportion of the tax.

We are now in a position to consider the case of a tax that is placed upon an article in some advanced stage of its production, or while it is in the hands of the merchant or importer on its way from the producer to the consumer. These advanced processes of production are the ones which, in general, produce the least rent and are affected most by changes in cost or value. Therefore, it is safe to conclude that such taxes are most certain to be shifted. The margin of profit which merchants, for example, make upon a given commodity of this class, is so small and so nearly uniform, that a tax upon that commodity would almost certainly cause them to stop handling it unless they could shift the tax. The question is: Will they shift it forward upon the consumer in the form of a higher price for the finished product, or will they shift it backward upon the producer of the raw material by paying him a lower price ? It is evident that the burden will be shifted in the direction of the least resistance. If the demand for the finished product is more elastic than the supply, the consumer has power to resist

---

[1] It has seemed expedient to avoid the use of such terms as consumer's rent; but to those who are familiar with that term it will readily occur that the elasticity of demand depends upon the amount of the consumer's rent which the commodity affords, just as the elasticity of supply depends upon the amount of producer's rent.

effectively the attempt to shift the burden upon him; but if the supply is more elastic, the producer has the greater power of resistance. Therefore, we conclude that the principle of the comparative elasticity of demand and supply, as determining the distribution of the burden of taxation between producer and consumer, applies to this as well as to other cases.

A tariff duty on imported commodities is no exception to the general rule that a tax can only affect the value of the thing taxed when it changes the relation of demand to supply. Since a tariff duty could scarcely be expected to add anything to the demand for the thing taxed, we must conclude that it must diminish the supply in the home market, if it is to be added to the price. In other words, the tariff cannot be shifted upon the home consumer, unless the effect of the tariff is to reduce the supply of the article in the home market. The question is: Under what conditions will a tariff duty on an imported commodity occasion a diminution in the supply of the commodity in the home market? Let us divide imported commodities into the following classes: (1) those which cannot be produced at home at existing prices; (2) those which are produced at home at existing prices, but whose production is subject to the law of diminishing returns; (3) those which are produced at home under the law of increasing returns.

Any commodity which is produced for a world-wide market tends to be distributed among different sections and political divisions, in such proportions, that the producer will realize as much net profit on that portion which is sent to one section as to another. If, at a given time, a larger net profit is generally realized on what is sent to one section than upon what is sent to another, manifestly the producers will, if they find it out, begin sending more to one section and less to the other, until the price is so reduced in the first and increased in the second, that the profits will be equalized. If a certain country levies an import duty upon the commodity in question, it would reduce the profit upon that part of the product which is sent to that country. Less would, therefore, be sent there and more to other countries until the equilibrium was again restored. This diminution in the amount sent to the tariff country would raise the price there unless the domestic product increased sufficiently to counterbalance the diminution in the amount imported. But if it should so happen that the import duty should occasion such an increase in the domestic product as to counterbalance the diminution in the amount imported, then no rise in the price would result, and the home consumer would not have to bear the burden of the duty.[1]

Under what conditions will the domestic product be increased by the import duty sufficiently to counterbalance the diminution in the amount imported ? The utility of the above classification will now appear. If the duty is levied upon a commodity which cannot be produced at home at the existing price, manifestly the home production could not increase sufficiently to keep the price from rising. The only condition under which it can be produced at home at all is that the price shall rise sufficiently to cover the cost of producing it under the unfavorable domestic conditions. In such a case the whole of the duty is almost certain to be added to the price. If the commodity is one which is produced at home, but under the law of diminishing returns, the results will differ only in degree, if at all. The price is certain to rise because the amount imported will diminish, and the domestic product cannot materially increase without

---

[1] This, of course, overlooks local conditions which sometimes exist on the border of the tariff country.

a rise in price.[1] The conditions are essentially the same as those illustrated in the diagram on page 421. We are safe in assuming that the domestic product has already increased as far as it could profitably at the existing price. Since it is an industry of diminishing returns, a larger production would involve a higher cost. Poorer land, poorer labor, poor managing ability, or all combined, would have to be called into use; or each existing establishment would have to be operated more extensively, and consequently, at a greater cost per unit of product.

Here, again, we may apply the principle of the comparative elasticity of demand and supply to determine the extent to which such a tax would affect the price, but it must be applied in a somewhat special manner. Paradoxical as it may seem at first, yet it is true that the more elasticity there is in that part of the supply which is produced at home the less elastic will be the whole supply. In other words, the more readily the home production will respond to a slight rise in price, the less an import duty will affect the whole supply on the home market. The reason is plain. If a slight rise in the price of the article will occasion a large increase in the amount produced at home, the home production will come more nearly increasing sufficiently to offset the falling off in the amount imported. That is, the total supply on the home market will be inelastic. This will give the consumer an advantage in the matter of shifting a tariff duty. He will, likewise, have an advantage if the commodity is one for which the demand is elastic.

If the duty is levied upon a commodity which is produced at home under the law of increasing returns, the result is

[1] It is needless to say that this can only apply to commodities which are imported in commercial quantities. It could not apply, for example, to a duty on corn and pork in this country; wool might serve as an example.

still worse for the foreign producer and correspondingly better for the home consumer. A diminution in the amount imported will open a larger market to the home producer and may enable him to produce cheaper, because on a larger scale. Where this holds true, the increase in the domestic product may be more than enough to counterbalance the diminution in the amount imported and actually increase the total supply on the home market. In such a case the consumer would have to bear no part of the duty. There are two possible exceptions to this conclusion. The first is that an industry of increasing returns always tends to be a monopoly. Where such is the case the monopoly will probably succeed in putting up the price after foreign competition is virtually shut out by the import duty. But where there is doubtless a tendency for industries of increasing returns to *become* monopolies, it can scarcely be maintained that all such industries *are* monopolies. The second exception is, that after the import duty had resulted in the enlargement of domestic industries, and consequent cheapened production, the price might be still further cheapened by removing the duty; and that consequently the consumers will be sharing the burden of the duty in that they could buy the article cheaper if the duty were removed. While this might be temporarily true, it is probable that the same forces which kept the price up before the duty was first levied would ultimately bring about the same conditions after the duty was removed.

This conclusion, as to the effect of an import duty upon the price of an imported commodity, which is also produced at home under the law of increasing returns, is apparently opposed to the orthodox teachings on the subject of the incidence of a tariff. It is a conclusion that has been reluctantly accepted by the writer, but one which has been logically forced upon him after mature deliberation.

Inasmuch as permanent taxes as permanent sources of public revenue should be levied in such a way as to repress productive enterprise as little as possible, and inasmuch as, — which means the same thing, — permanent taxes should be collected in such a way as to avoid as much as possible the shifting of the burdens, it follows that they should be levied mainly upon the land, incomes, and inheritances. Extraordinary or emergency taxes, such as war taxes, must of course be levied with regard to the immediate necessities of the case and not with too nice a regard for absolute justice. Every consideration, of course, must give way in the interest of national defence. The tax collected on the site value of land can have no repressive effect whatever on any productive enterprise. Its only effect is to reduce the selling price of land, not to change its rent in any way, nor to reduce its production in any way. From the standpoint of national interest, the selling price of land is a matter of indifference, provided its productivity is not affected. It is its productivity which enables it to support the nation. Its selling price is merely a means by which wealth is transferred from one citizen to another. Moreover, as already shown, the selling price of land once reduced by a tax, provided the tax is not thereafter changed, is reduced once and for all, and eventually becomes a burdenless tax, the whole burden of the future tax having been paid by the original owner.

A tax which represses productive enterprise weakens the state or the nation to that extent. A tax which does not repress any kind of useful or productive enterprise and still yields public revenue, strengthens the state, adds to its general power and prosperity, and is, therefore, just, according to our original definition of justice.